RaumFragen: Stadt – Region – Landschaft

Series editors

Olaf Kühne, Eberhard Karls Universität Tübingen,
Tübingen, Germany

Sebastian Kinder, Institute of Geography, Universität Tübingen,
Tübingen, Baden-Württemberg, Germany

Olaf Schnur, Research, c/o vhw Bundesverband e.V.,
Berlin, Germany

RaumFragen: Stadt – Region – Landschaft   Im Zuge des „spatial turns" der Sozial- und Geisteswissenschaften hat sich die Zahl der wissenschaftlichen Forschungen in diesem Bereich deutlich erhöht. Mit der Reihe „RaumFragen: Stadt – Region – Landschaft" wird Wissenschaftlerinnen und Wissenschaftlern ein Forum angeboten, innovative Ansätze der Anthropogeographie und sozialwissenschaftlichen Raumforschung zu präsentieren. Die Reihe orientiert sich an grundsätzlichen Fragen des gesellschaftlichen Raumverständnisses. Dabei ist es das Ziel, unterschiedliche Theorieansätze der anthropogeographischen und sozialwissenschaftlichen Stadt- und Regionalforschung zu integrieren. Räumliche Bezüge sollen dabei insbesondere auf mikro- und mesoskaliger Ebene liegen. Die Reihe umfasst theoretische sowie theoriegeleitete empirische Arbeiten. Dazu gehören Monographien und Sammelbände, aber auch Einführungen in Teilaspekte der stadt- und regionalbezogenen geographischen und sozialwissenschaftlichen Forschung. Ergänzend werden auch Tagungsbände und Qualifikationsarbeiten (Dissertationen, Habilitationsschriften) publiziert.

SpaceAffairs: City – Region – Landscape   In the course of the "spatial turn" of the social sciences and humanities, the number of scientific researches in this field has increased significantly. With the series "RaumFragen: Stadt – Region – Landschaft" scientists are offered a forum to present innovative approaches in anthropogeography and social space research. The series focuses on fundamental questions of the social understanding of space. The aim is to integrate different theoretical approaches of anthropogeographical and social-scientific urban and regional research. Spatial references should be on a micro- and mesoscale level in particular. The series comprises theoretical and theory-based empirical work. These include monographs and anthologies, but also introductions to some aspects of urban and regional geographical and social science research. In addition, conference proceedings and qualification papers (dissertations, postdoctoral theses) are also published.

Series Editors

Prof. Dr. Dr. Olaf Kühne
Universität Tübingen

PD Dr. Olaf Schnur
Berlin

Prof. Dr. Sebastian Kinder
Universität Tübingen

More information about this series at http://www.springer.com/series/10584

Olaf Kühne

Landscape Theories

A Brief Introduction

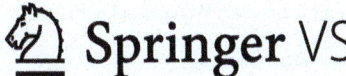 Springer VS

Olaf Kühne
Forschungsbereich Geographie
Eberhard Karls Universität Tübingen
Tübingen, Germany

ISSN 2625-6991   ISSN 2625-7009   (electronic)
RaumFragen: Stadt – Region – Landschaft
ISBN 978-3-658-25490-2   ISBN 978-3-658-25491-9   (eBook)
https://doi.org/10.1007/978-3-658-25491-9

Library of Congress Control Number: 2019935849

Springer VS

Verantwortlich im Verlag: Cori Antonia Mackrodt

This Springer VS imprint is published by the registered company Springer Fachmedien Wiesbaden GmbH part of Springer Nature
The registered company address is: Abraham-Lincoln-Str. 46, 65189 Wiesbaden, Germany

Acknowledgements

I would like to thank everyone who made this book possible. With the countless colleagues with whom I have repeatedly dealt with the subject of landscape over the past two and a half decades. Without your criticism, suggestions and support this book would not have been possible. I would like to thank Corinna Jenal in particular for the constructive review of the manuscript and Ted Cahill for the linguistic fine-tuning. My special thanks go to my wife, who always supports me in my research (and not only there).

Tubingen
January 2019

Contents

Introductory Remarks

The issue of landscape is of current interest, not only in science, but also in politics, economics, and civil society. As a result of rapidly occurring social transformation processes and the resulting changes in the demands placed on spaces (whether materially conceived or as social or individual constructions), traditional landscape interpretations are also challenged. Relavent examples being changes as outcomes of the expansion of regenerative energies, infrastructure projects, the extraction of raw materials, the expansion of settlements, the restructuring of settlements, etc. (see among many: Antrop 2000; Berleant 1997; Bourassa 1990; Cosgrove 2006; Daniels 1989; Jones 1991; Jorgensen 2011; Kühne 2018b, d; Paasi 2008; Schönwald et al. 2016; Kühne and Weber 2018 [online first 2017]; Lothian 1999; Pasqualetti 2001; Pasqualetti et al. 2002; Schein 1997; Selman 2010; Stiles 1994; Stobbelaar and Pedroli 2011; Terkenli 2001). To put it briefly, as does Schein (1997, p. 662)—"Landscapes are always in the process of 'becoming'".

'Landscape' describes a comparatively open semantical phenomenon for which there is a multitude of understandings as well as differing research approaches, from which it follows: "The landscape concept embodies several unresolved conflicts: between collective belonging and individual control, between the subjective and the objective, and between the mental and the material" (Jones 1991, p. 234). The conflicts among researchers that arise from dealing with landscape range from the 'right' theoretical approaches to the question of the constitutive level (material, individual, social or something in between) and adequate research designs, to the question of arrangements as well as the rights pertaining to the use of physical spaces (see for example: Gailing and Leibenath 2012, 2015; Kühne 2008c, 2018c, 2019; Olwig 2008; Olwig and Mitchell 2009; Walker and Fortmann 2003). At the same time, over the past decades, scientific research on the social significance of landscape in psychology, sociology, geography, medicine, planning, philosophy, archaeology, and environmental research has intensified (see also Berleant 1997) causing clear differentiation in the formation of landscape-theoretical approaches (among many: Bourassa 1991; Corner and Balfour 1999; Cosgrove

© Springer Fachmedien Wiesbaden GmbH, part of Springer Nature 2019
O. Kühne, *Landscape Theories*, RaumFragen: Stadt – Region – Landschaft,
https://doi.org/10.1007/978-3-658-25491-9_1

1985, 1997; Cosgrove 1998; DeLue and Elkins 2008[2001]; Franzen and Krebs 2005; Gailing and Leibenath 2015; Kaplan et al. 1998; Kühne 2018c; Manzo and Devine-Wright 2014; Weber 2016b). The developed theoretical references to landscape range from the inductive abstraction of empirical results to the deduction of general (social) scientific theory. In this book, 'landscape theories' is to be understood in the social scientifical tradition as the elaboration of statements that are as general as possible regarding conditions and developments of the relationship between 'landscape' and 'society' and the development of a practicable set of terms. Although landscape theories are fundamentally oriented, they are also bound to social and certain historical contexts, specifically scientific-historical. The temporal limitations of landscape-related theory formation also mean that a distinction can be made between theories which are more classical and those which are more contemporary. 'Classical' theory is a consolidated, partly canonized approach, while current theories are further developed by their representatives, on the one hand, even though their potentials and limits for landscape research are not yet fully determined on the other hand (cf. Treibel, Korte and Schäfers 1997). The boundary between 'classical' and 'current' theories may be fluid, e.g. 'classical' approaches may be further developed (such as currently engaged phenomenological landscape research; see Sect. 2.5.1), while 'current' approaches may mature into 'classics' (such as the possibility with social constructivist landscape research; see Sect. 2.4.1).

This book is not the first to deal with landscape theories. The overview works presented so far on the subject of 'landscape theory' refer either to the relationship between landscape and art or design (DeLue and Elkins 2008[2001]; Herrington 2016), landscape architecture (Corner 1999; Swaffield 2002), more generally landscape and (specifically psychological) aesthetics (Bourassa 1991), show a scientific perspective (e. g. Turner et al. 2001) or that of a discipline, such as geography (such as Wylie 2007). The work on 'environmental aesthetics' by Porteous (2013) clearly refers to the theme of landscape, but the object of his work is to develop an environmental aesthetic that goes beyond landscape aesthetics. Recently published in its second edition, "The Routledge Companion to Landscape Studies" summarizes the current state of (specifically Anglo-Saxon) landscape research and, ascribable to its detail and scope, is more suitable for people who have already gained an overview of the different theoretical approaches to landscape (Howard et al. 2018).[1]

The aim of this book is to present the diversity of currently discussed landscape-related theories and to place them in a scientific theoretical context. As already indicated, the focus is on the societal, as well as on the individual level; the natural scientific reference to the landscape is rather marginal. The representation of the different theoretical

---

[1]A synthesizing theoretical approach to landscape does not only take place in the Anglosaxion context but can also be found in French (Roger 1995), Polish (Myga-Piatek 2012), Italian (Raffestin 2005), and German (Franzen and Krebs 2005; Kühne 2018e).

positions is not (primarily) understood based on temporal sequences, as is often the case with disciplinary overviews (such as for geography in Wylie 2007 or Winchester, Kong and Dunn 2003). Rather, the structure of the presented theories is fundamentally organized in such a way that, starting from general scientifically theoretical basic positions (essentialism, positivism, and constructivism), more specific positions of landscape research are presented and related to each other from an interdisciplinary perspective (specifically sociology, psychology, geography, and philosophy). In the later sections of the book, the theoretical position treated in each case is again classified each time according to the basic positions of scientific theory. More generally: The chapters of the book build on each other, they do not simply juxtapose theoretical positions (which is why the newcomer to the subject should read them consecutively). In this form, it becomes possible to order the different approaches, to compare them within the created framework and to clarify how they relate to each other. At appropriate points throughout, where they facilitate the understanding of the theoretical approaches presented in each case, results from empirical research are also touched upon.

In addition to the English language state of the art of landscape theory formation, this book also aims to pay special attention to developments that have taken place in German-speaking countries.[2] In comparison to the English language-based literature, it has some specific characteristics. After many years of widespread abstinence (since the end of the 1960s; more details are given in Sect. 4.4) of the German-speaking spatial social sciences (specifically human geography, but also sociology, planning sciences) with regard to a reflective debate on the topic of 'landscape', a growing number of publications have been dealing with questions of landscape theory over the past two decades. These are—in international comparison—characterized by

1. a stronger focus on sociological and political scientific basics,
2. a more intensive study of the interpretation and meaning of terms,
3. a stronger focus on constructivist approaches.

These constructivist approaches are very strongly differentiated (e. g. into social constructivist, radical constructivist, and discourse-theoretical approaches) and terminologically sharpened by resorting to sociological (social constructivism and radical constructivism) and political scientific theory formation (discourse theory in the tradition of Laclau and Mouffe).

This book is generally aimed at people who are interested in questions that go beyond pure experience, immediate enjoyment, spontaneous rejection, simple description, etc. of landscape. This book is intended to be especially for people who have a professional

---

[2]Whereby this regional focus is also quite common in English-language survey works, such as Wylie (2007) with the focus on England or Winchester, Kong and Dunn (2003) on Australia.

interest in landscape, such as landscape planners, geographers, and landscape architects, but also philosophers, anthropologists, archaeologists, medics, sociologists, and psychologists who deal with spatial issues. In higher education, it is aimed more at students who are in their master's degree or about to complete a bachelor's degree. Here it is possible to build on the knowledge of subject-specific interpretations and methods in order to abstract them theoretically.

The book contains numerous text boxes, illustrations, and tables with the aim of presenting the different theoretical approaches to the reader as clearly as possible. There are two types of boxes:

> At the end of each chapter, there is a box in which the *main results of each chapter are briefly summarised*. These boxes have a grey surface colour.

> Boxes, on the other hand, in which *special theories or terms* are explained, are coloured blue.

The first box of the book deviates a little from this scheme, since it deals with a superordinate question, which always resonates in this introduction, but is only explicitly asked here (Box 1). The illustrations are either graphic abstractions of what is depicted in the text, graphically processed results from empirical research, photographs, or paintings. If they are better suited to provide an insight into the diversity of 'landscape' or structures and processes, a photo series will be used. The tables are used for the presentation of empirical results or for a compressed comparison of what is presented in the text.

The present book on landscape theory is divided—including this introduction—into seven chapters. Chap. 2 discusses current landscape theoretical positions according to the scientific paradigms of essentialism and positivism as well as different constructivist approaches, but also touches upon current approaches that have only had a minor impact on landscape research. Subsequently, Chap. 3 deals with different positions on the topics of landscape and aesthetics, whereby the scientific theoretical paradigms presented in the previous chapters serve as an analytical framework. Chap. 4 is devoted to the question of how landscape patterns of interpretation and evaluation are passed on to society and which different approaches to landscape are socialized. In particular, the systematic socialization (here on landscape) in the educational system, but also the manifestation of power in physical space (which in turn can be interpreted affirmatively in the educational system) is subject to diverse criticism, which is addressed in Chap. 5, but not without first having addressed the complex concept of power and the evaluation framework of critical landscape interpretations bound up in political worldviews. In

Fig. 1.1 Just as I wrote these lines sitting on the balcony of our house in Saarbrücken (Germany) at noon on August 9, 2018, after months of drought, a violent thunderstorm descended as a result of a highly unstable atmosphere (scientifically speaking), the course of which can be seen in the photo collage. If the depicted 'landscape' is generally given the predicates 'picturesque' or 'beautiful', although some people are disturbed by the pointed skyscrapers, the power line, and the wind turbines in the background which are not visible due to the weather, these lead us already to the question of different interpretations and evaluations of landscape. The thunderstorm caused the atmosphere (in the sense of mood) to drift towards 'sublimity', combined on the one hand with the relief of having survived the drought. On the other hand arises the personal concern of whether the fabric roof of the balcony would withstand the gusts of wind and whether the thunderstorm could develop in such a way as had the last thunderstorms in May, which flooded cellars in the surrounding area, destroyed a bridge, made roads impassable, etc. With the current thunderstorm the oppressive sultriness of the morning gave way to an afternoon of fresh coolness. These photographs can thus be used to create numerous cognitive, aesthetic, but also emotional and functional references to landscape theory. Nevertheless, they also show something that drives many who are concerned with the subject of landscape (and the theories associated with it): the fascination of landscape.

Chap. 6, the theoretical and aesthetic approaches to landscape that were previously used are related to empirical questions, such as the socialization of landscape concepts, the moral loading of landscape, and landscape conflicts. The conclusion (Chap. 7) undertakes the task of elaborating essential aspects and potentials, as well as research needs in relation to landscape theory.[3]

---

[3]This English textbook is an updated and extended synthesis of my research activities, which has been published mainly in German so far (with the exception: Kühne 2018c). In the first place, it concerns my textbook "Landschaftstheorie und Landschaftspraxis. Eine Einführung aus sozialkonstruktivistischer Perspektive" (Kühne 2018b; second edition), but also my contributions to the "Handbuch Landschaft" (Kühne et al. 2019) as well as numerous statements to questions of the landscape theory (e. g. Kühne 2005a, 2006a, b, 2008b, 2009a, 2014a, 2015a, 2018a).

Box 1: Why Landscape Theory?

For many people, landscape is the object of aesthetic enrichment or of daily work. Something self-evident, something everyday. So why take the trouble to deal with it theoretically? The answer to this question has several dimensions:

1. It is interesting (especially for social scientists) to deal with the question of how 'the normal', the 'self-evident', the 'everyday' emerges at all.
2. Theoretically dealing with an object (here landscape) facilitates abstraction from the multitude of individual cases, thus facilitating orientation.
3. Theoretical landscape reflections also make it possible to classify and compare a wide variety of research on the subject of the landscape, which often does not link itself directly, often only implicitly, to (scientific) theoretical justifications.
4. Dealing with the theoretical examination of landscape makes it easier to connect to different scientific disciplines (such as the social sciences, psychology, or philosophy).
5. The examination of landscape theories clarifies the multitude of possibilities for dealing with landscape and thus offers the possibility to contextualize one's own ideas (along with the theoretical ones) of landscape.
6. Conflicts over landscape developments often arise from different landscape-related (aesthetic or moral) norms, reflection on these norms facilitates understanding of these conflicts accordingly.
7. In research practice, theories are suitable for framing empirical research, while empirical research can test the degree to which theories can be generalized.
8. A very personal reason why it is worthwhile to study landscape theory: it adds another dimension to one's fascination with landscape (Fig. 1.1).

Currently Discussed Theoretical Perspectives on Landscape

The theoretical approach to landscape unfolds in the triangle between individual references, social conventions, and material objects. To which of these dimensions is assigned outstanding importance depends not least on the theoretical approach to science. These relationships will be discussed in this chapter, starting with the development of analytical terminology (Sect. 2.1) before introducing essentialist, positivist, and constructivist approaches (Sects. 2.2–2.4), followed by 'more-than-representational approaches', which are currently increasingly discussed in landscape research (Sect. 2.5). The chapter concludes with an examination of 'neopragmatism', which is less a theory of its own than an innovative form of dealing with theories.

2.1 Landscape Between Objectivity, Individual and Social Construction

The scientific discussion of what is meant by 'landscape' is largely stretched around the dimensions of society (1), the individual (2), and the dimension of physical objects (3), as well as their relationships, including superorders and subordinations (for the structuring of different approaches describing this relationship, see among others Bourassa 1991; Nassauer 1995; Zube et al. 1982). A fourth dimension—in the sense of an analytical abstraction—can be identified (specifically from the perspective of constructivist research; see more in Sect. 2.4). This refers to those physical objects that are viewed together as landscape according to the individual construction as based on social patterns of interpretation and evaluation (4). In reference to Bourdieu's theory of space (1991), Löw's reflections on the relational order of social goods and living beings (2001), and in an extension of the three-space approach (social space, appropriated physical space, physical space) to the individual world according to Popper's three-world hypothesis (1973) and the hybridization of the natural and the cultural (Latour 1996), these four

© Springer Fachmedien Wiesbaden GmbH, part of Springer Nature 2019
O. Kühne, *Landscape Theories*, RaumFragen: Stadt – Region – Landschaft,
https://doi.org/10.1007/978-3-658-25491-9_2

levels of landscape are named as follows: (1) social landscape, (2) individually actualized social landscape, (3) physical space, and (4) appropriated physical landscape.[1] In the following, the four levels of the understanding of landscape outlined here are presented in more detail:

1. The *social landscape* (German: 'gesellschaftliche Landschaft') comprises the interpretations and evaluation schemes of and about landscapes existing in societies. These are subject to both historical variability, i.e.—especially in the context of accelerated social development (see Rosa 2005) with its physical manifestations (Kühne 2007)— they are subject to a clear intergenerational change, are clearly differentiated with regard to cultural contexts (more on this in Sect. 4.3), and can be differentiated into socially differentiated special knowledge stocks (more on this in Sect. 4.2). The social landscape can be described as the socially available and retrievable stock of knowledge and 'emotional conventions'. It regulates the communicable and non-communicable aspects of landscape, as well as the conventions on who may communicate about landscape and how, and who may deviate from socially defined interpretation and evaluation schemes and in what form, without losing social recognition (in particular the relevant reference groups in the sense of Dahrendorf (1971[1958]) or at least having to fear this loss of recognition (a question which is dealt with in particular by discourse theory and critical landscape research; Sects. 2.4.3 and 5.3–5.5). Here the interface to the individually actualized social landscape becomes clear.

2. The *individually actualized social landscape* (German: 'individuell aktualisierte gesellschaftliche Landschaft') comprises individual knowledge, patterns of interpretation, and evaluation as well as personal emotional references to the landscape. These have a close feedback relationship to the social landscape: on the one hand, the individual picks out knowledge, patterns of interpretation and evaluation, and updates individual 'conventions of feeling' (Hasse 2000). On the other hand, the individual is also able to change social patterns by adding new interpretations, evaluations, and emotional references or by questioning traditional ones. Whether he or she can do this by gaining social recognition (especially from the reference group), i.e. the social landscape can be changed, depends on whether society grants him the right to deviate from the convention. As a rule, this is only the case for holders of special knowledge stocks, in this case landscape experts (whether in art or science; a subject to be dealt with in Sect. 5.4).

3. *Physical space* (German: 'physischer Raum') is the material basis for landscape. Material objects are observed under the mode of landscape observation (this is not only optical, but also contains elements which are acoustic, olfactory, haptic, etc.) and

---

[1]First considerations can be found in Kühne (2006a), further details later in Kühne (2008b, 2013c, 2018c, d). Hokema (2013) provides a comparison with other current landscape concepts. Operationalisations can be found, for example, for planning at Stemmer (2016), for tourism at Aschenbrand (2017), in the context of landscape simulations at Fontaine (2017a, b).

synthetisized to landscape (Sect. 3.7 elaborates this further). This means from a constructivist perspective (Sect. 2.4): Physical space *is not* landscape; it is rather a carrier of landscape attributions, because not every material object is part of landscape. This is where the interface to the appropriated physical landscape is defined. If virtual objects are added to the physical space, it can be described as 'external space'.

4. The *appropriated physical landscape* (German: 'angeeignete physische Landschaft') encompasses those material objects that are synthetized into landscape. Thus, as a rule, not every stone individually becomes part of the appropriated physical landscape, but rather a hill. The acquired physical landscape is highly individual, socially and culturally differentiated. The individually actualized physical landscape usually comprises a subset of the social landscape patterns; the same applies to partial social landscapes. These, in turn, can deviate greatly from each other: The landscape that an agronomist synthetizes in physical space according to a partial social pattern differs greatly from that of a conservationist (Kühne 2008b, 2013c). The acquired physical landscapes can differ greatly in diverse social contexts, depending on different cultural contexts. This also means that it is possible to design a 'global social landscape' that contains all landscape interpretation, evaluation, knowledge schemes, and emotional contributions as an analytical category, but which, due to its complexity, has only limited scientific and even less practical (e.g. planning) operationalizability.

The classifications of these four dimensions of landscape in relation to the social, the individual, and the material world can be found in Fig. 2.1. The above-mentioned appropriated

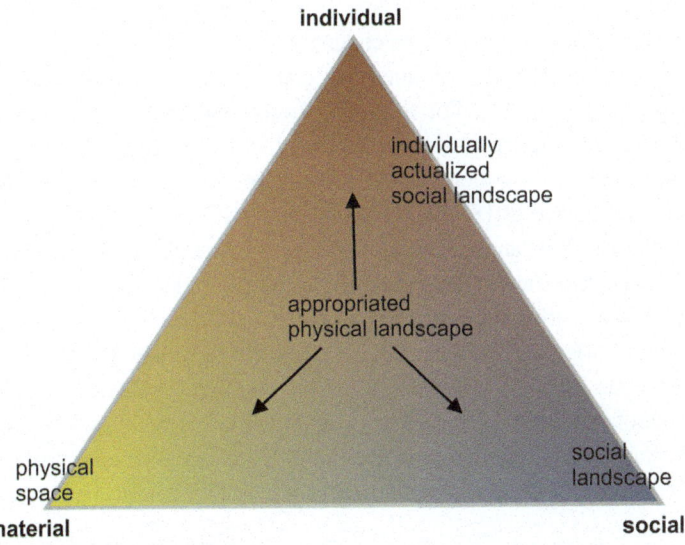

Fig. 2.1 The references of the social, the individual, and the material in relation to landscape. This figure forms the basis for the classification of the terms and theories presented in the following chapters in Fig. 7.2 and 7.3 in Chap. 7 (Conclusion; own presentation)

physical landscape occupies a special position, since the social (or partially social), the individual (as individually actualized physical landscape), or the material (if the landscape is thematized as material objects, but not the construction frame) is addressed.

All these levels are subject to a temporal change: the social landscape changes as new interpretations and evaluations take effect; the physical space is adapted to social and individual needs, the individually actualized social landscape changes through the appropriation of new patterns of interpretation and evaluation, developing emotional contributions, but also possibilities of influencing the physical space (Table 2.1). According to these changes the acquired physical landscape also changes. To put it briefly, as does Barbara Bender (2002, p. 103), in relation to the physical foundations of landscape: "Landscape is time materializing: landscapes, like time, never stand still".

2.2   Essentialism

The fundamental attitude of an essentialist (from Latin '*essentia*') assumes that things have necessary qualities that constitute their essence (Chilla et al. 2015). Accordingly, 'landscape' becomes a 'thing in itself'. This is equipped with specific properties and values. The outer appearance is not 'landscape', but merely an expression of its 'essence' (e.g. Kühne 2013c). In this way, different landscapes can be distinguished from such a perspective in a reciprocal imprint of nature and culture. The aim of an essentialist approach to landscape is to distinguish 'essential' and thus significant characteristics of a 'landscape' from those which are only 'accidentally' present (Albert 2005; see also Chilla et al. 2015). It is thus assumed that there is a definable core of landscape, with which landscape is attributed an independent reality, whose aesthetics are an inherent characteristic of it, which lends it value (thus connecting it to a pre-modern understanding of science; Kühne 2018e). For example, 'traditional' pre-modern farmhouse styles are understood as characteristics of the essential, whereas single-family bungalows in globally similar designed settlement extensions are not. They are declared accidental (Chilla et al. 2015; Kühne 2018e; Weber 2018).

This understanding of landscape was followed by 'traditional' geography of the 19th and early 20th centuries (and today continues to exist in landscape research in parts). For this geography, the world consisted of a well-ordered 'chambering' of natural and cultural entities (Blotevogel 1996; Egner 2010; Glasze 2015; Weber 2018). This geographical worldview becomes clear in Alexander Humboldt's (1769–1859) understanding of landscape. In the quotation attributed (since it is not found in his writings; Hard 1970a) to him of the 'total character of an earth region' (German: 'Totalcharakter einer Erdgegend'), three constitutive elements for the essentialist understanding of the landscape become clear:

1. Landscape is a whole ('totality').
2. This landscape is equipped with its own being ('character').
3. It is a distinct part of the earth's surface compared to other 'earth regions'.

Table 2.1 Empirical results on the temporal change of the social landscape: Results of the evaluation of four photos (survey years 2004, n = 455, and 2016, n = 436. Identical survey methodology: Saarland survey area, Germany, postal household survey, same questionnaire). The light gray highlighted area indicates a significant difference between the displayed values, the dark gray highlighted area a highly significant difference between the displayed values. Figures in percent. (One possible answer; according to: Kühne 2018d, p. 51)

	Survey year	Anxiety	Comfort	Indifference	Sadness	Happyness	Disgust	Love	Proudness	Attachment	Other	Don't know	Total
Half open	2004	0.2	45.3	2.4	0.0	22.4	0.0	2.2	0.4	16.0	4.8	6.2	100.0
	2016	0.3	33.6	1.0	0.0	33.6	0.0	1.8	2.0	23.5	3.8	0.5	100.0
Industry	2004	4.6	0.7	18.2	7.3	0.2	19.1	0.0	3.1	22.4	12.7	11.6	100.0
	2016	3.4	0.9	18.1	7.8	0.0	12.2	0.0	9.2	27.8	16.3	4.4	100.0
Wood	2004	1.3	33.2	7.5	1.3	29.9	0.4	1.8	2.2	11.4	7.3	3.7	100.0
	2016	0.7	23.5	14.6	1.2	26.2	0.5	0.5	3.9	16.7	6.3	5.8	100.0
Wind power	2004	3.7	2.4	32.3	7.7	4.2	17.1	0.0	4.0	4.8	11.0	12.7	100.0
	2016	7.4	1.6	24.7	11.1	3.9	14.3	0.0	3.2	11.1	14.5	8.1	100.0

This is associated with 'container' thinking (Thiem and Weber 2011; Wardenga 2002). Paffen (1973b, p. XXVI) considers landscapes decidedly as a "totality of physiognomically detectable 'geographical forms' (phenomena) in the 'geographical substance'"— explicitly in contrast to the 'experienced landscape' in the individual (Paffen 1973b, p. XXIV). Accordingly he defines landscape in an essentialistic way as as an expression of "mental inherent laws" and assumes an "integration of inorganic, biotic and, where appropriate, cultural-social complexes as causal networks and spatial structures" (Paffen 1973a, p. 76). Accordingly, the task of a geographer is to record the "essence of each landscape area" (Lautensach 1973, p. 31).

The term 'cultural landscape' is of outstanding importance for essentialist landscape geography. This term, which became popular in German geography in the second half of the 19th century (for more on the development of German-language geography see Sect. 4.4; a more detailed examination of the concept of 'cultural landscape' is given later in Box 5), was (and is) used to suggest an 'inextricable' connection between 'people and landscape' (Eisel 1982; Kühne 2013c). The relationship between man and landscape is not only interpreted as a research task for geographers, it also acquires a normative meaning: "If the transformation takes place quickly, it initially appears disharmonic, since the balance is disturbed for a long time" (Lautensach 1973, pp. 26–27). The physical manifestations of modernization (e.g. regenerative energies, the expansion of technical infrastructure or the extraction of raw materials) have challenged essentialist ideas of 'cultural landscapes' (see also Quasten 1997; Wöbse 1999). Accordingly, the essentialist understanding of landscape is often used today (implicitly or explicitly) as a justification for resistance to change in the physical space interpreted as landscape (e.g. Kühne and Weber 2018; Walter et al. 2013; Weber 2018; more on this in Sects. 6.1 and 6.2). Essentially oriented landscape research thus assumes that 'landscape' exists as a 'quasi-organismic entity with special characteristics', which has "an unalterable intrinsic value and its own identity" (Gailing and Leibenath 2012, p. 97). This in turn produces "a specific characteristic of 'land and people'" (Körner 2006, p. 6; see also Hard 2002) which must be preserved from an essentialist perspective.

The conservatism of essentialist landscape interpretation has far-reaching consequences beyond that: Immigrant populations are also considered accidental (not just bungalows), which adds a touch of 'blood and soil ideology' to this view. Another point of criticism concerns the normativity inherent in essentialist landscape theory. Assuming that there is a synthesis of landscape and people, it is not possible to derive normatively from this that there should be such a synthesis. This is a classical naturalistic fallacy, as Hume (2003[1738]) already criticized in the 18th century. Accordingly, this type of landscape geography was criticized at the end of the 1960s as "an apolitical, but ultimately conservative to reactionary, restorative geography was perceived as a discipline that particularly blatantly violated the standards of conceptual debate achieved in neighbouring disciplines of the humanities and social sciences" (Gebhardt 2016, p. 45). An essentialist understanding can be found not only in traditional landscape geography, but also where the 'essence' of man is to be derived from 'landscape characteristics'. Essentialist theory accordingly assumes that landscape preferences are historically created by environmental conditions (the so-called habitat theories, see Box 2). Compared to the other theories, it is able to provide norms for dealing with physical spaces, since the 'essence of landscape' is to be preserved, which makes it (often implicitly) attractive for planning. Planning is strongly norm-based, for example, the 'conservation of historical cultural landscapes' (e.g. in Germany) becomes a legal task of spatial and landscape planning.

Box 2: Habitat Theories

The habitat theories, which are still popular today (especially in psychological landscape research), postulate "that we still instinctively prefer landscapes with elements and structures that enabled early humans to survive and develop" (Hunziker 2010, p. 35). Constitutive for the family theory of phylogeny is the fear of prehistoric man of being surprised and injured/killed, as well of striving for physical security (Gold and Revill 2003). The following theories find a broader discussion:

1. According to the savannah theory (Orians 1980, 1986) human beings prefer half-open landscapes (understood as material objects), because the origin of mankind would be in savannahs (with grasslands, embedded shrubs, and water areas as well as higher vantage points). A confirmation of this theory is seen in the preference for semi-open landscapes in the settlement of North America, in higher prices for real estate with a distant or water view, and in the effort of humans to create savanna-like landscapes in the form of gardens and parks themselves or to paint them in a preferred manner (Orians 1980, 1986; Wilson 1984).

2. The Prospect Refuge Theory (Appleton 1975, 1984) assumes that the preference for semi-open landscapes arises from the need to 'be seen and not seen' (Appleton 1975). Open view is offered by the savannah through its wide grasslands, the trees standing alone or in groups provide privacy or could also serve as a hiding place (see also Hunziker 2010).

3. The Information Processing Theory (Kaplan and Kaplan 1989; cf. also Kaplan and Kaplan 1982; Kaplan et al. 1998) is probably the most developed, and most empirically tested and used approach in biological theories contemplating primeval influences (Hunziker 2010). Accordingly, people prefer rooms that facilitate the gathering of information and whose information is intellectually connectable. They differentiate four different criteria for classifying the quality of information (Kaplan and Kaplan 1989): complexity (as a multitude of different objects and interdependencies), mystery (not all information is immediately understandable, but offers the possibility of becoming understandable), coherence (simple structures and contexts) and legibility (the possibility of finding one's way back to the starting point; for more details, see a. o. Gimblett 1985; Hunziker and Kienast 1999; Kaymaz 2012; van der Jagt et al. 2014; Wohlwill 1968).

Eventually, these theories assume that a stimulus (a certain environment) would provoke a certain reaction (preference of a 'landscape'; Tuan 1976) that determined the actions of today's humans. The 'Gestalt-Theorie' (Köhler 1969; see also Antrop and Van Eetvelde 2000) goes so far as to produce a finally isomorphism (= alignment) between certain formal aspects of environmental objects and neurological processes. In order to prove the validity of the respective theories, empirical (usually quantitative) studies are used, which in turn can be assigned to a positivist understanding of the world (see Sect. 2.3). Irrespective of whether such preference patterns can also be found today, the inference of conditions from the early days of mankind on today's preferences represents an analogy.

2.3 Positivism

To this day, the positivist understanding of landscape dominates large parts of science, but also of public discussion and of those administratively concerned with landscape (planners). In the following, the main features of a positivist understanding of the landscape will be presented. Subsequently, its integration into the planning will be discussed, especially with regard to the challenges that arise.

2.3.1 Positivism and Landscape

According to the mathematician and philosopher Auguste Comte (1798–1857), who wanted to establish a 'positive science', the focus of scientific research is on those objects "which exist in the world outside human consciousness and which can be experienced and discovered through measurement and perception" (Egner 2010, p. 30). The aim of this focus is to generate verifiable certainties with the help of empiricism. 'Space' in general, and 'landscape' in particular, becomes here an observable, measurable, and countable quantity—and thus analysable (Egner 2010, p. 98). In contrast to essentialist landscape research in pursuit of essentialities, positivist research measures individual phenomena and divides them into 'layers', such as distribution of enterprises, population, land use, soils, climate, visual landscape, and technical infrastructure which are fed into Geographic Information Systems (GIS) nowadays. The information collected in this way and divided into levels is subjected to abstraction (Chilla et al. 2015). 'Spaces' are differentiated, juxtaposed, inductively generalized, while at the same time the notion of 'spatial entities' does not disappear, even though the essential link between culture and nature is rejected (Eisel 2009). Like 'space', 'landscape' can also be defined as a container—as "genuine reality" (Schultze 1973, p. 203)—'filled' with various elements that can be located and related (Gailing and Leibenath 2012). This access—in conjunction with technical innovations—had a considerable influence on the scientific work "quantification, mathematization and computer modelling seemingly offered unlimited potential for unravelling the spatial fix of human affairs" (Tilley 1997, p. 9).

A positivist understanding of the world also dominates in sciences with spatial and landscape references, beyond the 'classical spatial sciences', such as geography, landscape architecture or planning sciences: in large parts of psychological landscape research, landscape is understood as a given material object that can be perceived and cognitively processed by humans. These cognitive patterns, in turn, are the subject of experimental research, so attempts are made to examine the theories presented in Box 2 (for more details, see e.g. Thompson 2018). This also shows the difference between social and natural science theory formation (which includes large parts of psychology): Social science theories are linked with the goal of developing a framework of general statements on the conditions and developments of society (as in this case, also society and landscape) on the one hand, and to develop a practicable set of terms on the other hand. The goal of natural science theory formation is to generate (empirically) verifiable and thus falsifiable statements (see more precisely: Chalmers 2013; Treiben et al. 1997).[2]

2.3.2 Positivism and Landscape-Related Planning

The positivist landscape research does not only deal with the analysis of the object landscape, which it understands in this way. In co-evolution with new computer technologies models of landscape are generated, forecasts are made (e.g. Gebhardt 2016). If 'landscape' is not only analysed, modelled and predicted for future developments, but is also to be intervened in this development, the analyses, modelling and predictions must also be evaluated. This challenge is taken up by landscape-related planning. Consequently, in spatial planning, 'landscape assessment procedures' are still centrally anchored today (e.g. Roth 2012; Roth and Bruns 2016; Stemmer 2016; Weber et al. 1999; cf. also Kearney and Bradley 2011). Such procedures pursue the aim of decomplexing 'landscape' into an objectified and thus politically operationalisable numeric value or pictogram (Kühne 2013c). This is based on an analytic frame by measuring and counting 'landscape elements' and their spatial arrangement such as biotope types (Kühne and Weber 2017 are examples of this). Also landscape preferences (if possible in the form of mean values) of people are measured and/or modeled, for example as "landscape viewing qualities" (Loidl 1981, p. 14–17) are clarifying the "impairments of the landscape" (Weber et al. 1999, p. 352; of positivist approaches to the positivist evaluation

---

[2]In scientific practice, this relationship is not in the form of a strictly separated dichotomy, but rather in the form of a polarity. This means that empirical studies are also based on social science theories, and natural science theories are used to form concepts. A juxtaposition nevertheless seems to make sense, in order to become clear about specific scientific logics.

of landscape among many: Frank et al. 2013; Howley 2011; Schirpke et al. 2013). Subsequently, they are spatially identified distinctly using a Geographical Information System (GIS; such as Sahraoui, Clauzel and Foltête 2016; in this context e.g. Konermann 2001; see also Antrop 1997). The criticism that these evaluation methods are the reproduction of aesthetic preferences of experts (Burckhardt 2004) is countered by the survey of landscape preferences of landscape users (Stemmer and Bruns 2017; see Sects. 4.2 and 5.5). The result of this approach is that the positivist fundamental position is extended by constructivist interpretations (Stemmer 2016).

Positivist landscape research (also in relation to aesthetic attributions)—due to its scientific tradition of thought—is particularly effective in planning processes, whereby ultimately the empiricism of 'landscape' is very important (preferably processed in GIS layers; see Kitchin 2015). It is often used for framing and an 'essentialistic' attribution of an 'intrinsic value' of 'cultural landscape' is made as a justification context for measures. The procedure of spatial planning with positivist basic understanding to integrate not only essentialist but also constructivist plantings poses challenges. One concerns the naturalistic fallacy: With regard to essentialist greening, this is conservative (see above), because just because something was, it does not mean that it should be so in the future (in this case landscape). With regard to the collection of opinions from users, there is a majorisation problem: Just because the majority is of one opinion does not mean that this should be binding for all. Planning ultimately means deciding in favour of one alternative and rejecting all other alternatives after weighing up the arguments. However, due to the naturalistic misconceptions, there is no weighing up, since in the end they only lead to an alternative that cannot be weighed up. Another concerns the problem of argumentative inconsistency, since arguments are made at different levels of scientific theory. The fact that this is forced by the fact that data and models are value-neutral, whereas planning is normative, makes the dilemma understandable, but no less virulent. This problem of different logics will be discussed in more detail in the context of autopoietic systems theory in Sect. 2.4.2 (the topic of landscape concepts is discussed in more detail in the planning in Sects. 5.4 and 5.5; a more detailed discussion of the topic of participation can be found in Sect. 6.2).

2.4   Constructivist Approaches

If in positivist approaches the constitutive dimension of landscape lies either on the level of the material objects, i.e. landscape is understood as a physical object, or in essentialist approaches as 'essence' 'behind the objects', in constructivist approaches the constitutive level of landscape is found in the individual or social construction. If individual or social ideas of landscape are examined, it is not (as it is often the case in psychological landscape research, for example) the perception (level of the individual or generalized of a social structure) of landscape as a real object that is spoken of, but rather the construction of a landscape (basing on social conventions). This construction takes place through an individual, socially predetermined synthesis of certain material and immaterial objects and aspects.

With this strong focus on construction processes, constructivist approaches (more in the social sciences and humanities tradition) clearly distinguish themselves from classical (positivist and essentialist) approaches, to which an 'object fetishism' (Duncan 1990, p. 11) is attributed. Three constructivist theories relating to landscape are discussed below: social constructivism, autopoietic systems theory, and discourse theory. The scope of the explanations on social constructivism and autopoietic systems theory is somewhat more comprehensive than on discourse theory, since in the section on social constructivism fundamental aspects of constructivist world view are explained and the theoretical foundations of autopoietic systems theory can neither be assumed to be trivial nor generally known.

2.4.1   Social Constructivism

According to social constructivist landscape research, the construct 'landscape' is the result of socially formed patterns of interpretation and evaluation, on the basis of which an internal synthesis of observed material objects and their connection with symbolic meanings takes place (for example, a stop sign is not merely a collection of metal and paint but communicates a general social expectation of action). The social constructivist landscape theory is (in its current interpretation) strongly based on the roots of the phenomenological sociology of Alfred Schütz (1960[1932], 1971[1962], 1971) and its further development from Peter Berger and Thomas Luckmann to social constructivism (Berger and Luckmann 1966). In English landscape research, precursors of social constructivist landscape theory date back to the middle of the 20th century (Hoskins 2005[1955]), on which Denis Cosgrove (1984, 1993) based his studies on 'symbolic landscapes'. Social constructivist landscape research received a significant impulse from the 1994 essay 'Landscapes: The Social Construction of Nature and the Environment' by Thomas Greider and Lorraine Garkovich (1994), in which they refer decisively to the social constructivist sociology of knowledge by Berger and Luckmann. Since the beginning of the 2000s, the number of works based on social constructivist landscape theory has increased significantly (among many: Aschenbrand 2016, 2017; Fontaine 2017b; Kühne 2008a; Trudeau 2006).

The process of 'construction', which is central to social constructivism, is described as "not an intentional action, but a culturally mediated pre-conscious process" (Kloock and Spahr 2007[1986], p. 56), which is based on the fact that abstractions in the form of prior knowledge of the world flow into every perception (Schütz 1971), whereby "nowhere is there anything like pure and simple facts" (Schütz 1971[1962], p. 5). Consequently, perception is not an isolated incidence, but rather the result of "a very complicated process of interpretation in which contemporary perceptions are related to earlier perceptions" (Schütz 1971[1962], pp. 123–124). But there is not only a reference to one's previously possessed perceptions, after all we are born into a world whose conceptual frameworks and categories used by humans already exist in our culture (Burr 2005). Substancial patterns of interpretation and evaluation with which we confront the world (including ourselves) are thus socially defined and conveyed to the individual in the process of socialization (see Sect. 4.1). In addition to this internalization, externalization has a central significance for symbolic communication: here, material objects are assigned certain symbolic meanings by means of which they communicate with others (this becomes particularly clear in the context of traffic signs; Berger and Luckmann 1966). Language is particularly of importance with regard to the social standardization of interpretations and evaluations: Language produces realities, structures perceptions, and thus does not represent an 'objective instrument of the representation of reality', but rather a social "system of signs and rules" (Werlen and Weingarten 2005, p. 192).

From a social constructivist perspective, social science studies can be understood as "constructions of the second degree: constructions of those constructions which are formed in the social field by the actors whose behavior the scientist observes and attempts to explain in accordance with the procedural rules of his science" (Schütz 1971[1962], p. 7). Social constructivism pursues a research program that—also empirically—"investigates the question of which interpretations of reality become socially binding" (Kneer 2009b, p. 5). Questions dealt with by social constructivist research are not 'what-is' questions, but questions of *who constructs the* world *and how*, how world interpretations and world evaluations differ, and how they acquire social commitment, in this case in relation to the social construct landscape.

Even if everyday space in general and everyday landscape in particular are experienced as self-evident and objectively given and understood as a "property of physical nature" (Läpple 1992, p. 201), it is nevertheless a historically developed and abstracted achievement that arose from an intersubjective synchronization of egocentric spatial understandings related to one's own body and the co-presence of objects.

According to the central aspects of social constructivism, externalization and internalization, social constructivist landscape research deals, on the one hand, with the questions of how physical objects possessing symbolic meaning are charged. Accordingly, they are "interpreted as concrete, material 'embodiments' of the social, e.g. of ideas, social relationships, habits, lifestyles, etc. The social is thus made accessible through interpretation from its physical embodiments" (Hard 1995, p. 52; Fig. 2.2). On the other hand, social constructivist landscape research is oriented towards the relationships between socially shared notions of landscape and individual constructs of landscape, because like all other systems communicating via symbols, social patterns of interpretation and attribution of landscape must be learned by the socializing individual: "There is no naive relationship to the landscape before all society. The naive cannot see the landscape because he has not learned its language" (Burckhardt 2006, p. 20). According to the high importance of the written rendering of the world in particular, and landscape in general, it can also be understood as text (see Box 3).

Fig. 2.2 The Watts Towers in Los Angeles, California, are an example of the difference and tempo-ral variability of the symbolic connotation attached to a material object. They were built by the Italian roofer Simon Rodia between 1921 and 1954 from arm-thick steel pipes which were covered with cement and provided with all kinds of ornaments (predominately shards and shells; Olessak 1981). They were called—in connection with the origin of Rodia—'Italian Garden' (Ipsen 2006). The Watts Towers are a result of the Californian social norm 'to do something big', to which Rodia explicitly referred. According to Banham (2009[1971], p. 111), they can be understood as a physical manifesto of "an innocent fantasy", which originated independently of historical models in "self-absorption". Morris (2002[1976]) associates with them a protest against the future tyrannies of the electronic age with its short-term regime, its constant reversibility and its virtuality. At the time of its creation, Rodia and his towers were exposed to various hostilities, from the neighborhood, but also from the city administration, which considered the towers not earthquake-proof (Rolle 1997[1968]). Today the assessment of the towers has changed. Ipsen (2006: p. 101) focuses his work on the Watts Towers on their social and cultural connotation in their environment: "Although Watts is still associated with crime and social unrest, it is also a work of art and a symbol of a transcultural place that connects Los Angeles with the regions from which one or one's parents immigrated". In addition, the Watts Towers will be marketed as a tourist attraction. (For more details see Kühne 2012b). (Photo: Kühne)

> **Box 3: Landscape as Text**
> What we know about landscape is based on different texts (in the content-wise sense of a coherent sequence of visual and linguistic signs, such as books, maps, Internet videos, documentaries, newspaper articles, the stories of acquaintances, etc.), which also form the basis for the individual construction of landscape (see e.g. Duncan and Duncan 1988; Winchester et al. 2003; Duncan 1990; Lindström et al. 2018). Texts in turn also form the basis for the inscription of (scenic) ideas in physical spaces,

for example in the form of plans (Dunn 1997). In the course of the linguistic turn, the meaning of language increases: "Society is a text. Nature and its representations are discourses. Even the unconscious is structured like a language" (Mitchell 1992, p. 89). Accordingly, the physical foundations of the synthesis 'landscape' can also be read according to their symbolic contents and translated into a linguistic terminology (such as metaphor, synecdoche, metonymy, etc.; as specifically in Duncan 1990). As a result of the cultural, social, and individual approaches and interpretations of the landscape texts, it becomes difficult to speak of a 'landscape'. 'Landscape' therefore takes place primarily in the plural. Nevertheless, this social and individual interpretation is only one side of the metaphor: the physical foundations of landscape, which ultimately represent the 'written text', are the other side. This page in turn is characterized by a different authorship, which can be deciphered by knowledge of historical contexts, especially in relation to everyday and working worlds (Muir 2000; Franke 2008). However, this also involves deciphering the discourses of different social powers inscribed in physical spaces (Duncan 1988; see also Chap. 5 on the subject of power and landscape).

One element of the supersubjective connection of landscape are narratives "Narrative is a means of understanding and describing the world in relation to agency" (Tilley 1997, p. 32). Narratives represent sense-giving established storylines, which on the one hand offer orientation and on the other hand are culturally and temporally variable. The relationship between people and the objects synthesized as landscapes (such as forests, mountains, cathedrals, etc.) generate narrative connections, "creating aesthetic and moral guidance for activity" (Tilley 1997, p. 33). Narratives form instructions, such as how which physical spaces are to be interpreted and evaluated ('no go areas' are regarded as dangerous and uninviting, regardless of whether individual experiences with them exist or not), but also how behaviour is to be organised in certain places (at a vantage point another behaviour is regarded as adequate than in a football stadium).

Critics such as Richard Peet (1996) accuse the concept of landscape as text of ignoring the world of material objects. Rather, landscape is also text, but not only text.

Different modes of landscape construction are designed for various aspects of society (e.g. regarding education, place of residence, etc.; see Chap. 4 for details). These are also reflected in the individually actualized social landscape: the cognitive mode refers to knowledge about landscape, the aesthetic mode to the patterns of evaluation of an external space as a beautiful, ugly, sublime or picturesque landscape, the emotional mode is particularly effective in referring to it as home, the economic mode refers to the question of whether an external space designated as landscape can be used to generate income, the functional mode refers to the extent to which a physical space is suitable for personal appropriation, e.g. for personal appropriation, the fitness of a physical space for the purpose of personal use, the symbolic mode refers to the possibility of charging physical objects with meanings, as well as the normative mode, which refers to the definition of target states based on general social assessment patterns (see Ipsen 2006; Kühne 2018e; Schein 1997; Stotten 2015). Appleyard (1979) sees landscape as an element of this symbolic communication; it thus serves as an instrument for defining normality (and thus also non-normality) and as a spatially pronounced symbol of belonging and strangeness. Another evaluation scheme is that of the 'typical' as presented by Purcell (1992; Box 4; on the relationship between the 'typical' or 'stereotype' and the familiar or 'homeland', see Sect. 4.2).

Box 4: The 'Typically' Approach

Purcell's 'typically approach' (1992) is based on the human being's ability to combine complex information into 'types', thereby reducing their complexity and maintaining his own ability to act. If a physical space is constructed as a landscape, it is compared with already formed—socially mediated—landscape types, whereby the deviation from the 'typical' is rejected. According to Purcell (1992), four central evaluation criteria of landscape can be found:

1. The expansion of the section of space constructed as a landscape;
2. the degree of (attributed) naturalness or anthropogenic transformation;
3. the relief;
4. the occurrence of water (for a more detailed discussion of this approach see Hunziker 2000).

Here the synthetic meaning of landscape becomes clear: Different elements are related to each other, to which a meaning is then ascribed.

A crucial potential of social constructivist landscape theory lies in the 'construction of the second degree' of landscape. It allows the investigation of different understandings of landscapes, their comparison, and also the mechanisms of their evolution. The social constructivist perspective, however, is also associated with the renunciation of the attempt to determine the 'true' landscape, which represents an observer-independent 'reality', whereby the intersubjectively binding determination of a 'value' of landscape also becomes an impossible undertaking. Finally, values are the result of discursive negotiations between different social and individual interests and not a characteristic of an object or constellation of objects (the issue of the moralization of landscape is explored in more detail in Sect. 6.1). From a constructivist perspective, there is no 'thing in itself' (in this case 'landscape in itself'), but only individual interpretations of one 'thing' (or more) in the context of socially produced and mediated interpretations (Blumer 1969; Kühne 2015d).

In comparison to the other constructivist landscape theories, which refer more strongly to communication processes, the social constructivist landscape theory assigns great importance to material objects (here specifically in the form of externalization). Although this has led it to be accused of insufficient 'theoretical purity' (Leibenath 2014a), it also makes it suitable of being connected to physical spaces understood as landscapes for planning approaches (Bruns and Kühne 2013; Kühne 2009a; Stemmer 2016). In the context of spatial planning, the potential of social constructivist landscape theory lies not in concrete statements with regard to material objects (what is to be built or preserved, where, and how), but rather—due to its sensitivity to power—with regard to questions of procedural justice or the generating of life opportunities (in the sense of Dahrendorf 1979; see Kühne 2014b, 2017b with regard to spatial developments; see Box 13 for understandings of justice). Concisely summarized, social constructivist landscape theory does not answer 'what' questions ('what is landscape?', 'what is to be built?'), but 'how' questions: 'how is landscape socially constructed?', 'how do social and individually actualized social landscapes relate to each other?', 'how is process-oriented planning to be designed?' and much more.

2.4.2 Autopoietic Systems Theory

Although Niklas Luhmann's systems theory has so far been used sporadically for the investigation of specific communication logics in relation to landscape, no extensively elaborated autopoietic systems of theoretical landscape theory has yet been developed. The radical constructivist approach to landscape-related topics has so far been limited primarily to some facets of the complex of topics, such as planning (van Assche and Verschraegen 2008), cultural and ecological adaptation (Van Assche 2010), energy system transformation (Kölsche 2015), nature conservation (Heiland 1999) or ecosystem services (Kühne 2014a), which, however, show the potential of Luhmann's systems theory for landscape research. In comparison to landscape research, the systems theoretical approach of the Luhmann type to space has a greater tradition (among many: Egner 2006; Goeke and Lippuner 2011; Lippuner 2007, 2008; Redepenning 2006, 2009).

Based on the autopoietic systems theory of Niklas Luhmann (1984, 1986, 1989, 1993, 1996, 2001[1997]), the following will deal with the communicative construction of landscape. For Luhmann, communication is the only genuine social action. Communication takes place in the threefold selection of information, communication, and understanding. Ex-post can be determined: Communication has then taken place if an understanding of Y follows the formation of a difference between information and communication from X (e.g. Luhmann 2017). In order to make the relationships between communication and landscape more comprehensible, some basic features of Luhmann's systems theory are first presented, followed by the communicative construction of landscape, before an interim summarizing conclusion is drawn in which the potentials of autopoietic systems theory for landscape research are presented.

In his formulation of autopoietic systems theory, Luhmann essentially draws on two strands of theory: firstly, radical constructivism, and secondly, structural functionalism. The neurological basis of radical constructivism is represented by the investigations of Maturana and Varela (1987): The nervous system is a self-contained, closed system[3] that has no direct access to its environment. Accordingly, consciousness is described as autopoietic (=self-producing): The consciousness is closed as regards its organization and thus autonomous, although it does not act self-sufficiently. In terms of its components, it has neither an input nor an output, although in terms of its biotic prerequisites it is both material and energetic (Maturana and Varela 1987). As a result of the impossibility of a direct reference of consciousness to its environment (Glasersfeld 1995; Maturana and Varela 1987; Steffe and Thompson 2000), the production of knowledge is described—according to radical constructivism—as a circular and closed, i.e. 'autopoietic' process. This ultimately means that knowledge is only produced from knowledge, communication from communication. The prerequisite for the construction of its environment by consciousness is the observation of this environment. Due to the autopoietic unity of consciousness, however, this observation does not take place directly, but on a biotic level (via sensory impressions that are transformed into nerve impulses). By observation Luhmann (1984), following the request of Spencer Brown (1971, p. 3), understands "draw a distinction" as a designation-on-the-use-of-a-distinction (for more details see: Kneer and Nassehi 1997). A prerequisite for observation is a perceptible difference. First, at the level of the observed environment, i.e. in relation to landscape, the objects observed as landscapes must differ from each other. Secondly, the sensory equipment of the observing organism must be able to detect the differences in the objects (which is not possible for humans pertaining to different infrared wavelengths). Third, the consciousness must be able to grasp the sensory perceived differences and place them in the context of the knowledge produced to this point, which in relation to landscape means: without the knowledge of which sensory distinctions can be identified in which spatial and social contexts, such as landscape, 'landscape' cannot be formed within consciousness (in this context among others: Burckhardt 2006; Kühne 2008d; Watzlawick 1995). Alongside radical constructivism, Luhmann's autopoietic systems theory is based on Talcott Parson's structural functionalism (1991[1951]). He describes modern society as a functionally differentiated society. Society thus differentiates itself into subsystems that take on specific tasks for the entire society, although these tasks cannot be taken on by other subsystems of society (Parsons 1991[1951]): The system of economy is responsible for the

---

[3]A system is understood to be a structure of effects whose elements are more closely connected to one another through direct mutual influences than with elements of their environment (Sachsse 1971).

production and distribution of scarce goods, the system of politics for the basic orientation of society, the system of social community for the transmission and maintenance of social roles, norms and values, the system of cultural trust for the preservation of social values (for details see e.g. Treibel, Korte and Schäfers 1997). The formation of systems and subsystems is associated with a reduction of complexity: Some of the many possible references are selected, but the vast majority of relations are excluded, which is why there is always a complexity gap between the system and the environment (Luhmann 1984).

Luhmann connects the two strands of theory by understanding society as subdivided into self-referential, i.e. autopoietically operating subsystems. Societal subsystems operate based on specific binary codes (the economy, for example, with the code have/do not have, politics: have power/do not have power), but are not in a position to grasp their environment 'as it is' (Luhmann 1984, 1986, 2001[1997]). In systems theory, the term environment is used to describe everything that is not the observing (sub)system, i.e. this also applies to other social subsystems, which is why, for example, the subsystem economy is environment to the subsystem politics. The observation of the environment according to the specific system codes means that the subsystem of the economy is observed with regard to the question of whether money can be earned with it or not, only those aspects of the environment which are connected with the profit or loss of money are observed, others lie outside the observation horizon (e.g. the extinction of species becomes relevant for the subsystem economy if economic losses, e.g. because economically exploitable species are affected or there exists a risk of loss of reputation/goodwill). The subsystem of politics, on the other hand, observes its environment based on the concept of power/non-power, i.e. in a democracy, whether voters can be won by dealing with a topic or not. The legal system is thereby resonated if there is a violation of existing law. For the subsystem of science, those parts of the environment that promise the production of new knowledge become relevant. From the perspective of autopoietic systems theory, the social construction of the world is always carried out selectively and according to the respective subsystemic logics, which means that it is not possible to grasp the world 'as it is' because a construction is always carried out on the basis of specific logics. This also means that processes can take place in the world that do not receive any attention in social communication because they do not resonate with any of the social subsystems, i.e. they do not exist in society. The ability of society to observe by de-complexing and de-differentiating the system reduces its stability and adaptability (e.g. when political or scientific questions are dealt with according to economic considerations, or when economic questions are dealt with politically; see Luhmann 1988, particularly, on the dangers of de-differentiation). As a result, the system of society is destabilized because society's ability to deal with challenges in a differentiated way is reduced (for more detailed introductions to Niklas Luhmann's sociology, see Kneer and Nassehi 1997; Reese-Schäfer 1992 and Fuchs 2004).

In the sense of systems theory, the construction of landscape can be understood as a systemic construction (Kühne 2006b): the construction of landscape within the consciousness means a reduction of complexity, because certain elements are selected from a multitude of spatially arranged elements and placed in relation to one another, while other elements are not considered in the construction of the landscape. With this complexity-reducing system formation, because not all elements are added to the system formation 'landscape', a segregation of meaning is connected, because the selected elements—in summary—are attributed the meaning 'landscape' on the basis and in relation to social ideas of 'landscape'. This interpretation is often made using adjectival additions such as 'beautiful', 'old industrial', 'sublime', 'historically grown', and 'typical'.

The construction of landscape takes place in the social subsystems according to the codes described above, provided that the social subsystems are set in resonance (Fig. 2.3). The social subsystems are particularly resonant when changes in the status quo are observed, either in relation to the material level (here often mediated by the science subsystem), or in relation to the communication of other social subsystems (such as evaluation by the mass media). The economic construction of landscape takes place according to the difference scheme of have/do not have, i.e. the question of whether and to what extent money is earned or lost with what is understood by landscape (e.g. in the form of agriculture, tourism, locations for industrial, or service enterprises). The relevance of landscape references for the economy increases when new possibilities for generating money emerge or when the loss of these very possibilities threatens; for the former, the energy system transformation is an example, for the latter, the second condition in land use. Here the interferences with the political system are already evident, which is then put into resonance when, for example, the promotion of the use of renewable energy sources promises an increase in power, whereby communication with the 'social soundboard' (Weber 2008) is primarily carried out through the mediation of (mass) media, which in turn are put into resonance when current changes can be observed (such as citizen protests or new scientific findings).

But not only the social construction of landscape follows (in large parts) the specific logics of the respective logic of the social subsystems; its inscription in the 'physical and biotic systems' also follows these patterns according to the codes of the individual social subsystems (Kühne 2006b, 2008b; Läpple 1992): The subsystem of the economy (particularly present in terms of area in the form of agriculture and forestry) is, according to the system's own code Have/Not-Have, interested in arranging material objects in a form that promises a particularly high yield (for example in the form of large farmland or age-group management; see also Ipsen 2006). The social subsystem of politics (especially environmental politics) intervenes in the design and arrangement of material objects on the basis of the power/non-power code (using laws, ordinances, guidelines and statutes; cf. also Warnke 1992), for example by modifying the unrestricted implementation of the logic of the economic system by legal requirements (for example, by linking the payment of subsidies to certain ecological standards). The subsystem also makes use of spatial planning, which—although bound by instructions—strives for the physical manifestation of its own disciplinary logics, for example in the sense of the model of the

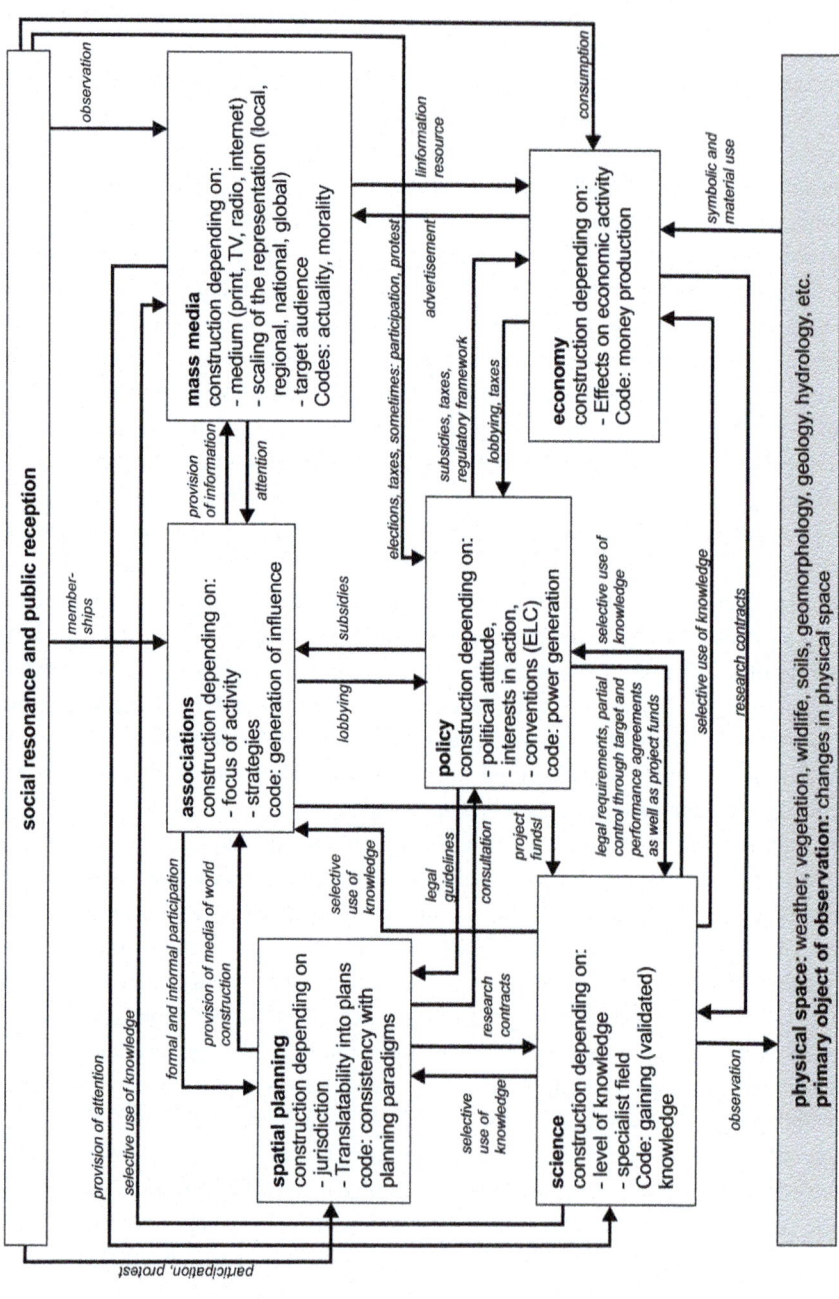

Fig. 2.3 Simplified scheme of the social subsystem specific observation of the respective environment and interferences between the different subsystems. (Based on Kühne 2014a; Weber 2008)

'compact city', on the basis of which an 'urban sprawl' is then to be prevented, whereby these planning specifications in turn are translated into the specific logics of the other subsystems, for example in the form of additional costs (van Assche and Verschraegen 2008). From this, it becomes clear how the different subsystemic logics of society inscribe themselves in the material world. These in turn (especially when changes occur) are observed and (re)constructed by the individual social subsystems according to their own codes (Kühne 2005a, 2014a). The expansion of a partial social code to the detriment of other codes is associated with the loss of a differentiated construction of the world—in this case landscape. Against this background, the attempt to understand the world in the form of 'ecosystem services' (among many: Grunewald and Bastian 2013; Schröter-Schlaack 2012; TEEB 2009) can also be understood: biotic and abiotic, cultural, social, etc., as well as the role of the world in the development of ecosystem services. Structures and functions are subordinated here to an expanding economic logic, independent of other possible sub-systemic observation and evaluation patterns.

Autopoietic system theory has the potential to comprehend subsystemic logics and their interferences. With regard to planning, Luhmann's theory of systems can be used to derive the objective from within Luhmann's theory of systems which is not to strive for central control of the design and placement of material objects, but to enable spaces for the self-control of the various social subsystems (also as the object and result of subsystemic interference) or to strive for control by stimulating the self-control of other social subsystems (van Assche and Verschraegen 2008). Here the limits of autopoietic system theory also become clear: Concrete statements about the design and arrangement of the material foundations of landscape cannot be derived from it—as with other constructivist theories. Through the macrosociological approach of autopoietic theory, i.e. it is oriented towards society as a whole and its subsystems, individual constructions of landscape fall out of its focus, i.e. if the relationship between the individual (who is not familiar with autopoietic systems theory) and society in relation to landscape is to be investigated, a theoretical framing with social constructivist landscape theory is more advisable.

2.4.3 Discourse Theory

Discourse-theoretical landscape research can be carried out to a large extent in the tradition of Jürgen Habermas, Michel Foucault, and that of Ernesto Laclau and Chantal Mouffe. Jürgen Habermas (1981) represents the normative concept of discourse, he sees discourse as the process of a nondominated discussion that is intended to make 'true' consensus possible. This understanding of discourse is specifically present in the discussion on participatory planning (see for example Heales 1997; Tewdwr-Jones 2002). Michel Foucault's discourse-theoretical approach, on the other hand, is analytical, i.e. it merely attempts to describe and fathom what exists. Central to Foucault (1977) is the deconstruction of discourses by means of historical genealogy. In the style of archaeological excavations, Foucault wants to uncover buried discourses that were considered 'natural' at the time. He thus shows how perfectly legitimized social 'truths' were created by temporally bound interpretations of the world. In relation to landscape, this means that social constructions, especially the norms for their interpretation and evaluation, are expressions of historical social conditions (see e.g. Wylie 2015). The following explanations follow the discourse theory of Laclau and Mouffe (Laclau and Mouffe 1985; Mouffe 2000, 2005). This discourse theory is based, among others, on Foucault (as well as on Saussure, Barthes and a non-economic Marxism), but it differs from the discourse theory of Foucault in two causal points: for Laclau and Mouffe there is no area of the non-discursive or pre-discursive, which means: all social relations are the temporary results of discursive confrontations. In comparison to Foucault, they focus on the limitations of discourses (Glasze 2008). In terms of landscape, this means: The discursive negotiation about landscape is not characterized by a temporal sequence of interpretation and evaluation patterns, but by the temporally variable competition of discourses.

The introductory remarks on the discourse theory according to Laclau and Mouffe make clear the temporary anchoring of meanings (see Kühne et al. 2016; Leibenath and Otto 2013, 2014; Weber 2015a, b, 2017b, 2018; Weber et al. 2017). The fundamental focus of the theoretical approach is the emphasis on the constructional character of our social negotiations and thus the rejection of an ultimately founded basis—an anti-essentialist approach (Laclau and Mouffe 1985). This means that there is no basis on which a specific interpretation of landscape would be based. What is understood as 'landscape' is reversible and the result of social negotiation processes (Weber 2015b, 2016b). A final fixation of landscape understandings is accordingly impossible. From such an impossibility "of a final fixation of meaning it follows that identities, social relations and 'spaces' are ultimately always contingent. Decisions that are made could therefore also turn out differently" (Weber 2015a, p. 101). However, the changeability of meanings is not reflected in everyday life, meanings and evaluations are usually understood as given and 'normal'.

This results in a temporary fixing of difference relationships. Differential relationships are understood to be linguistic signs "which are all fundamentally different from one another, but which are put into relation by being arranged in a row" (Weber 2015a, p. 104). Laclau and Mouffe (1985) describe this temporary fixation of differential relations as discourse. This excludes or suppresses alternative discourses and meanings. If 'landscape' is discursively closed as mesoscale space, interior spaces, for example, form the 'outside' of the discourse. If a discourse is organized around a central point—a node point—external borders are set at the same time: there is a demarcation from what the 'inside of the discourse' is *not*. *The more* 'self-evident' the connections of the inner discourse appear, the more powerful the discourse becomes—a 'hegemonic discourse'. If landscape is defined hegemonially as a 'beautiful, natural, and valuable area', trees are included in this area, while an antagonistic boundary is drawn to wind turbines for example (Leibenath and Otto 2012, 2013, 2014). In recent years, independent discourse-theoretical landscape research has developed with regard to the analysis of power processes, with which application-related issues such as the expansion of wind power and electricity grids are also taken into account. While in moderate social constructivism the level of physical objects has its own meaning, from a discourse-theoretical perspective, elements of 'external space' only become socially relevant through linguistic mediation. As a result, discourses *on* landscape are analysed, but fewer statements are made concerning the 'compelling' development of, physical foundations—such as the preservation of 'historically grown cultural landscapes' (for discussion on the construction of 'natural landscape' and 'cultural landscape' see Box 5). In an application-oriented way, discourse-theoretical alternative patterns of interpretation can be brought to the fore and thus show that other views than currently established meanings appear possible. When standards such as procedural fairness are formulated, they concern the rules of discursive processes that must be negotiated 'openly'.

Box 5: The Concepts of 'cultural landscape' and 'natural landscape'

In the professional dealing with landscape, the term 'cultural landscape', which appeared in German geography in the 1830s (Potthoff 2013), is updated, accentuated and discussed (among many: Antrop 1997; Bloemers et al. 2010; Czepczyński 2008; Henderson 2003; Jones and Daugstad 1997; Vervloet et al. 2010). The discussion about the definition of cultural and natural landscape is dominated by essentialist and positivist positions, while constructivist approaches dominate in the reflection of this discussion. Carol (1973, p. 147) understands the cultural landscape as "organised in contrast to the natural landscape". For Siekmann (2004, p. 32), this view means to distinguish "human […] action […] from non-human, natural events". In his classical definition Carl O. Sauer (1969[1925]), p. 46) writes: "The cultural landscape is fashioned from a natural landscape by a cultural group. Culture is the agent, the natural area is the medium, the cultural landscape is the result". Schmithüsen (1973, p. 167) focuses on the historicity of 'cultural landscape' in a positivist tradition of thought by defining cultural landscapes as "historically shaped entities in which the way of life and ideas of earlier societies are still effective reality in a variety of ways, even in the present".

The (dichotomous) separation of cultural and natural landscape, however, is also subject to intense criticism, whereby the critique makes use of the constructivist and sometimes the positivist perspective: Haber (2000) criticizes (relying on constructivist interpretation) that landscape is an expression of culture and is only expressed in cultural perception (similar to Winchester et al. 2003). Termeer (2007) argues in his etymologically justified rejection of the concept of 'cultural landscape': "The syllable '-schaft' [in German; in English: -scape;] already refers to human activity, in this respect a preposition of 'culture' before 'landscape' creates a pleonasm". Konold's criticism (1996, p. 5) is positivistically justified when he states, "in Central Europe almost all landscapes are cultural landscapes, shaped by man according to his needs and his respective possibilities". Tress and Tress

(2001, p. 55) also argue positivistically by emphasizing the hybrid character of landscape: "Since humans have existed, they have influenced and changed landscapes. The landscapes are the visible product of this influence. Landscape is neither created solely from nature nor from culture".

In consideration of the arguments, Heiland (2006)—constructivistically informed—pleads for the further use of the terms, after all, in landscape research it is by no means exclusively a question of describing current states, but rather of depicting "past and future states and phenomena, or even states and phenomena that can only be imagined or desired (otherwise there would hardly be the concepts of good, truth, freedom, God, etc.)". (Heiland 2006, p. 49). Schenk (2011, p. 14), on the other hand, sees the use of the phrase 'cultural landscape' as a 'strategic pleonasm' "in order to mark the spatial effectiveness of man in a historical perspective at the centre of [the] interest" (Schenk 2011).

2.5 'More-Than-Representational' Approaches

With the development of constructivist approaches, there has been a strong shift of focus towards the dimension of the social and partly individual construction of landscape. Since the turn of the last century, this focus has increasingly led to a counter-movement that is striving to bring the material back into the focus of scientific investigation (e.g. Duineveld et al. 2017; Waterton et al. 2013; Wylie 2003).

In comparison to the other presented theoretical approaches to landscape, which assume a strong subject-object-separation, the following will deal with approaches that take an 'intermediate' position in this respect, i.e. that want to abolish this separation. In contrast to representational (positivist or constructivist) theories, the focus of "more-than-representational" theories (Lorimer 2005, p. 85; cf. also Ingold 1993; McCormack 2003; Thrift 2008; Waterton 2013) lies specifically in focusing on the mutual influence of man and non-humans, which also removes the dichotomous separation between man/society and environment (Krauss 2018). To this end, the phenomenological landscape research will first be focused on somewhat more extensively, since on the one hand these essential features of the more-than-representational-approaches' will be made clear, and on the other hand, since a comprehensive state of research has been achieved here. In one sense, the approaches discussed here show a close connection to social constructivism, on the foundations of which these 'more-than-representational-approaches' are ultimately based by extending them (Waterton 2013), and in another sense they take essentialist borrowings. Subsequently, the actor network theory and the assemblage theory will be presented, which enable an integration of the material into (social science) landscape research (in the spatial sciences: Färber 2014; Mattissek and Wiertz 2014; Murdoch 1998; van Wezemael and Loepfe 2009).

2.5.1 Phenomenology

Social constructivist and phenomenological landscape research—as already mentioned—are closely related to each other, since they have the same phenomenological
roots. Nevertheless, the approaches have clearly diverged so that a separate presentation seems to make sense. Phenomenology is associated with thinkers such as Edmund
Husserl (1913), Maurice Merleau-Ponty (1962), Martin Heidegger (2005[1927]), but also
with Alfred Schütz (1971), already mentioned in the context of social constructivism.
Phenomenology can be understood as the study and description of phenomena. All units,
things, and events that present themselves to the world (Moran 2002; Tilley 1997, 2005)
and present themselves to the subject are understood as phenomena: "Phenomenology
involves the understanding and descripton of things as they are exprienced by a subject"
(Tilley 1997, p. 12). The starting point of the phenomenological conception of the world
are sensual experiences, behind whose phenomena its 'essence' is sought (Sokolowski
2000), through which it essentially pursues an essentialist world view and can certainly
be seen in the tradition of romantic science (Wylie 2018), which sought to form a unity
of cognitive, moral, and intuitively aesthetic ideas (Eisel 2009). Phemomenology chooses
a third path between an empirical-inductive (as is characteristic of positivism) and a
theoretical-deductive approach (such as autopoietic systems theory). Phenomenology
takes thought, speech, and action as its object, in which starting from a concrete case
(whether imaginary or real), something essential and fundamental is intuitively deduced.
This basic principle refers to the experience of the world (not its analysis), which must be
described. The phenomenologically oriented landscape researcher thus becomes a "story-
teller" (Tuan 1989, p. 240): "His or her description is inexpungibly mixed with exegesis
and intepretation, for ordinary language not only contains interpretative conjunctions that
invite use (since, for, because, therefore, etc.), but is also very rich in words that rever-
berate—that hint at relationships—beyond their literal meanings". In contrast to artistic
description, this description is based on explicit terms whose understanding she formulates (cf. Moran 2002; Sokolowski 2000). Accordingly, the goal of a phenomenological
turn to the world does not lie in the collection of objective data or in the definitive and
irrevocable recognition of the 'essence' of the subject of the concern (e.g. landscape).
Rather, this goal is to achieve a subjective gain in knowledge in which perception and
affect take on an outstanding significance, which Wylie (2005, p. 236) characterizes as
follows: "A percept is a style of visibility, of being-visible, a configuration of light and
matter that exceeds, enters into, and ranges over the perceptions of a subject who sees.
An affect is an intensity, a field perhaps of awe, irritation or serenity, which exceeds,
enters into, and ranges over the sensations and emotions of a subject who feels".

From a phenomenological perspective, landscape can be understood as a space that
is lived through in both individual and collective everyday action. People accordingly
live in, with, and from the landscape, they become "existential insiders" (Bourassa 1991,
p. 3) of this landscape. Landscape is experienced by living in it, by using it, by moving
in it (Grömer et al. 2012). On the other hand, this means, as Berleant (1997, p. 11) makes
clear: "Landscapes, too, bear the mark of their inhabitants". The familiar environment is

not made up solely of material objects, but includes the relationships, community activities, traditions, spatial norms of action, world views, etc., experienced there (Forbes 2007). A "landscape understood in this way is the space of human life appropriated by human work and human action" (Piepmeier 1980, p. 38). A landscape understood in this way emerges from the meanings given to spatial arrangements, for without these meanings landscape would be a mere environment (Forbes 2007). Tilley (1997) states that meaning in turn arises from human confrontation with the material world, whose medium is the human body. Using one's own body as a medium, being in the world can be understood by other people both in the present and in the past (see also Berleant 1997, Barrett and Ko 2009; Rebay-Salisbury 2013). Accordingly, phenomenology accepts different interpretations of landscape (Johnson 2012), which are different and interrelated in conflict. Thus, the experience of landscape is not only dependent on its character, but also on the personal knowledge and moods of the person experiencing it, as well as their changes. For Berleant (1997), this is the difference between environment and landscape: environment is thus understood—as a more general expression—as objectively given space; landscape, on the other hand, is a special space with which individual experience is associated. "The key concern in this approach is the manner by which places *constitute* space as centres of human meaning, their singularity being manifested in the day-to-day experiences and consciousness of people within particular lifeworlds" (Tilley 1997, pp. 14–15; emphasis in original). 'Place' is inseparably linked to the experiences and meanings of a location, while 'Space' is a more abstract construct, based on the experience of 'place', which brings it together and separates it from its immediate meanings (see for example Relph 1976 and Tilley 1997).

From a phenomenological perspective, the relations between subject and object are to be understood relationally (Gibson 1979; Chemero 2003). The resolution of the (construct) of the subject-object dichotomy takes place on both sides: On the one hand, a constant change of the 'subject' takes place by dealing with 'objects', whereby artefacts are to be understood as part of the human cognitive system (DeMarrais et al. 2004; Renfrew and Zubrow 1994; Rebay-Salisbury 2013). On the other hand, knowledge inscribes itself so intensively into the human body, becoming so firmly anchored in it, that it can hardly be articulated on a cognitive basis (Sørensen and Rebay-Salisbury 2012). In the landscape context, this can mean on the one hand that buildings, corridors, infrastructures, etc. can be understood as externalised cognitive artefacts, and on the other hand that landscape (as a material object) is shaped by habitualised and no longer reflected knowledge, such as certain (traditional) tree pruning, irrigation and drainage methods, etc. In the context of the landscape, this can mean that buildings, corridors, infrastructures, etc., can be understood as externalised cognitive artefacts. Lorimer (2005, p. 85) summarises the mutual interpenetration of landscape and man as "embodied acts of landscaping" and Berleant (1997, p. 109) summarises: "A landscape, an environment, even more, is embodied experience". Phenomenological landscape research by no means focuses solely on a rational approach: "Emotions are [...] closely connected with material culture, places in the landscape as well as human actions, practices and rituals" (Rebay-Salisbury 2013, p. 63). This emotional attention to landscape as well as its multisensory experience focuses phenomenological landscape attention on atmospheres (Kazig 2007, 2013; detailed in: Nogué i Font 1993 Sect. 2.5.1), replacing distanced observation of what is called landscape (as in constructivist approaches) with an in-the-landscape observation (Wylie 2007). It is thus not a social or individual construction, instead becoming the starting point for a mental and physical integration (Ingold 2002).

The current phenomenological research focus is not free of predecessors within landscape science, for example Passarge (1929) or Hellpach (1950[1911]) pursued a phenomenological research program, but without the decided theoretical foundation that current phenomenological research exhibits. Historical precursors in the first decades of the 20th century and humanist geography in the 1970s, put human action, human consciousness, and human creativity into the focus of their reflections, such as Tuan (1976), Buttimer (1980) or Relph (1976). As a result, Wylie (2007, p. 140) calls the reapplication of phenomenological approaches a "re-emergence" (see also Wylie 2018). Hard (1995, p. 133), for example, expresses criticism of the phenomenological approach: "The limitations of the phenomenological approach are clear: as an intersubjective empirical test, there is nothing available to it but the reader's consenting understanding on the basis of related life experience in this area of life".

As a result of the close 'relationship' between social constructivist and phenomenological landscape research, the differences are briefly outlined below: While social constructivism has established itself as a social science theory, phenomenology is primarily a philosophical approach to the world, which has an effect on landscape research: Whereas social constructivist landscape research focuses on social processes of landscape construction, phenomenological landscape research is more concerned with the effects and meanings of 'landscape' for the individual human being. In this context, another substancial difference between social constructivist and phenomenological landscape research also becomes clear: While social constructivist research focuses on the construction processes of landscape concepts, phenomenological research is more strongly oriented towards questions of practices, appropriations, meanings, and changes of 'landscape', whereby its understanding of landscape is strongly materialized and not—as in social constructivist landscape research—taking place on the level of social (and thus connected: individual) processes.

2.5.2 Actor Network Theory

The 'actor network theory' (abbreviated ANT), which is already widespread in geography (Bosco 2015), is based on the work of the French sociologists Michel Callon and Bruno Latour as well as the British scientist John Law (Kneer 2009a; Law and Hassard 1999). Its aim is to break down the common distinctions in science (but also beyond that in politics and administration or in everyday use) especially those between society and nature as well as between society and technology with the help of the network concept (Bosco 2015; Castree 2002; Haraway 1991; Murdoch 1998; Schulz-Schaeffer 2000). The ANT transcends the classical understanding of social theory; after all, it is characterized precisely by a dissolution of the boundaries between the understanding of the social and the dimensions of the world previously defined by it. 'Natural' and man-made, animate and inanimate objects are regarded as part of the social world, and no longer the societies and communities of man alone. Social, technical and natural units, and factors are treated "as explananda rather than explanans by the actor network theory" (Schulz-Schaeffer 2000, p. 188). Thus the "explanation of nature with the help of social factors or conversely of society with the help of natural-technical factors [...] is explicitly excluded" (Kneer 2009a, p. 19). In the understanding of ANT, the world is made up of a network of references that can be material or immaterial. Acting human and non-human objects are called 'actants' in the ANT. The references of different actants in the network are quite variable, as Latour (2002[1999], p. 218) vividly illustrates: "With the weapon in your hand until you hold someone else, and even the weapon in your hand is no longer the same. You are another subject because you hold the weapon; the weapon is another object because it maintains a relationship with you. No longer is it the weapon in the arsenal or the weapon in the drawer or the weapon in the bag, no, now it is the weapon in your hand, aimed at someone who cries out for his life". Instead of the separate conceptualization of distinct subjects and objects, of societies and things, of people, animals, and plants, the investigation of networks takes place: Each 'thing' is understood as the result of networked relationships, landscape correspondingly as a network of 'things' (e.g. trees, houses, people) that stand in different relation to other 'things' (streams, other people, other houses), whereby these relationships are always subject to a certain contingency (i.e. can be changed in certain frames, e.g. by other people).

The equal, but always contextualized, treatment of human and non-human actants can be regarded as connectable and fruitful for landscape research, since here the reciprocal influence cannot be examined and theoretically framed in an abstract form as 'nature' or 'culture', but in relation to individual 'actants', i.e. something that acts without which it would be subject to the specific logic of an acting human being (in more detail in Bosco 2015). The ANT can be understood as a radicalization of social constructivism: It integrates the 'outside' of social constructivism, namely 'nature', into the contemplation. Social constructivism, on the other hand, focuses on the understanding of social contexts (Schulz-Schaeffer 2000); non-human objects are not excluded theoretically, but they only become relevant if they experience a symbolic, emotional, aesthetic connotation. In this respect, there are possibilities for extending and shifting the focus in relation to social constructivist landscape research. Accordingly, non-human actors are ascribed the possibility to determine landscape independently.

Through the integration of science into the network of actants, a self-observation problem arises that is already inherent in the constructivist approaches (in the form of the observation of society in which scientists are integrated). ANT makes this problem even more virulent: That scientists no longer look at their objects from an elevated perspective but are themselves entangled in the networks of the actants (and not only, as in social constructivism, in those of the human!). Another criticism made of the ANT is the creation and use of its own terminology, which makes 'spontaneous connectivity' more difficult (autopoietic systems theory was also confronted with such a criticism). This terminology follows from the formulation of an own research program and facilitates interdisciplinary

work; after all, none of the participating disciplines can make use of the ancestral terminology; rather, the participating researchers must acquire the theory, including their own
terminology, from the participants (cf. Bosco 2015; Färber 2014; Schulz-Schaeffer 2000).

In addition to being able to connect specifically to social constructivist approaches
(this does not apply to radical constructivist approaches that strongly emphasize the
level of communication), the ANT proves to be able to connect to critical research, so
the asymmetrical distribution of power can be reconstructed when dealing with networks
(Färber 2014). The wide thematic range that can be worked on with the ANT as a theoretical framework (without classical pre-categorization such as city and country, nature
and culture) makes it attractive for interdisciplinary landscape research (Färber 2014).

2.5.3 Assemblage Theory

The spread of constructivist approaches in spatial social sciences was associated with a
departure from the consideration of the material (Kazig and Weichhart 2009). Assemblage
theory attempts to give greater consideration to materialities in this scientific context
(Landa 2006). The aim is to integrate materiality into a principally constructivist thought
structure using the French authors Gilles Deleuze and Félix Guattari. The aim is to avoid
falling into essentialist or geodeterminist interpretations (Mattissek and Wiertz 2014).
Assemblage theory can be understood as an approach "that addresses social ensembles
on the basis of the processes they generate. It conceptualizes processes of creation and
transformation of social ensembles called assemblages and proposes an approach to the
analysis of generative processes" (van Wezemael and Loepfe 2009, p. 108).

Assemblage theory focuses on the types of relationship between social constructs and
the material substrates of the world. Material things become socially relevant when they
are negotiated discursively (Mattissek and Wiertz 2014). It is not the essentialist question
of what is material 'in the core' or 'in essence' that is negotiated, but how material (social)
can work (van Wezemael and Loepfe 2009). The material is thus also understood as a consequence of discursive negotiations (Mattissek and Wiertz 2014), for example by deciding
in spatial planning which claims may materialise and which may not (e.g. nature reserve or
industrial estate). In addition to the connection to the discourse theory, the assemblage theory can also be made fruitful for critical spatial and landscape research (Färber 2014). In this
context, the theme of 'inverse landscapes' could also be taken up, even if these were formulated out of social constructivist tradition, i.e. those contingent offers of materialization that
did not materialize because alternative interests had greater assertiveness (Kühne 2013a, b).

2.6 Neopragmatism

Neopragmatism is already spreading in urban and regional development research (e.g.
Chilla, Kühne et al. 2015; Chilla et al. 2016; Eckardt 2014) and offers less a new theoretical
basis for landscape research than a more object-oriented approach to theoretical principles.

The first approaches to philosophical pragmatism date back to the 16th century, to Francis Bacon, but philosophers such as William James, Charles S. Peirce, and John Dewey formulated them in the last third of the 19th century. The central statement of philosophical pragmatism lies in the superiority of practical criteria over theory. Thus, pragmatism assumes that the practical consequences and effects of action, meanings, and truths should determine action, not moral principles or great theoretical buildings. Truth is thus constituted by usefulness and usability. This means, for example, that from a pragmatic perspective it is sufficient to assume the 'existence' of the city of Bielefeld if—even if the person dealing with the subject has visited a place with this name—acquaintances have visited a place called 'Bielefeld', media reports exist about 'Bielefeld', publishers indicate the place of publication 'Bielefeld', and this place is listed on street maps and atlases (even if the 'Bielefeld conspiracy' that has been circulating for some time claims the opposite).

Philosophical pragmatism has had a major influence on research at the Chicago School (Joas 1988; Schubert et al. 2010), which has had a strong impact on the social sciences. The 'Chicago School' is characterized by a strongly empirical research program, dealing with urban processes of change, later (especially after the Second World War) with symbolic communication. Research in a pragmatic tradition is characterised by a 'medium' research horizon. In the social science context, they are neither limited to the micro-level (such as the family) of society, nor are they aimed at macro-sociologically exploring the development of 'society as a whole', for example in order to develop comprehensive theories on the development of society (such as systems theory). The focus—in the tradition of the Chicago School's 'community studies'—is on neighborhoods to entire cities (Eckardt 2014), in the context of regional studies rather than (partially) regional units.

Neopragmatic space research (whether with reference to city or region, landscape or general space) differs from pragmatic approaches by its meta-perspective and—associated with it—by a stronger inclusion of theoretical elements. Insofar as a gain in understanding of social developments and contexts can be expected, different constructivist and empirical (or positivist) approaches (and research methods) are combined (Eckardt 2014; Fine 2000). Neopragmatic research is primarily concerned with looking at an object of research from different perspectives in order to obtain a differentiated picture of it by means of 'theoretical' and empirical 'triangulation'. Accordingly, neopragmatic research also accepts (partial) contradictions between theoretical approaches and the relationship between theory and empirical method. Thus, a constructivist theoretical perspective can also be combined with methods of quantitative social research, which are usually assigned to a positivist basic understanding; if it is reflected that quantitative results also ultimately represent an element of social construction of the world (Kühne 2018d).

Compared to 'classical' theoretical approaches, there is another difference in neopragmatic approaches: If the former focus primarily on 'world explanation' (as in particular in the context of positivism or essentialism), neopragmatic approaches can also be related to generating action guidelines for political or administrative practice (Chilla et al. 2015, 2016; Weber et al. 2016). Neopragmatic landscape research is therefore suitable not only for combining different interdisciplinary research disciplines, but also for combining science and practice in a transdisciplinary way. Neopragmatic landscape research thus has great potential in questions that are characterized by a reference to application and by a certain explorativity (in terms of both empiricism and theory). This theoretical as well as empirical openness in the search for 'useful' knowledge contradicts teleological thinking (for a focused comparison of the different approaches: Box 6).

Box 6: Current theoretical accesses to landscape-a brief summary
The theoretical approaches to landscape research presented here have different potentials and restrictions, which means that they are suitable for different questions in a differentiated way.

Essentialist landscape research, in its search for the 'essence of landscape' expressed through material phenomena, is difficult to operationalize empirically or to connect with constructivist approaches. However, with its strong normativity (the 'essential' of a landscape must be preserved!) it is able to give planning processes a goal. Positivistic approaches, which understand landscape as a material object, are aimed at analyzing this object or its 'perception' in a dissecting way. Normative statements are not in the foreground.

In constructivist approaches, the social dimension is the constitutive one for landscape. Depending on the theoretical orientation, questions of the emergence and dissemination of patterns of interpretation and evaluation in relation to landscape (social constructivism), the question of specific system logics in the construction of landscape (autopoietic systems theory) or the question of the striving for discourse sovereignty (discourse theory) are in the focus of consideration. Phenomenological approaches, assemblage theory, and ANT fill a gap in scientific theory that gapes between constructivist and positivist approaches to the world by addressing the question of how material, social, and ultimately individual are interwoven. Neopragmatism does not offer such a new approach; it places a theoretical triangulation alongside the classical methodological triangulation in social research by aligning theoretical focuses primarily with the (initially assumed) usefulness of results. The difference between a neopragmatic approach and a simple combination, e.g. a positivist and essentialist perspective, to support essentialist landscape theories with empirical research (such as savannah theory, see Box 2) lies in the conceptual reflectiveness of the combination, in which opportunities, contradictions, and problems are weighed against each other in a documented way.

With regard to scientific disciplinary orientations, different theoretical preferences can be identified: An essentialist approach can be found specifically in classical geography, but also in landscape architecture and planning; positivist approaches are present specifically in scientific landscape research as well as in the majority of environmental psychological spatial research; constructivist approaches dominate in social science and new cultural geography research, while more-than-representational approaches can be located specifically in more recent cultural science-oriented landscape research (more on this in Sect. 4.4 and also in Jorgensen 2011).

A brief comparison of the presented theories can be found in Table 2.2.

Table 2.2 Comparison of the presented theories. (According to: Chilla et al. 2016; Kühne et al. 2018)

	Word origin	Landscape understanding	Constituent level	The Self-Conception of Landscape Scientists	Focus	Aims	Sample publications
Essentialism	From Latin: *essentia*	'landscape' as a 'wholeness' in the sense of an 'independent being'	The 'essence' of 'landscape' lies at the core of perceptible phenomena	'landscape' can only be grasped by reasonable persons	Exploration of essential properties of 'landscape' in the object itself	Formulating normative assertions about landscape	Lautensach (1973), Orians (1980, 1986)
	Word origin	Landscape understanding	Constituent level	The Self-Conception of Landscape Scientists	Focus	Aims	Sample publications
Positivism	From Latin: *positivus* (set, given)	'landscape' as a real object that can be empirically explored and generalized by counting, measuring, and weighing individual phenomena.	Physical space	'landscape' can be captured by people trained in empiricism	Objective description of 'landscape' using empirical methods	Reconstruct a picture of the landscape as exact as possible, analyse structures and processes	Bastian and Schreiber (1999), Kearney and Bradley (2011), Sahraoui et al. (2016)
Social constructivism	From Latin: *construere* (assemble, layer)	'landscape' is not understood as a physical object, but as a social or individual construction.	Social level	Focus on 'landscapes' as social constructs with multiple perspectives	'landscape' as a result of social negotiation processes	Explore processes of landscape construction	Cosgrove (1984), Greider and Garkovich (1994), Kühne (2018b)

(continued)

Table 2.2 (continued)

	Word origin	Landscape understanding	Constituent level	The Self-Conception of Landscape Scientists	Focus	Aims	Sample publications
Autopoietic systems Theory	From ancient Greek: *autos* (self) and *poiein* (create, make, build)	'landscape' is the result of communication processes.	Social level	'landscape' as a possible object of social communication, observed by the scientist trained in autopoietic systems theory	Investigation of different system logics with regard to the construction of 'landscapes'	Understanding of the system-specific communication of landscape and the interferences between the social subsystems	Heiland (1999), Van Assche (2010), Kühne (2014)
Discourse theory after the	From latin: discursus (walking around)	'landscape' emerges from competing discourses.	Social level	Scientists trained in discourse theory strive for a hegemonic interpretation of 'landscape'	Constitution and transformation of diacursive formations into 'landscape'	Understanding the power structures underlying 'landscape' discourses	Leibenath and Otto (2013), Weber (2016, 2018)
Phenomenology (also other more-than-representational theories)	From ancient Greek: *phainómenon* (apparitional); *lógos* (doctrine	'landscape' emerges from the meanings that a space acquires.	Between individual and material level	Individual attention to 'landscape', in reflection of one's own knowledge, moods and preferences	Effects and meanings of 'landscape'	Individual approach to 'landscape'	Tuan (1989), Tilley (1997), Wylie (2005)
Neopragmatism	From ancient Greek: *néos* (new, young), *pragma* (action, thing)	The understanding of the 'landscape' depends on the respective question.	Tends to be at the social level, but depends on the question posed	In theoretical accesses to 'landscape' trained scientist selects well-founded theoretical approaches	Usually: Interactions between the individual, society and physical space	Maximizing knowledge through a multi-perspective approach to the theme of 'landscape'	Eckardt (2014), Chilla et al. (2015, 2016)

Aesthetic Approaches to Landscape

The question of aesthetic qualities (in essentialist and positivist thought traditions) and aesthetic ascriptions (in constructivist approaches) of landscapes (as social constructions, in constructivist perspectives) belong to central aspects of landscape research (among many: Augenstein 2002; Berleant 1997; Berr 2008; Brady 2003; Brook 2018; Bourassa 1990, 1991; Burckhardt 2006; Dettmar 2004; Duncan and Duncan 2004; Fontaine 2017a; Gobster et al. 2007; Hartz and Kühne 2009; Hauck and Hennecke 2017; Hauser and Kamleithner 2006; Hoisl et al. 1987; Jedicke 2013; Jongen 2008; Jorgensen 2011; Kaymaz 2012; Kazig 2016; Krauss 1974; Kühne 2012b; Kühne et al. 2017; Linke 2017a; Nohl 2001a, 2001b, 2015; Parsons and Daniel 2002; Porteus 2013; Sahraoui et al. 2016; Schirpke et al. 2013, 2013; Schönwald 2017; Tuan 1989; Wöbse 2002). Different interpretations and meanings of the relationship between aesthetic judgements and landscapes have developed, from which very different normative consequences can be derived. However, before these developments are discussed, a brief introduction to aesthetics is given, with a focus on philosophical aspects, supplemented by social science approaches (more detailed introductions to different scientific approaches to aesthetics can be found, for example, in Dickie 1973, 1997; Graham 2005; Liessmann 2009; Majetschak 2016; Reicher 2015; Scheer 2015[1997]; Schneider 2005; Schweppenhäuser 2007).

3.1 Aesthetics: Between Philosophy and Experiment

The term 'aesthetics', derived from ancient Greek, refers to the doctrine of sensory perception (*Aisthetical Episteme*) and is thus complementary to the doctrine of thinking (*Logical Episteme*) and morality (*Ethical Episteme*). Here, also, the old European—and to this day still influential—(often normatively understood) idea of the unity of truth, beauty, and good becomes clear that only that which is also true and good can be beautiful or the thought vice versa: What is true and beautiful must also be good or

© Springer Fachmedien Wiesbaden GmbH, part of Springer Nature 2019
O. Kühne, *Landscape Theories*, RaumFragen: Stadt – Region – Landschaft,
https://doi.org/10.1007/978-3-658-25491-9_3

the beautiful and good must also be true (e.g. in Augustinus 1962[390] and Psyeudo-Dionysius Areopagita 1988[around 500]). Nevertheless, it was not until Alexander Gottlieb Baumgarten's 'Aesthetica' (2009[1750–1758]) developed into an independent philosophical sub-discipline (Gilbert and Kuhn 1953; Reicher 2015), which "increasingly displaces the paradigm of an ontologically founded theory of beauty that has survived from antiquity and the Middle Ages" (Schneider 2005, p. 7). Baumgarten conceives a complementary relationship between aesthetic art and logical science, which Ritter (1996, p. 43) outlines as follows: "Where all of nature, which belongs to our existence as heaven and earth, can no longer be expressed as a concept of science, the sentient sense aesthetically and poetically produces the image and the word in which it can present itself in its belonging to our existence and assert its truth". The complementarity of (analytical) science and aesthetic observation results from the different but complementary directions of investigation: while (analytical) science divides structures, functions and processes into individual parts in order to then subject them to investigation, the philosophical-aesthetic approach brings together different phenomena—starting from a sensory perception—to form its synthesis (e.g. Hahn 2017; Peres 2013). Since the second half of the 19th century, however, an analytically oriented empirical or experimental aesthetic has developed (Gustav Theodor Fechner 1871). Empirical aesthetics draws analytically on the experience of individual subjects, using different methods of empirical social research (quantitative as well as qualitative). Experimental aesthetics, on the other hand, can be defined as that part of empirical aesthetics that "investigates causal hypotheses with the help of experiments, guided by theory" (Kebeck and Schroll 2011, p. 15). As regards landscape, the empirical approaches discussed in Sect. 2.3, which depict the 'aesthetic quality' of landscapes understood as objects in numerical values, can be found. As a result of the changeability of both social interpretations and sensual impressions from physical arrangements, aesthetics (as well as the social sciences) "do not completely and permanently succeed in the theoretical recording of their objects" (Pfütze 2016, p. 87).

According to Majetschak (2016, p. 87), Baumgarten, Kant and Hegel are of central importance for the fundamentals of (specifically philosophical) aesthetics, as they have since served to form theories on aesthetic questions "either as motivic quarries or as a foil for critical debate". In this respect, these authors will be given more intensive attention subsequently. Following (and extending) Kühne (2018e), six central threads of discussion on aesthetics (and landscape) are outlined below.

3.2   Aesthetic Judgements Between Beauty, Picturesqueness, Sublimity and Ugliness

Beauty, often conceived as a "unity in diversity" (Schweppenhäuser 2007, p. 63), forms the central concept of aesthetic reflections; accordingly, the development of aesthetics can also be understood as a history of "a constant reinterpretation of the concept of beauty" (Borgeest 1977, p. 100). Thus Kant (1959[1790]) understands the beautiful as something that is generally pleasing without a term, i.e. there would be no direct (e.g. economic) individual or social interest in an object described as 'beautiful'. A classic example from landscape research: Only persons with sufficient distance (in terms of economic interests, but also—and this will have to be discussed in Sect. 3.6—education) are in a position to perceive a physical space called landscape as 'beautiful', not the farmer who earns his living with the physical foundations of landscape. John Dewey (1958, 1988[1934]) contradicts the Kantian separation between the aesthetic and the practical world by describing 'beauty' as thoroughly consuming (e.g. in the practice of tourist attention to 'landscapes'), whereby a reference to objects guided by individual interests takes place. In other words, he contradicts a conceptual separation of aesthetic experience and ordinary life processes by stating a continuum between everyday experience and aesthetic experience. In a formulation that focuses more strongly on the hybrid, the aesthetic attention can then always be understood as a hybrid of life-worldly and aesthetic experience. In relation to landscape, this means that its production falls back on aesthetic as well as life-worldly (e.g. individual-functional, emotional, and cognitive) patterns of interpretation and evaluation, so that the individual (but also the social) construct landscape is always the result of a hybrid approach (the subject of hybridization is dealt with in more detail in Sect. 6.3). According to Seel (1985), the patterns of aesthetic access to the world that have been shaped are again dependent on experience, whereby aesthetic experience has become a "self-reflexive experience of the world in which we live, in other words an 'experience of experience'" (Lehmann 2016, p. 31). Aesthetic experiences, on the other hand, "are connected with direct generation of meaning, since they convey the supposedly simple feeling of existing and of affirming this existence" (Bosch 2018, p. 25). With the expansion of the aesthetic, at the latest since the designed formation of everyday objects, that which is useful can also be regarded as aesthetic (see e.g. Dorschel 2002). This also opens up new patterns of interpretation and evaluation for the aesthetic attention paid to landscape: not only is the 'romantic landscape' aesthetically charged, but everyday or industrially transformed physical spaces are also subjected to an appreciative aesthetic charge (see Box 7).

Box 7: Post-industrialization and landscape

In the context of phases of social upheaval and their physical manifestations, there is an intensification of the focus on the theme of landscape. With the transition from an agricultural to an industrial society, the wild respective of the agrarian landscape was constructed as aesthetically pleasing and worth preserving by an ever-increasing proportion of the population. Today, in the countries of Western Europe and North America, as well as in Japan, post-industrialization processes have been taking place since the 1960s (Bell 1999[1973]), i.e. the importance of the secondary economic sector (industry) is declining compared to that of the tertiary sector (services). From a spatial point of view, we can speak of a change from "industrial space" to "post-industrial space" (Lash and Urry 1994, p. 193; Harrison 1994). This is particularly evident in the old industrial regions of Western Europe and North America (such as the Central English industrial region, the Ruhr area, the so-called 'Rust Belt' of the United States). As the spatial representations of the pre-industrial era (such as castles, but also agricultural land) experienced a symbolic and aesthetic charge with increasing industrialization, such a new connotation takes place in the phase of post-industrialization with the objects of the industrial era (among many: Hall 1995; Hauser 2001, 2004; Herrington 2006; Hoppmann 2000; Liessmann 1999; Pregill and Volkman 1999; Schwarzer 2014). Traditional patterns of interpretation and aestheticization from the phase of industrialization are taken up and transferred. Old industrial cityscapes "associate baroque ruin aesthetics with decaying blast furnaces and memories of the picturesque garden of the eighteenth century" (Hauser 2004, p. 154; see also Herrington 2006; Howard 2011). In a romantic tradition, ruins symbolize doubts about the success of progress (Trigg 2009) and—here using the example of the Duisburg Nord Landscape Park (Fig. 3.1)—are connected with elements of classical park design (Chilla 2005, p. 184): "Park elements and the diverse use of plants alienate the old industrial heritage, at the same time enhancing it visually and making it usable for local recreation". With the abandonment of the industrial uses of objects, these—provided they are not torn down—are subjected to connotative recoding, although the former functions remain latent (Dettmar 2003, 2004; Hasse 1993; Ipsen 2006). Old industrial objects become symbols of the "simple, hard working life" (Vicenzotti 2005, p. 231). On the one hand, this symbolic charge follows the evaluation scheme of the 'simple, hard, and rural community life' of the time of transition from the agricultural to the industrial social order; on the other hand, it represents a reaction to the de-standardization and fragmentation of post-industrial society (cf. Eisel 2009; Höfer 2001). In addition, old industrial properties offer an opportunity to experience new landscapes (Herrington 2006; Schönwald 2015). This process can be influenced by the idealization of industry, the experience of the specific nature of old industrial sites and the offer of the interpretation pattern of old industrial ensembles as wild nature (Höfer and Vicenzotti 2013; Schwarzer 2014).

The concept of beauty is supplemented by the concept of sublimity: while beauty—according to Edward Burke (1989[1757])—inspires love, sublimity inspires admiration. Accordingly, the experience of sublimity is associated with large, impressive or horrible objects, such as volcanoes, forests that are difficult to penetrate, mostly with objects from the realm of the 'natural', to which Berleant (1997, p. 28) refers. The experience of beauty, on the other hand, follows the perception of small and pleasant objects. Kant moves away from Burke's strong fixation on objects in his understanding of beauty and sublimity by founding the 'beautiful' "in the harmonic interplay of mind and sensual imagination ('imagination')" (Peres 2013, p. 38; see also Graham 2005; Lothian 1999), while "he attributes the 'sublime' to a disharmonic interplay of reason

Fig. 3.1 The Duisburg Nord Landscape Park (Germany), built on the site of the Duisburg-Meiderich iron and steelworks, which closed down in 1985, combines the old industrial heritage with classic garden design, thus combining the sublime of industrial culture with the beautiful of the garden to create a picturesque setting. (Photos: Kühne)

and sensual imagination" (Peres 2013, p. 38). The understanding access to the sublime is quite difficult (in comparison to the beautiful), so "the feeling of the sublime includes the powerlessness and questioning of the subject in view of the overpowering nature, the storming 'too much'" (Pries 1989, p. 10), which resists the effort of intellectual control (Pries 1989, following Kant). The sublime resists the effort for control, since it resists a different and mutually excluding disjointed thinking: "In the feeling of the sublime not only listlessness and lust coincide, but it contains […] almost all manifestations of the occidental dichotomy: Irrationality and rationality, passivity and activity, empiricity and transcendentiality, negation and affirmation, detachment and connection, nature and culture, physical and techne, crisis and megalomania, critique and metaphysics, abyss and transition, chaos and order, revolution and restoration—this series, too, could be continued at will" (Pries 1989, p. 11; see also Castree 2002; Scherle 2016). This ambiguity and contradictoriness caused the concept of sublimity to lose its meaning in the context of modernity striving for dichotomous classifications of the world (Pries 1989). It was not until the emergence of the postmodern discussion in the 1970s that it experienced a renaissance (Lyotard 1987; see also Welsch 1987; the topic of postmodernism is dealt with in detail in Sect. 6.3). In the context of the landscape, 'sublimity' experienced a special updating in the context of reference to (modern) technology, such as the combination of size, heat, and danger, e.g. in a steelwork (cf. Bartels 1989). Berleant (1997, p. 78) characterizing this transition of the experience of sublimity as follows: "No longer is it nature, then, that exemplifies the sublime, as it did from the mountaintops and stormy coasts in the eighteenth century; it is the human environment". On the other hand, in the second half of the 20th century, beauty fell into a crisis, after all, the "aesthetics of beauty [...] had uncritically degenerated into mere 'design' and in consumer society had been reduced to a commodity" (Friesen 2013, p. 90). The near omnipresence of designed objects and object constellations "the threat of oversaturation, anaesthetization and social desensitization" (Recki 2013, p. 229) becomes the subject of both conservative and (neo) marxist contemporary criticism (see Sects. 5.2 and 5.3). The anaesthetic "eludes perception and for this reason does not evoke an aesthetic experience" (Linke 2017a, p. 28; for more details see Welsch 1993).

Another category of aesthetic judgement is formed by the ugly. In comparison to the sublime, the ugly, similar to the beautiful, does not evoke "too strong emotions—one pleases, the other does not, one creates pleasure, the other aversion, which is probably stronger than its positive counterpart, may give rise to immediate reactions, but is seldom perceived as dramatic" (Liessmann 2009, p. 72). In Karl Rosenkranz's (1996[1853]) 'Aesthetics of the Ugly', the ugly is conceived as the 'negative beauty'. Thus, Rosenkranz assigns the ugly a "secondary existence" (Rosenkranz 1996[1853], pp. 14–15), in which it appears in three manifestations: First, in the form of amorphia, which denotes a shapelessness or an indeterminacy of form. This amorphism lacks a 'nature-corresponding' limitation or unity in the necessary difference, whereby it cannot be 'beautiful' (see also: Pöltner 2008). Second, in the form of asymmetry, which denotes the inequality of opposites, i.e. the unformity. Thirdly, the disharmony, which describes the mismatch between the part and the whole, at the point of agreement, gives rise to a mismatch which creates false contrasts (Fig. 3.2).

The 'aesthetic three-pole' formed from beauty, ugliness, and sublimity (Seel 1996) can be extended to include the ugly, the picturesque, and the kitschy (this is described in more detail in Sect. 3.6): According to Rosenkranz (1996[1853]), the ugly can experience an aesthetic revaluation through transformation into the comic, whereby the comic unites "the beautiful and the ugly by liberating both from their respective (pseudo-ideal) one-sidedness" (Hauskeller 2005, p. 61), whereby the caricature characterized by exaggeration and disproportion is regarded as the highest form of this transformation of the ugly into the comic. If the comical refers to an abolition of the ugly and the beautiful, the picturesque forms an intermediary between the beautiful and the sublime: Through this mediation, the picturesque has a comparatively high complexity, irregularity, and differentiation (Carlson 2009; see Fig. 3.3). In the context of landscape experience, the picturesque is created by the combination (widely used in landscape painting) of 'beautifully' connoted objects and object constellations in the foreground (classical: flowers) with objects in the background (mountains or thunderclouds) that are regarded as

Fig. 3.2 If Karl Rosenkranz's criteria are applied to landscape, 'ugly' aspects can also be seen in more or less nature-influenced spaces, the yellow colour created by sulphur deposits contrasts with what is usually expected under 'beautiful' natural landscape (Lassen Volcanic National Park, CA). However, what is shown could also be interpreted under the aesthetic mode of sublimity, provided that a subject-oriented aesthetic is represented (see Sect. 3.4). (Photos: Kühne)

Fig. 3.3 A Californian cliff in fog. A more 'sublime' scenery receives the impulse through lighting by the setting sun to be interpreted as 'picturesque' or—if sunsets are understood as popularised aesthetic attention—also 'kitschy'. (Photo: Kühne)

'sublime' (e.g. Büttner 2006). Thus Carlson (2009, p. 3) describes the picturesque as follows: "Picturesque items are typically in the middle ground between those that are beautiful and those that are sublime, being complex and eccentric, varied and irregular, rich

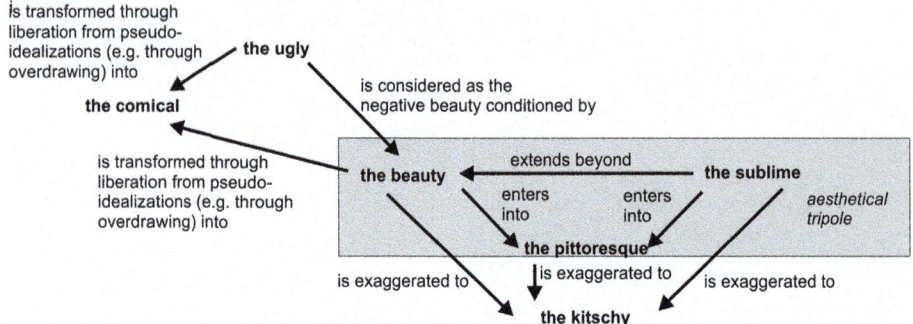

Fig. 3.4 The mutual references of aesthetic judgement (in extension of: Kühne 2018e)

and forceful, and vibrant with energy". By (unconscious) exaggeration (which in turn depends on the observer), the beautiful, the picturesque, and the sublime can be transformed into the kitschy (see Sect. 3.6 and Gelfert 2000; Illing 2006; Liessmann 2002; on the connection between the different dimensions of aesthetic judgement, see Fig. 3.4).

3.3 All Dichotomies? First: Art Aesthetics Versus Natural Aesthetics

The references to the art aesthetic and the natural aesthetic were for a very long time characterised on the one hand by a dichotomous separation, and on the other by an effort towards hierarchization. Kant (1959[1790]), for example, assigns a higher value to natural beauty than to artistic beauty, which he justifies with the fact that the aesthetic of nature arises unintentionally. Thus, this corresponds more to his understanding of beauty, which—as shown in the previous section—constitutively contains an uninterested pleasure (and at least the artist may be assumed to have an interest; cf. Mayechak 2016). In contrast to Kant, Hegel (1970[1835–1838]) assigns a greater value to artistic beauty than to natural beauty, which is ultimately a "beauty born and reborn out of the spirit, and the more the spirit and its productions stand above nature and its phenomena" (Hegel 1970[1835–1838], p. 14). In keeping with this focus, Hegel's aesthetics can therefore be understood exclusively as a philosophy of art (Peres 2013). Croce (1930, p. 32) sharpens this argument by taking beauty as an expression. Expression is again bound to mental activity, but since nature is passive and spiritless, it is also excluded from beauty. Arnold Gehlen (1960) is less concerned with the contextualization of modern art in relation to the comparison with nature, to which he attributes a "need for comment" (Gehlen 1960, p. 162) by drawing attention to the fact that "in many cases works of modern art cannot be received at all or at least not adequately without comment" (Majetschak 2016, p. 105).

With an intensified discussion about nature (and more generally about environmental) burdens as well as the challenge of protecting nature and the environment, the conceptual version and the way in which nature and cultural aesthetics are referred to each other is becoming more topical (cf. Lundmark 1997; Tiezzi 2005). In the current re-focusing of natural beauty, a strong reference to human beings with their nature-related needs can still be noted, but nature is no longer understood as a pure resource for the aesthetic edification of man alone (cf. Haber 2006; van Noy 2003). There is also a successive deconstruction of the modern dichotomy of natural aesthetics and art aesthetics: art and nature are increasingly being attributed "to the fact that they are both 'unity phenomena' of the aesthetic" (Seel 1996, p. 269). These 'phenomena of unity' generate 'moods' that arise between the human and the object, but which are mostly ascribed to the object (Hartmann 1953). These two developments are particularly relevant in landscape research: The deconstruction of the antithesis (connected with superiority and subordination) of nature and art aesthetics can be understood in feedback with the dissolution of the dichotomy of the construction of nature and cultural landscape, the engagement with the mediation between subject and object with the increasing engagement with 'atmospheres' to be addressed in the following section.

3.4 All Dichotomies? Second: Object Orientation Versus Subject Orientation

A discussion that continues having an effect to this day (cf. the explanations on essentialist/positivist and constructivist landscape theories in Sects. 2.2–2.4) deals with the question of whether the aesthetic is a property of an object, or whether it is a subjective (or social) attribution (in more detail on landscape in Lothian 1999). Shusterman (2001) describes the first understanding as 'naturalism', the second as 'historicism'. The naturalistic position of an 'objective aesthetics' can already be found in Plato's work (2005[in the 4th century B.C.]), in which he ascribes to each object an underlying idea, whereby this object is all the more beautiful as the more clearly an idea can materially develop, i.e. the form underlies the 'essence' of the object. Francis Hutcheson (1694–1747; 1986[1725]) promoted the subjectivist concept of aesthetics: although the emergence of beauty—as an idea—is based on the combination of uniformity and diversity of material objects, the ability to perceive beauty is a position that also dominates Baumgarten, in which "beauty essentially refers to knowledge as such" (Majetschak 2016, p. 30). In this tradition, Friedrich Theodor Vischer (1807–1887; 1922, p. 438) focuses on the processuality of turning to objects described as 'beautiful': "Beauty is not a thing, but an act". From this subjectivist point of view beauty becomes the "product of the subject and his mental faculties and abilities" (Hartmann 1924, p. 3). However, these 'mental faculties and abilities' are not determined solely by the subject (as was already made clear in the introductory remarks in 2.1 on landscape) but are subject to social foundations. Immanuel Kant (1959[1781], 1959[1790]) already referred to such a conditionality of aesthetic judgements in the social, that aesthetic interpretation was finally based on "socio-cultural values, learned norms, personal experiences, character traits, and desires"

(Frohmann 1997, p. 175). This social conditionality also becomes clear in the nature of the judgment: According to Kant (1959[1790]), the aesthetic judgment is not a judgment of cognition (i.e. not a logical judgment), rather it is a judgment of taste to which he denies any cognition function; at this point he bases taste judgments on "a judgment power that reflects exclusively subjectivity" (Peres 2013, p. 35; cf. also Liessmann 2009; Lothian 1999). Taste can be understood as the ability to make aesthetic judgements (Kant 1983[1793]; from a sociological perspective: Bourdieu 1987[1979]; Illing 2006; Kühne 2006c, 2008b), the basis of which is an individual engagement with social aesthetic conventions; accordingly, a new aesthetic interpretation of an object means the 'constitution of a new work' (Danto 1981). Whereby this constitution is indeed contingent, but not arbitrary, because taste is subject to discursive social negotiation processes (see also e.g. Eickelmann 2016; Majetschak 2016), as Borgeest (1977, p. 100) clarifies with the example of the 'point of orientation of aesthetics', the 'beautiful': "There is no point of orientation for the determination of the beautiful, which may hope for all-round and all-time acceptance and of which the opposite could not be claimed with the same right". Thus, if an essentialist basic position is adopted in landscape research, landscape 'beauty' is understood as part of its essence (naturalism), which is to be fathomed, whereas in a constructivist position in the sense of subjectivism questions come to the centre of consideration as to who, in which social contexts, can provide physical arrangements described as landscapes with a taste judgment according to which social conventions, without losing their recognition in certain social contexts (and last but not least: what significance taste judgements have for the social and individual construction of landscape). If, in this context, the objects of aesthetic reference (following Reicher 2015) are assigned to the different levels of landscape reference (Sect. 2.1; Fig. 3.5), material objects and virtual objects can be assigned to external space, physical objects of the individually actualized social landscape and abstract objects whose origin is to be found in social conventions, both the social landscape and its individual updating, if these abstractions are in turn individually reflected or related to one's own living environment.

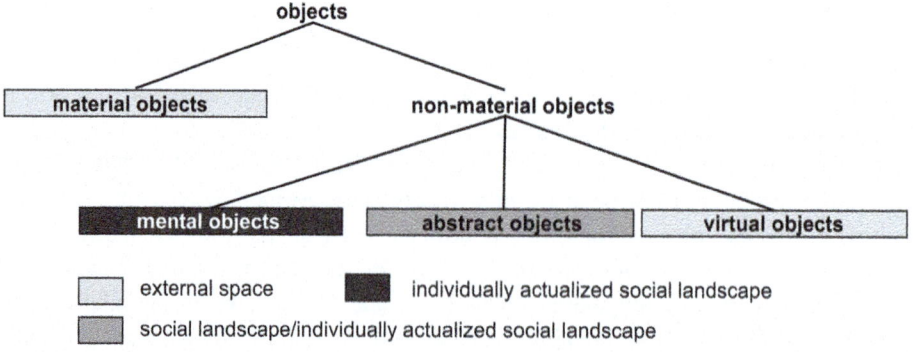

Fig. 3.5 Objects related to the allocation to the different levels of landscape. (Own visualization according to Reicher 2015)

Fig. 3.6 The references of society, individual, material objects, and the medium of the atmosphere in a hybridity-sensitive aesthetic

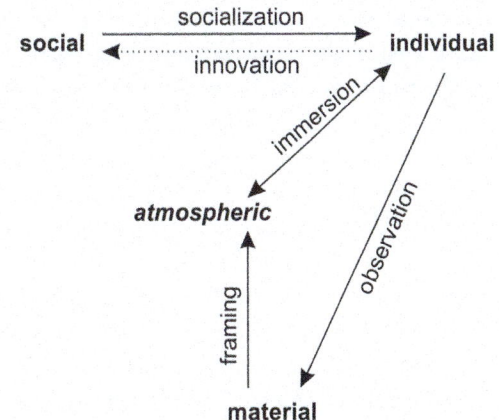

Atmospheres can be conceived as a fleeting transitional phenomenon between the perceiving subject and the world of material objects (Kazig 2007, 2013, 2016). Atmospheres are created by sensually perceived constellations of the material environment and influence the subjective perception of humans (among other things: Forkel and Grimm 2014; Gebhard 2013; Kazig 2007, 2008; Weber 2017a). Atmospheres can be understood as a medium of sensual relations between the sentient human being and his environment (Thibaud 2003). Gernot Böhme (1995) goes even further by assigning an independent reality to atmospheres, which is based specifically on the fact that atmospheres cannot be limited to the symbolic. The temporality of atmospheres is not only influenced by weather conditions, times of day and seasons, structural arrangements, density of vegetation, etc., but also by other people and the artefacts moved by them, as can be seen from the example of a 'slightly dangerous atmosphere': "A slightly dangerous atmosphere occurs when other road users than pedestrians are on the road in the pedestrian area of a square" (Kazig 2008, p. 154; on the interaction of the social, the individual and the material, including the atmospheric, see Fig. 3.6).

With the medium of the atmosphere, the dichotomy of subject and materiality in parts can be eliminated. The inclusion of man's emotional access to his environment through atmosphere leads to the question of the relationship between rationality, sensuality, and emotionality, which will be discussed in the following section.

3.5 Approaches to Rationality, Sensuality, Emotionality, and Atmospheres

The aesthetic access to the world by means of 'taste' takes place between two poles. On one there are emotions in the form of an individual 'sense of taste', on the other cognitive judgements of taste. In one aspect, it requires the ability to let oneself be touched by atmospheres (or to perceive certain arrangements of material objects in connection with social relationships as 'Heimat' which means in English a synthesis of home, homeland, native land, home town, strong social bonds, cultural belonging and others; cf. Kühne 2009c; Kühne and Spellerberg 2010; Rose 1995; Sopher 1979). From a different aspect, it requires the ability to deal cognitively with the question of aesthetic effect (for example in connection with painting, music, literature, geography, etc.). Especially in the modernist tradition of thinking, the cognitive approach is ascribed a higher value than the emotional one (as Satter 2000 explains using the example of music). In the context of the development of postmodern interpretations, the modern dichotomous view has changed into a perspective of the above-mentioned polarity that takes hybridities into account; on the other hand, the superiority of the cognitive over the emotional has been abolished (for more on this, see also Sect. 3.6 and Kubsch 2007; Kühne 2006a; Vester 1993).

The emotional attention to material objects and object constellations, e.g. in the form of atmosphere and emotional occupation, as well as the cognitive approach to aesthetic effects are based on sensual perceptions. Thus, an aesthetic judgment (as a cognitive act) becomes possible only through the mental engagement with sensual perceptions. Aesthetics is more than just 'sensual perception' or a taste judgement, but becomes the 'science of sensual perception' or the 'science of sensual knowledge' (according to Alexander Gottlieb Baumgarten; Satter 2000), i.e. it is the instance of reflection on taste judgement, just as ethics is the instance of reflection on morals, thereby also opening the sensual relation to the world to the judgement of knowledge (according to Kant). The word aesthetics thus denotes "the theory or philosophical discipline that reflects on a meta-level on beautiful, ugly, impressive phenomena and their corresponding recording and evaluation and on artistic works as their subject" (Peres 2013, p. 16). In this sense, we use aesthetics when this reflective level is to be addressed. The adjectival or adverbial use of 'aesthetic' in turn refers to the object level of taste judgment (cf. Peres 2013). Georges Bataille (1985) understands an aesthetic approach to the world as a sensual-affective appropriation that eludes cognitive attention and thus ultimately means a refuge for an individual, sovereign approach to the world. Nelson Goodman (1992), in contrast, calls into question an aesthetic reference to the world in the form of a purely emotional implementation of sensory perception: Any idea of the aesthetic experience as a kind of emotional bath or orgy is idiotic. Compared to the fear, sorrow, depression, or enthusiasm that triggered a real battle or loss, withdrawal or victory, the emotions that played a role are usually suppressed and indirect. Moreover, they are generally no more pronounced than the excitement, despair or joy of scientific research and discovery. The reciprocal penetration of emotional and cognitive—i.e. hybrid—approaches to the world is not limited to aesthetic reference; Goodman (1990) extends it to art and science by not understanding these two approaches to the world as clearly separable. Rather, both were mutually conditioned, which means that aesthetics can be interpreted as a special form of epistemology. The aesthetic attitude (here understood as a synthesis of art and science) is interpreted as restless, inquisitive, as well as examining (Goodman 1973). Knowledge, which is produced from such a synthesis of art and science, is not directed towards unambiguous truths (like modern science), but rather has the goal of "producing different world designs (in science as in art)" (Gethmann-Siefert 1995, p. 110).

Whereas in Sect. 3.4 the construction of the modern dichotomy of subject and object was annulled by viewing atmospheres as mediums, in this section the modern dichotomy and hierarchization of cognition (high-quality) and emotion (inferior) was deconstructed and presented in a postmodern approach of the hybridization of cognition and emotion as well as science and art—with principle equivalence of the poles. This postmodern deconstruction of modern dichotomies is concluded in the following section with an examination of the constructs of high and trivial culture.

3.6   Social Operationalizations: High Culture (Art)—Trivial Culture (Kitsch)

The dissolution of the dichotomy of high and trivial culture takes place in the context of a postmodern self-understanding as a 'constitution of radical tolerance' (Welsch 1988; a more intensive relationship between landscape and postmodernism is established in Sect. 6.3). The dichotomy of high and trivial culture in modern thought is linked to the existence of "universally binding authorities" (Kastner 2002, p. 232), while in postmodernism "authoritative hierarchies" are leveled (Kastner 2002, p. 232). Instead of the stigmatizing aesthetic judgement 'Kitsch', the bearer of 'bad taste' by the representatives of high culture, which means a distinctive attribution of a lack of knowledge or applicability as generally valid defined aesthetic standards (Illing 2006; cf. in the context of architecture: Stevens 2002), a culture of 'interpretative polyvalence' takes its place (Kastner 2002, p. 232). As a result of increasing social differentiation, aesthetic (and moral) standards are also pluralized, making a uniform basis for assessing what is 'high culture' and what is then 'trivial culture' absurd. Thus 'kitsch' no longer functions "as a false expression of false needs, nor as an expression of right needs, but kitsch, at least the tolerance aesthetics of our days want it, is regarded as a right expression of right needs" (Liessmann 2002, pp. 26–27). With the associated levelling of the (generally binding) artistic and philosophical avant-garde, these have "either become classics or rearguards" (Liessmann 2009, p. 11). The prevailing postmodern aesthetic is an expression of the increasing realization that thinking "has increasingly moved towards the insight that the basis of what we call reality is of a fictional nature since Kant" (Welsch 2006, p. 8). The hybridization of science and art described in the previous section results in 'reality' being constructed 'aesthetically' rather than 'realistically'" (Welsch 2006, p. 7; cf. also Liessmann 2009; Trigg 2006). The delimitation of the aestheticizing also concerns the merging with the economic to form an "aesthetic economy" (Reckwitz 2012, p. 133). The dissolution of the dichotomy between art and audience (Reckwitz 2012, also Liessmann 2009) also expresses the dissolution of aesthetic boundaries: visitors are involved in art projects, in Disneyland visitors dress up as Disney figures, among others (see Eickelmann 2016; Fontaine 2017b; Henning 2016; Kebeck and Schroll 2011). This dedifferentiation of art and other social subsystems is flanked by an expansion of social 'aesthetic competences', i.e. the consequence of the 'expansion of education' since the

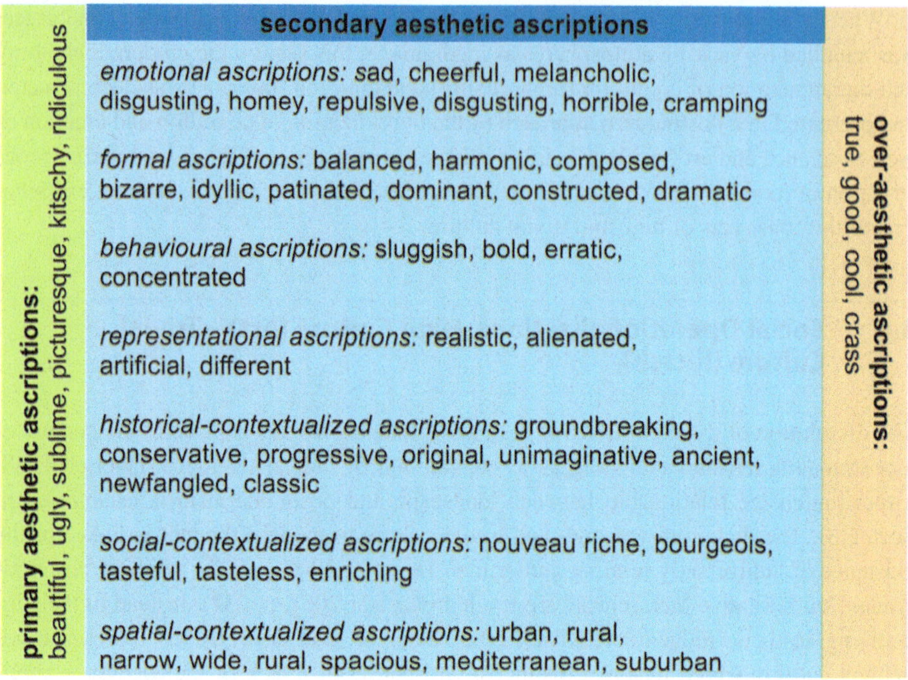

primary aesthetic ascriptions: beautiful, ugly, sublime, picturesque, kitschy, ridiculous	**secondary aesthetic ascriptions**	over-aesthetic ascriptions: true, good, cool, crass
	emotional ascriptions: sad, cheerful, melancholic, disgusting, homey, repulsive, disgusting, horrible, cramping	
	formal ascriptions: balanced, harmonic, composed, bizarre, idyllic, patinated, dominant, constructed, dramatic	
	behavioural ascriptions: sluggish, bold, erratic, concentrated	
	representational ascriptions: realistic, alienated, artificial, different	
	historical-contextualized ascriptions: groundbreaking, conservative, progressive, original, unimaginative, ancient, newfangled, classic	
	social-contextualized ascriptions: nouveau riche, bourgeois, tasteful, tasteless, enriching	
	spatial-contextualized ascriptions: urban, rural, narrow, wide, rural, spacious, mediterranean, suburban	

Fig. 3.7 Examples of (landscape) aesthetic attributions. Primary aesthetic attributions refer to the classical (presented in Sect. 3.2) aesthetic references, secondary aesthetic attributions form connections to other categories, supra-aesthetic attributions denote judgements that often include aesthetic ones (following: Reicher 2015)

late 1960s (cf. Müller 1998). Because of such an aestheticization of life, the aestheticized view of physical space as landscape also gains in social significance (cf. Fontaine 2017b). However, this gain in significance is often not accompanied by an application of the 'constitution of radical tolerance', but rather by a modernist-residual hierarchical appreciation of one's own taste judgement in relation to alternative ones (Kühne and Weber 2018[online first 2017]; Weber et al. 2016; a more differentiated collection of aesthetic attributions in relation to Fig. 3.4 due to the further explanations can be found in Fig. 3.7). These taste judgments often refer not only to visual sensory stimuli, but also to those that were not at the centre of scientific and planning attention in modernity, as will be discussed in more detail below.

3.7 Back to the Beginning: Meaning of the Senses

While in space research before the 20th century non-visual phenomena received a great deal of attention (Faure 1993), modern science was strongly oriented towards optical phenomena in its attention to physical spaces. This is not least shown to advantage by the use of optical metaphors, for example when it is formulated that "scientists see the world 'through certain glasses', that they have prejudices that 'distort' their 'view' of an object, that with their 'worldviews', 'paradigms', 'ideas' or 'categories' they 'interpret' the procurement of the world" (Latour 2002[1999], p. 165).

Raab (1998) justifies the disregard of the other senses with the 'quality criteria' of Western science, which is characterized by scientific thinking (freedom of value, general validity, and comprehensibility): For example, visual perception could be assigned both optical qualities (colors) of a physically measurable dimension (wavelength of light) and a manageable subjective category system for classifying these qualities (e.g. basic colors). On the other hand, "in the olfactory domain, there are neither consistent relationships between the chemical-physical characteristics of fragrances and their discernable sensations, nor systematic classification aspects according to which subjective fragrance qualities can be classified, discernible" (Raab 1998, p. 16). Even acoustic components of sensory perception cannot be reduced to volume in decibels, and even the decomplexing transformation from sound to noise is "more than a physical effect on our hearing organ; it is a source of information; and the sum of sounds forms our acoustic environment" (Burckhardt 2004, p. 205). Sounds and smells are particularly fleeting and "removed from descriptive and formative access" (Winkler 2005, p. 85; see thus: Botteldooren, De Coensel and De Muer 2006). Both require that "the place of man as perceiver and creator always remains recognizable" (Winkler 2005, p. 86). Nevertheless, both have a specific spatial connection, so that one can speak of 'soundscapes' and 'smellscapes', which—in analogy to 'landmarks'—are characterized by certain 'soundmarks' and 'smellmarks' (for more details see: Porteous 1985; Schafer 1993; Thompson 2004). The tactile dimension of the appropriation of the physical foundations of landscape exhibits a high degree of sensory intensity: it is not limited to the recording of distances, geometries (extension), and surfaces (which become particularly concise through the visual dimension), but also conveys information about materiality, the energetic state (e.g. temperature, electric charge), and dynamics (such as vibration or current; Rodaway 2011).

In comparison to the scientific and planning access to landscape, persons without expert knowledge combine visual aspects "with an acoustic, olfactory, tactile and gustatory dimension" (Bischoff 2005, p. 9; cf. also Porteous 1982; on the empiricism of the meaning of non-visual components of such constructs see Kaymaz 2012; Kerney and Bradley 2011; Kühne 2006a, 2018d; Rodaway 2011; Vining 1992). In this respect, phenomenological landscape research focuses intently on the interrelationships of non-visual landscape experience (Berleant 1997; Kazig 2013, 2019; Revill 2018). In the course of the postmodern hybridization of art and science, the multiplication of social foundations for aesthetic judgements, the recognition of the hybridity of cognitive and emotional scientific approaches to the world, and more generally the expansion of aestheticization (and thus multisenosoric attention to the world; see detailed Sect. 6.3) of different social functional systems, the increased inclusion of non-visual stimuli in the space-related sciences appears to be necessary (as in the recent past, for example, in Edler and Lammert-Siepmann 2017). Particularly regarding the representation of

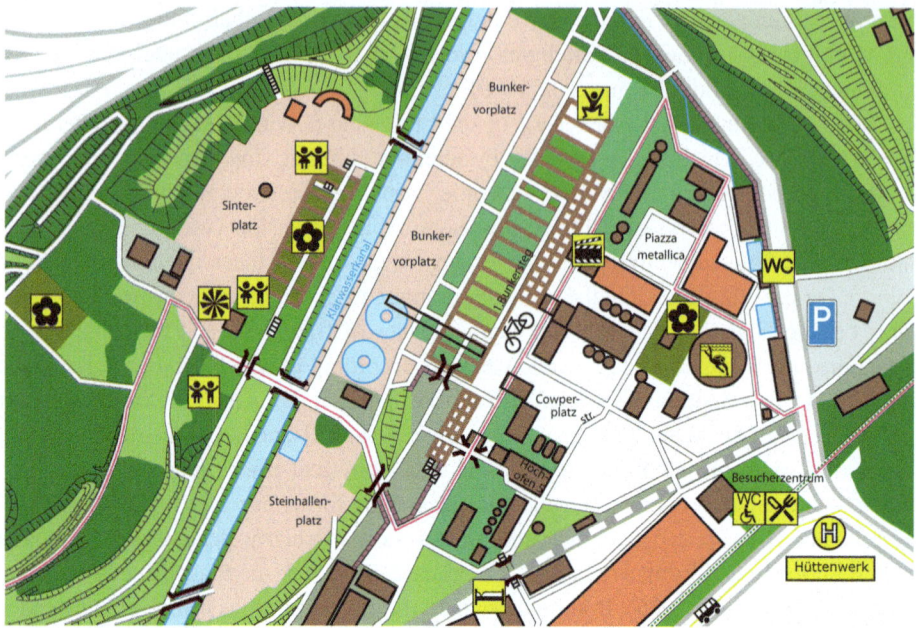

Fig. 3.8 Excerpt from an audiovisual map of the Duisburg Nord Landscape Park (Germany) based on the didactic method 'living map'. The acoustic signatures (audiorealistic sound sequences from freesound) served to appropriate the acoustic dimension of landscape (from: Edler et al. 2015, p. 262; with permission to be reproduced by the authors)

landscape heritage, there are great challenges in making historical non-visual stimuli accessible to experience (Fig. 3.8).

The ability to make (landscape) aesthetic judgements (summarizing this chapter, see Box 8) does not grow out of the individual, but is a process of socializing social conventions and of dealing with them individually, which is the subject of the following chapter.

Box 8: Aesthetic approaches to landscape—a brief summary

Aesthetics can be described briefly as the instance of reflection of aesthetic judgements. In this respect, landscape aesthetics means the instance of reflection of landscape-related judgements. Theoretically and methodically, this topic area is approached from different perspectives. Philosophical aesthetics focuses on the examination of the conceptual connections between aesthetic judgements and landscape, social science on the emergence and function of social aesthetic conventions, psychology on landscape preferences (the intensity of the references or the potentials of these are summarized in the Table 3.1). As with landscape research, different preferences are also given to the individual, the social and the material in aesthetics, whether for example the 'beautiful' quality of an object, or a social or individual attribution. In relation to landscape, the aesthetic assessment is not limited to the 'aesthetic tripole' (Seel 1996) of the beautiful, the ugly, and the picturesque, but is extended to other contexts—up to a connection to moral and ontological references. A further peculiarity of a landscape-aesthetic turn to the world lies in its multisensory nature, although optical stimuli dominate in the perception/construction (depending on the chosen theoretical access) of landscape, acoustic and olfactory stimuli in particular have a special significance—which has so far received comparatively little attention in landscape research—with the exception of phenomenological landscape research (Sect. 2.5.1).

Table 3.1 The references of philosophical, psychological, and social-scientific landscape aesthetics to the landscape theories presented in Chap. 2, structured from ++ (very large references or potentials) to – (very small references or potentials)

	Philosophical land-scape aesthetics	Psychological land-scape aesthetics	Social scientific land-scape aesthetics
Essentialist approaches	++	–	–
Positivistic approaches	±	++	+
Social constructivist approaches	+	–	++
Autopoietic systems theory	–	–	++
Discourse theory	–	–	++
Phenomenological landscape research	++	–	±
ANT and assemblage theory	++	–	+
Neopragmatism	++	++	++

The Differentiated Socialization of Landscape

4

The relationship between society and the individual—in the landscape context of the social landscape to individually actualized social landscape—is characterized by a considerable dynamic; after all, the aim is to synchronise individual ideas of landscape with social (or partially social) ones. An essential process here is that of (landscape) socialization. In landscape socialization, patterns of interpretation and evaluation are developed based on "one's own experiences, others through the mediation of parents and friends, through books and films, i.e. through commandments and prohibitions or simply through certain labels as beautiful or edible, as ugly or inedible" (Kruse-Graumann 1996, p. 172). The question of the socialization of landscape patterns of interpretation and evaluation focuses on the direction from society to the individual, a question that has been intensively addressed over the past decades (e.g. Herzog et al. 2000; Kook 2008; Kost 2017; Kühne 2008a; Lindström 2008; Lyons 1983; Miller 1984; Stern et al. 1993; Stotten 2013; Wattchow and Prins 2018). Socialization theory in general and landscape theory in particular follows strongly the constructivist (especially social constructivist) theoretical approaches (see Sect. 2.4 for the basics).

This chapter first provides an insight into the main features of the process of socialization, and then looks at the question of the landscape references in this process. This was followed by an examination of the cultural differentiation of landscape concepts as a result of different socialization. The chapter concludes with a comparison of Anglo-Saxon and German-language geographical landscape research.

4.1 Main Features of the Process of Socialization

The necessity of socialization is based on the poverty of the human being in instincts and a low degree of innate behavioural patterns. This in turn resulted in his great 'cosmopolitanism' (Berger and Luckmann 1966; Gehlen 1956; Plessner 1924). Accordingly, people

© Springer Fachmedien Wiesbaden GmbH, part of Springer Nature 2019
O. Kühne, *Landscape Theories*, RaumFragen: Stadt – Region – Landschaft,
https://doi.org/10.1007/978-3-658-25491-9_4

are dependent on *learning* patterns of interpretation, action, and evaluation from other people in order to make them members of the society of other people. The introduction of the individual into society (socialization) is correspondingly associated with the internalization of social values, norms, and roles (internalization) (Dahrendorf 1971[1958]). The function of the socialization process is a double one (Fend 1981):

1. In the process of socialization, people acquire the skills that make them accepted members of society.
2. Through this process, society is reproduced through the transmission of values, norms, patterns of action, etc.

For the socializing individual, society is (also) restriction, because it is "so omnipresent and at the same time so resistant that we constantly bump into and rub against it; society is an annoying fact" (Dahrendorf 1968b, p. 50). Society does not seem to us all to be an 'annoying fact' because its norms and role patterns, its interpretations and evaluations of the world are uncomfortable, "society is an annoyance because, although it relieves us of our burden through its reality and perhaps even gives us the expressive possibilities of life in the first place, it surrounds us always and everywhere with impassable ramparts in which we can establish ourselves, which we can paint colourfully and think away with our eyes closed, but which remain immovable" (Dahrendorf 1968b, p. 50). However, the socializing human being is not solely a "victim of the circumstances" (Nissen 1998, p. 151), which dictate interpretations, values, norms and roles to him; after all, there is an area "in which the individual is free to shape his roles himself and to behave in this or that other way" (Dahrendorf 1968b, p. 151). Such an understanding of socialization clarifies the possibilities of the individual to also develop deviant understandings of the world. These can then (of course under certain conditions, such as sufficient power in certain social contexts) represent a starting point for changes in socially shared patterns of interpretation, evaluation, and role expectation. In this sense, socialization can also be understood as "the process of the emergence and development of the personality in mutual dependence on the socially mediated social and material environment" (Geulen and Hurrelmann 1980, p. 51).

In the previous section, reference was made several times to the processuality of socialization. Thus, Berger and Luckmann (1966, p. 130) divide this process into a primary and a secondary socialization: "Primary socialization is the first socialization an individual undergoes in childhood, through which he becomes a member of society. Secondary socialization is any subsequent process that inducts an already socialized individual into new sectors of the objective world of his society." In primary socialization an everyday and thus 'normal' access to the world (but also to oneself) is established, while in secondary socialization new, specialized, institutionalized "subworlds" are introduced (Berger and Luckmann 1966, p. 138). As a result of social differentiation, flexibilization and individualization of biographies, socialization has developed into a lifelong process.

Socialization includes—as briefly discussed—not only the introduction to immaterial worlds of meaning and the socially accepted way of dealing with them (e.g. with the content of social norms of action, role expectations, and shared patterns of interpretation and evaluation), but also the reference to physical objects, especially when these have a guiding and symbolic function (Blumer 1973; Geulen 2005). This reference of man to his material as well as immaterial environment is usually actively shaped by him (Hahn 2017, p. 24): "Man does not only live his life, he must also lead his life. Moreover, he leads this life—he can't help it—in the direction of an environment, an environment, an environment that he has to accept".

4.2   The Differentiated Socialization of Landscape

In the context of the socialization of 'landscape'—following what has been said in the previous section—the person becomes introduced into social landscape-related patterns of interpretation and evaluation, into norms for dealing with what is called 'landscape', and thereby can communicate in appropriate role and via 'landscape' without loss of social recognition taking place. In doing so, a reference is made not only to the social environment, but also to the material environment and its handling (Wattchow and Prins 2018). From this perspective, the constitutive level of landscape—following a construc- tivist understanding—is not a section of a physical space, but individual attributions and views based on social conventions (and possibly a critical examination of them). These social conventions for the interpretation and evaluation of landscape are conveyed in the process of socialization. This means: As a result of the socialization of 'landscape', ego learns what alter means when alter refers to a certain constellation of objects and sym- bols as 'landscape'.

In the process of socialization, cognitive, emotional, functional, and aesthetic action competences relating to landscape are developed (with varying intensity; Ipsen 2006; Kühne 2018c, e; see Fig. 4.1). For example, certain knowledge about geology, vegeta- tion, cultural-historical objects, etc. is imparted, how a space described as a landscape can experience an emotional affection as 'home', how such a space can be used for the fulfil- ment of one's own needs (for sport, contemplation, etc.), and which object constellations can be described as 'beautiful', 'uglier', 'sublime' or 'picturesque'. With socialization,

Fig. 4.1 Cognitive, emotional, functional, and aesthetic competences in relation to landscape and its interpenetration. (Own presentation in further development of Ipsen 2006; Kühne 2018e)

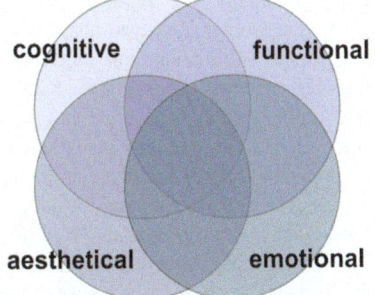

socially desired/permitted/unwanted actions are also conveyed in certain spatial constellations and their social commitment tested (Proshansky et al. 1983; Somerville, Power and Carteret 2009; Visscher and Bouverne-De Bie 2008). The social construction of landscape is—as shown—subject to considerable temporal (see Table 1), social (e.g. according to age and gender; Fig. 4.2), place of residence (urban, suburban, rural), and cultural differentiations (Bruns 2016; among many: Bruns and Kühne 2015; Bruns and Münderlein 2017; Bruns and Paech 2015; Dietz and Kalof 1993; Herzog et al. 2000; Kearney and Bradley 2011; Kühne 2006a, 2015a, 2018d; Miller 1984; Stern et al. 1999). This means that, on the one hand, certain contents of social landscapes are selectively conveyed on a partial social level and, on the other hand, that social concepts of landscapes differ culturally.

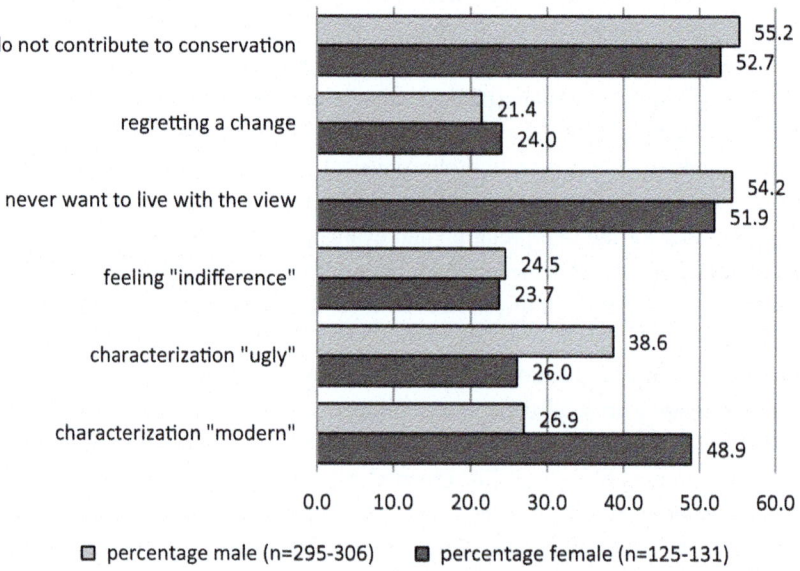

Fig. 4.2 The evaluation of an 'open landscape with wind turbines' differentiated by gender, evaluation of a photo. Female respondents characterized them significantly more frequently as 'modern' and significantly less frequently as 'ugly' than male respondents. In contrast to the other references, the women surveyed also show a much less critical attitude than the men surveyed (survey year 2016, Saarland survey area, Germany, postal household survey, data in percent, several possible answers; according to: Kühne 2018d: p. 60). (Although quantitative social research, as the results presented here are based on, is generally associated with a positivist understanding of science, while qualitative social research is regarded as an empirical approach to constructivist understanding of science, quantitative methodology can also be reconciled with constructivist approaches if the results are not understood as an 'image of social reality', but as 'expressions of social construction processes'. In a neopragmatic framing of research, the integration of different approaches takes place via the question of the expected progress in knowledge and not from the principle of the chosen [exclusively chosen] perspective.)

The socialization of landscape cannot be understood as a continuous process of medi-ation and internalization of a generally valid pool of social interpretations and valuations of landscape as well as norms, values, and roles in dealing with what is called 'land-scape'. The process of landscape socialization can rather be divided into phases in which specific appropriations and internalizations are carried out. Landscape socialization takes place in two phases, sometimes supplemented by an optional third: In the first phase the 'native regular landscape' (German: 'heimatliche Normallandschaft') is created, in the second phase the 'stereotypical landscape' is formed. In the third (optional) phase, land-scape-related (professional) training involves the internalization of certain landscape-re-lated special knowledge stocks (cf. Kühne 2008a; Stotten 2013; see also Sect. 4.4). The term 'phases' is not to be understood in the sense of a strictly opposed temporal sequence. Rather, it suggests a dominant pattern of appropriation of scenic interpreta-tions and valuations. This means that even in the phase in which the internalization of stereotypical knowledge and interpretations dominates, it is still possible to establish home-normal references to the landscape (Kühne 2006a).

The 'native regular landscape' arises in childhood, especially through the personal appropriation of one's own living environment, mediated by parents, if available by (especially older) siblings, grandparents, later also in the peer group, etc. The native regular landscape is "filled with first memories of regional language, sounds, smells, colours, gestures, moods and speaking things and deeply anchored in the memory" (Hüppauf 2007, p. 112; see also: Hunt 2016; Tuan 1974). The native regular landscape is particularly characterized by emotional occupations, from which specific norma-tive demands are derived: A physical space interpreted as a landscape does not have to meet (stereotypical) beauty norms, it does have to be familiar. The norm of the stability of physical structures is derived from this, i.e. changes in the physical foundations of a normal home landscape are interpreted as 'loss of homeland' (Kühne 2009c, 2011b; cf. also Hammitt 1981). The patterns of interpretation and evaluation internalized in the context of the emergence of 'stereotypical landscape', on the other hand, are based less on familiarity than on socially divided norms, especially aesthetic (Kühne 2008a, b, d). The creation is also not primarily carried out by one's own view, but on the basis of secondary information through school lessons (especially school books), films, Internet, picture books, with the increasing importance of the Internet etc. Thus, the general stand-ards are conveyed and internalized, how (normatively) a space interpreted as a 'beauti-ful' landscape has to look like (and how not), which spatial differentiations apply to a 'desirable landscape' (a metropolis should not present itself like a village, a desert not like a semi-open landscape). In addition to these aesthetic norms, ideas of individual use-fulness (as a functional dimension, e.g. for walks or as a backdrop for sporting activities) are also formed in this phase of adolescence. Already in children—according to Tapsell (1997) and Tunstall et al. (2004)—a functionally motivated differentiation of preferences according to interest in use can be determined. They prefer object constellations that invite to play, while aesthetic and ecological aspects are of secondary importance.

In the interpretation and in particular (re-)evaluation of a physical space under the mode of the stereotyped landscape, those elements that do not correspond to these stereotyped ideas are labelled negatively. A possible revision of these negatively labelled objects is accordingly advocated, while under the mode of the 'native regular landscape' these objects can also be subject to a positive-emotional reference (Kühne 2018d). In comparison to the 'native regular landscape', stereotypical landscape concepts exhibit a comparatively high degree of stability: The 'native regular landscape' is formed individually to locally for a specific—narrowly defined—period of time, i.e. a subsequent generation can—after revision of physical structures—develop a 'native regular landscape' with a different content on the basis of these changed structures. Stereotypical notions of landscape, on the other hand, are based on the updating of historically developed social patterns of interpretation and evaluation (Kühne 2015b, 2018e; Schenk 2006, 2017) (in German-speaking countries since the Middle Ages), which accordingly show a stronger supraindividual commitment and persistence.

These native-regular landscape and stereotype landscape conceptions are selectively supplemented by expert special knowledge stocks, which are acquired in vocational training and in particular scientific study. On the one hand, these are strongly cognitively influenced, on the other hand they are subject to a subject-specific deficit orientation: the interpretations and valuations consensualised in subject-specific discourses are used for the analysis and evaluation of spaces described as landscapes—combined with a specific terminology in each case. As a rule, deficits are named in the sense of a comparison of being and target, with the result that indications for the approximation of 'being' to the 'target state' are expressed. Even these subject-specific, expert special knowledge stocks are not stable, but are subject to competing paradigmatic basic orientations (such as successionism in distinction to the preservation of 'historical cultural landscapes'; cf. Hokema 2015; Kühne 2008b; Leibenath 2014b; Wojtkiewicz 2015).

4.3   The Cultural Diversity of Landscape Constructs

The question of the extent to which different cultural contexts affect the construction of 'landscape' can be examined in terms of the result in the form of preference analyses (as in Herzog et al. 2000; Zube and Pitt 1981), for example by presenting photos for evaluation of people from different cultural backgrounds, or it can be examined genetically with regard to the emergence of cultural differences in access to the material and immaterial environment. This does not involve quantitative psychological tests to identify differences and similarities (positivistic understanding of science), but linguistic research or qualitative interviews. The latter research strand, being social science and humanities, will be dealt with more intensively in the following. After all, the culture-specific construction processes investigated in this way form the basis for the numerically recorded valuation differences of quantitative research.

The construct, which is looked into on the basis of social conventions into the material (increasingly also virtual) world—called 'Landschaft' in German-speaking countries—deviates markedly in other cultural contexts, whereby 'culture' is under-stood to mean the sum of the various classification systems and discursive formations from which social practices are derived, which in turn update the classification sys-tems (Berleant 1997; Hall 1994). In a landscape context, this means that if we ascribe the attribute 'landscape' to certain object constellations on the basis of certain socially divided, culturally anchored patterns of interpretation and evaluation, and then apply the adjective 'beautiful' to this attribute, we update the underlying classification system and perpetuate it (cf. e.g. Cosgrove 2006; Kook 2008; Kühne 2008b; Weber 2017a). Since these classification systems are always formulated differently in terms of language, there are clear differences in what is subsumed under 'landscape' or there is no linguistic equivalent to what is understood in the German language under 'landscape', in which the term first appeared and then (among numerous transformations) made a global career (see Box 9).

Box 9: The meaning of the word 'Landschaft' in German

In the Germanic languages, the word 'landscape' is a verbal abstract derived from numerous other -skapjan ('shafts') (similar to: *skapi-, *skapja- and *skafti-), which were characterized by a uniform spectrum of meanings: It included the meanings of shape, form, texture, nature, condition and manner. The roots of the conceptual history of the word 'Landschaft' in German go back to the early 9th century (Gruenter 1975[1953]). In Old High German it meant something "which in the vast majority of cases has the quality of a larger settlement area" (Müller 1977, p. 6). As a derivation of person or group names, it had a basic meaning of the behaviour and social norms of residents living in an area, but without a direct reference to the physical space. In the course of the 12th century, this meaning was supplemented by a double political component: landscape was understood as a politically and legally defined space, which in turn was a constitutive part of a larger political unit (Müller 1977). In addition, the politically capable (i.e. not the farmers) of a region were summarised as "representatives of the 'whole land-scape'" (Hard 1977, p. 14). In the High Middle Ages, the term was extended by a figurative component of the cultivated space dominated by a city (Müller 1977), a meaning that anticipates the later dichotomous separation of cultural and natural landscape. Based on the style of Dutch painting, the element intending to convey a meaning of 'scenery' was added to the German 'Landschaft' (Antrop 2018; Büttner 2006). This created the 'double character' of the concept of landscape, which was intended to make a career across the German-speaking world (see Sect. 4.4): 'land-scape' denotes both a physical space and the act of aesthetic construction. This tradition also includes the interpretation of the 'total character of an earth region' attributed to Alexander von Humboldt: in addition to visual (aesthetic) aspects, the (educated) observer recognises the 'character' of a space (in the sense of an essentialist 'being'). The construction of landscapes in Romanticism and in the

Biedermeier epochs, that were particularly intense and persistent in Germany, took a special path compared to other European languages (Safranski 2007). In Romanticism, landscape experienced "its highest revaluation in that mythological and historical contents merge into an expanded concept of 'Landschaft'" (Hohl 1977, p. 45; see also Piepmeier 1980). For Romantic painters—Caspar David Friedrich (1774–1840) should be highlighted—painting was no longer merely a question of artistic practice, but "one of the inner and moral and religious constitution of the artist" (Büttner 2006, p. 262; Fig. 4.3). In the Biedermeier era, landscape became a symbol of humanity, which was seen as threatened in particular by the development of civilization and tendencies towards technical usability and general utility thinking, which in physical space became symbolized by the expansion of cities and industrial facilities (Kortländer 1977). Landscape thus became the medium of social criticism, a tradition that is updated today in current discussions

Fig. 4.3 The picture 'The Wanderer above the Sea of Fog' (German original: 'Der Wanderer über dem Nebelmeer') by Caspar David Friedrich (painted around 1817). Today (at least in Germany), the painting, with its innovative large-scale back view of a human being, is regarded as the epitome of Romanticism. The picture is interpreted as an expression of man's desire for unity with nature, but also as a presentiment of death on the part of the (middle-aged wanderer) as well as a political commitment to the German nation (the wanderer wears the 'Altdeutsche Tracht' (old German costume) which was forbidden at the time; Grote 1950; Hoch 1996; Hofmann 2013; Lankheit 1978; reprint with permission of the Hamburger Kunsthalle)

about 'landscape and justice'. At that time, 'pre-modern rural landscape' was ide-alised as a homeland that had to be protected by the 'Heimatschutzbewegung' (homeland protection movement; Eisel 1982; Lekan and Zeller 2005). This specific connection, "i.e.—according to the idea—always individual and organic harmony of culture and nature can then be read in the 'Landschaft'" (Körner 2006, p. 6). This diversity of interpretation and evaluation of the word 'Landschaft' shaped (more or less unreflected) its use in German geography, especially in the form of 'Landschaftskunde' (landscape studies) for the change of the 19th to the 20th cen-tury and its conceptual export to international science (see Sect. 4.4).

A more detailed description of the concept of landscape in German can be found in Hard (1977), Müller (1977), Kühne (2015b), Schenk (2013).

Such differentiations can already be found in different European languages. Common to the English *landscape*, the French *paysage*, the Hungarian *taj* and the Polish *krajo-braz,* for example, is the aesthetic component with the German *Landschaft*; however, the material dimension contained in Hungarian and German (i.e. landscape as an object) is separated from this in English and French. This dimension is covered in French by the words 'pays', 'campagne' and 'terroir', whereby the word *terroir* also contains the gus-tatory charms that are only marginally linked to the German concept of landscape, and in English the material dimension is defined by the terms *land* and *country*, which in turn form further 'semantic courts' (Hard 1969, 1970b), such as 'country' as a political term. The German 'Landschaft' and the Hungarian taj show a special emotional charge in the context of 'Heimat', while the Polish 'krajobraz' is literally translated: View-in-the-country, has a stronger subjective component (Cosgrove 2006; Drexler 2009a, b, 2013; Hernik and Dixon-Gough 2013; Olwig 2002). Arabic, on the other hand, has no equiv-alent to the German 'Landschaft', here the Arabic word for 'garden' is used as a make-shift (Makhzoumi 2002, 2015), while in Turkish the word *payzaj* as a fiefdom word from French follows the French content (Türer-Baskaya 2013). Pursued further, the references in Japan and China to material and symbolic spaces are on the one hand clearly more differentiated (among other things, social ideas and material design are conceptually sep-arated); on the other hand, the juxtaposition of nature and culture, as it characterizes the Western concept of landscape, is not found; people are regarded as part of nature (Taylor and Xu 2018). The concept of 'landscape' as a comprehensive aesthetic synopsis and of the underlying objects and object constellations was only introduced as a scientific term through contact with Western science (especially German geography; see the following section; Gehring and Kohsaka 2007; Taylor and Xu 2018; Ueda 2009, 2013; Zhang et al. 2013). From this short synopsis the diversity, the different intersections, as well as the reference contexts of 'landscape' become clear (for more details see: Bruns 2013; Bruns and Kühne 2015; on the implications of landscape and colonialism see Box 10).

Box 10: Landscape and colonialism

With the colonization of large parts of the world, landscape consequences were also implied in the various dimensions of landscape. On the one hand, the interests of economic use (e.g. in the form of plantations) and political and administrative power (e.g. in the form of forts or entire settlements and parts of settlements according to European ideas) were inscribed in physical space; on the other hand, an aesthetic appropriation of physical spaces took place, including those that were transformed by colonial influence and are still present today as representatives of the sometimes brutal foreign rule. At the same time, literature, paintings, and photographs from the colonial era have shaped the image of the global South to this day (for more details, see Barnett 2015).

The colonization was also associated with a cartographic survey of the colonized world. As Harley (1992, p. 528) shows, cartography in the 16th and 17th centuries was "simultaneously a practical instrument for colonial policy, a visual rhetoric for fashioning European attitudes towards the Americas and its people, and an analogue for the acquisition, management and reinforcement of colonial power." In addition to cartographically mapping the areas, scientists from the colonizing countries also researched them, seeing in the colonized objects of research or aids for simple work (such as carriers) and denying them the ability to (aesthetically) capture physical spaces interpreted as landscapes (Gräbel 2015). Accordingly, the geographical descriptions of the spaces interpreted as landscapes were not the result of precise observation, let alone systematic recording, but rather of personal preferences filtered by colonial values (Mitchell 1994). The relationship between landscape visions and colonialism can therefore also be understood as "the dreamwork of imperialism" (Mitchell 1994, p. 10). Connected with the colonialist view of the world is the dichotomous (i.e. modernist) construction of 'us and them' as well as 'here and there', connected with the revaluation of one's own against the foreign (Said 1978). The worldwide spread of a western concept of landscape (strongly influenced by classical German geography) in the landscape-related sciences can also be interpreted as an element of the colonization of the world (and its consequences that continue to this day).

From a critical perspective (see Sect. 5.3), the principles of colonization, such as unequal exchange or aesthetic standardization, can be found not only in the context of processes on a global level, but also within a state or a region—for example, when the rural hinterland produces raw products that are then centrally processed and marketed, or when the rural environment is gentrified and the demands on a picturesque environment stand in the way of rational land management by the population that has already settled there (see, for example, Ipsen 1991, 1997; Walker and Fortmann 2003).

4.4   Historical Developments: Landscape as a Topic of Comparison Between Anglo-Saxon and German Geographical Research

The development of the 'expert special knowledge stocks' on the topic of landscape is not globally uniform, rather there are both culture-specific influences (through certain landscape concepts), national research traditions, differentiated influences of certain personalities, but also specific discursive developments and (scientific) political framework conditions (such as the priority given to certain disciplines). In this section, the developments in Anglo-Saxon and German geographical landscape research over the past 100 years are presented in their main features. This comparison appears to be of interest as far as, at the beginning of the scientific examination of landscape, research by German-speaking researchers was of great importance, whereas today Anglo-Saxon landscape research (also as applies to the number of researchers in this field) is of outstanding importance. The sub-division of Anglo-Saxon geography into a British and a North American tradition is less emphasized in the following, since the intention of the comparison is different. The main stages and developments of the respective developmental traditions will be discussed (more detailed descriptions of the respective traditions can be found in Hard 1970b, 1977; Kong and Dunn 2003; Schenk 2013; Wardenga 2006; Winchester, Wylie 2007; in a summary in Antrop 2018; Duncan and Duncan 2009; Cosgrove 2004 provides a comparison of Anglo-Saxon and German understandings of the landscape).

Common roots of Anglo-Saxon (especially North American) and German landscape research can be found in the understanding of landscape which is represented by Carl O. Sauer (1889–1975). He was a German geographer who built the Berkeley School of Geography into one of the leading Institutes of the United States in the 1920s and 1950s, internationalizing the concept of landscape of the 'classical' German geography during the turn of the 19th to the 20th century (Price and Lewis 1993; for his definition of landscape, see Box 5). In this essentialist tradition, he understood landscape as a 'superorganism', in which culture had a strong influence on physical space, thus setting himself apart from the previously dominant geodeterminism (which assumed that natural factors determined culture). Like the 'classical' German cultural geography, the Berkeley School was strongly fixed on the investigation of cultural inscriptions into physical space understood as landscape (Mathewson 2009; Wagner and Mikesell 1962). A specific focus of 'traditional' geography was the investigation of traditional material elements, such as the mapping of house, roof, and corridor forms (e.g. Born 1977; Kniffen 1965). The access to the physical spaces interpreted as 'landscape' was a more expert one, typical for essentialists. According to Wylie (2007, p. 41), the expert understanding of Sauer and his successors could be described as follows: An "expert, someone one who stands apart from the phenomena in question, the better to objectively scrutinise it".

The classical geographical concept of landscape arose from two traditions of thought (Hard 1977, p. 15): "(1.) the 'physiognomic' tradition of the versatilely interested traveller combined from a 'naïve' world view and 'scenic eye' and (2.) the 'regionalist' tradition of 'thinking in earth spaces' and earth space divisions". The criticism of this paradigm was similar in the Anglo-Saxon region and in Germany, although the consequences were completely different. Criticized were, firstly, the holistic-organistic understanding of landscape and culture, which, for example, left no room for individual developments (e.g. Duncan 1980); secondly, the already thematized 'object fetishism' (Duncan 1990, p. 11), i.e. the focus on material aspects of culture; thirdly, the focus on the exploration of 'traditional' and 'exotic' landscapes (Winchester et al. 2003) with extensive suppression of urban developments (Mathewson 2009). The result of the worldview of 'traditional geography' is a "well-ordered mosaic of spatially segmented natural and social units" (Blotevogel 1996, p. 13), which "structurally excludes both the increasingly important spatial interdependencies and the conflictual nature of spatial formations" (Blotevogel 1996, p. 13). In North American landscape research, J. B. Jackson, with his focus on vernacular landscapes since the 1950s, has formed an alternative discourse to traditional cultural landscape research (which, however, was only received more intensively in German-language landscape research in the first decade of the 21st century; for example, in Franzen and Krebs 2005; Prominski 2004). Jackson (1997, p. 343) focuses his considerations on the vernacular landscape, landscape is not a work of art for him: "It is a temporary product of much sweat and hardship and earnest thought". In this way he not only differentiates himself from an aesthetically fixed perspective on landscape, but also from ideas of a harmonious and ultimately stable 'organism' by referring to the changeability of the materially understood landscape.

In English speaking scientific communities, criticism of the Berkely School reached a (provisional) climax in the development of the 'new cultural geography' (Cosgrove 1989; Cosgrove and Jackson 1987; Duncan 1990). Although new cultural geography also dealt with historical contexts (although contextualized and theoretically framed), it considered not only spatial but also of social aspects as well as urban and rural spaces and is "interested in the contingent nature of culture, in dominant ideologies and in forms of resistance to them" (Cosgrove and Jackson 1987, p. 95). Here a transition is made from an essentialist basic attitude (and approaches of empirical approaches) to a view dominated by social constructivism. So, for Cosgrove (1984), 'landscape not simply the world we see; it is a way of seeing the world'. In the 'new cultural geography', 'landscape' always remained present, conceptualized as 'text' or as an everyday construction. In Germany, on the other hand, criticism of the largely essentialist 'landscape paradigm' of German geography culminated at the Kiel Geographer's Day in 1969. Geographical landscape research was replaced by a positivist-empiristic paradigm with almost no resistance to empirical evidence, methodological justification, and ideology, and with consideration to an "all too simple realism" (Kaufmann 2005, p. 102). This had differentiated consequences for the sub-areas of geography, such that in the "mainstream in anthropogeography it was hardly career-promoting to speak of landscape" (Schenk 2006, p. 17). While 'landscape', conceived as a material object in physical geography oriented towards the natural sciences, was conceptually preserved and perpetuated there in connection with ecosystem approaches (in ecology also referred to as 'ecosystematic') as geoecology or landscape ecology (e.g. Eisel 2009; Kirchhoff and Trepl 2009). With the 'quantitative revolution' and thus quantitative approaches (Arnreiter and Weichhart 1998; Gebhardt 2016; Glasze 2015), positivist approaches were established, with a focus on the category 'space'. On a medium scale, the concept of 'region' made a career, especially in German-speaking geography, which was deemed more positivistic than the 'essentialistically burdened concept of landscape' (Chilla et al. 2016).

After 1969, Historical Geography in Germany remained the refuge for dealing with landscape in human geography, which specifically dealt with the material (partly immaterial) heritage of landscape, understood as a 'historically grown cultural landscape' (Fehn 1976; Schenk et al. 1997; Schenk 2001, 2006, 2011), a focus that has been increasingly developed in Anglo-Saxon geography since the 1970s (Harvey and Wiljinson 2018). In terms of discourse theory, German human geography can be described as the replacement of one hegemonic discourse by another (Weber 2018; cf. Sect. 2.4.3 of the Discourse Theory). In Anglo-Saxon (specifically North American) geography a strong Marxist geography developed, which in part connected with the 'new cultural geography' (e.g. Cosgrove and Daniels 1988; Harvey 1996). In this understanding of landscape, unequal possibilities of manifesting one's own interests in the physical space described as landscape is ciritized as well as the development of existing relations of perpetuating landscape-aesthetic conceptions (using the example of Disneyfication; Warren 1994), which contribute to eradicating economic inequalities (such as the unequal distribution of property in space) from consciousness by means of aesthetization (Bermingham 1989; Cosgrove 1998). The resonance of Marxist ideas remained restrained in West German geography, only in the 1990s—after the German Democratic Republic had been annexed to the Federal Republic of Germany (the designation 'reunification' appearing somewhat euphemistic, since the political, administrative, economic, etc., system of the FRG was simply extended to the former GDR)—did the 'critical geography' strengthen, but without making use of the term 'landscape'.

Presently in English-speaking geography, in addition to the perpetuation of (neo) Marxism (more so in the United States than in England; see Wylie 2007), there is also an increased focus on phenomenological approaches (see Sect. 2.5.1), as well as a discourse-theoretical perspective based on the approaches of Michel Foucault (1977) and the making available of actor network theory (see Sect. 2.5.2), while at the same time continuing to devote socio-constructivist attention to geographical landscape research (cf. Wylie 2007; here we can also speak of discourse pluralization), German geography has been increasingly concerned with constructivist approaches since the first decade of the 21st century (see also Sect. 2.4). However, this approach is based more on sociological theory formation (social constructivism and radical constructivism) than on Anglo-Saxon geography or political science discussion (in discourse theory, in which Laclau and Mouffe are more likely to be followed than Foucault as in Anglosaxion world; Wylie 2015; see Sect. 2.4.3). Approaches to 'critical landscape research' are influenced more by Bourdieu's sociology (Sect. 5.4) than by a Marxist orientation (more detailed: Gebhardt 2016; Kühne 2018e). Constructivist landscape research has established itself in German geography to such an extent that it presents itself as a 'New Landscape Geography' (Kühne et al. 2018), quite self-confidently, in a human geography environment that is still rather sceptical of the concept of landscape today. The strong discursive demarcation of humangeographic landscape research on the part of 'mainstream geography' has in turn led to a lesser inner struggle for discourse sovereignty, so that within German-language humangeographic landscape research both constructivist, phenomenological, and positivist approaches coexist. In view of the renewed focus of parts of German human geography on the subject of landscape with a theoretical framing beyond essentialist and positivist approaches, it is today again internationally connectable and certainly also able to enrich these as a result of the development of specific perspectives (cf. detailed Kühne 2015b; a résumé on the subject of landscape socialization can be found in Box 11).

Box 11: The socialization of landscape—a brief summary
In order to understand the question of how social and partial social notions of landscape are perpetuated, it makes sense to examine the different forms of socialization of landscape. Landscape socialization research is able to contribute to the understanding of why and in what way certain interpretations of landscape are similar (especially with regard to stereotypical patterns of interpretation and evaluation) or different (especially with regard to native regular landscapes, but also with regard to the differentiation of expert, technically bound special knowledge). It becomes clear how closely this interconnects with other thematic fields of landscape research, such as the question of social power structures, landscape aesthetics, and also the examination of landscape paradigms as well as the investigation of the historical development of landscape concepts (specifically in cultural differentiation). Theoretically, landscape socialization research can be connected in a special way to the constructivist family of theories (especially to social constructivism and discourse theory). From this perspective, research questions arise as to how, for example, technical paradigms from the expert special knowledge stocks affect systematic components of the emergence of stereotypical landscapes ('landscape education'), how individual contradictions between native-normal landscape ideas and stereotypical and special knowledge stock ideas are interpreted. If the cultural ties and also the social differentiation of landscape interpretations and valuations are taken serious scientifically, the focus of research is increasingly on the specific and special. This can also be applied to the investigation of scientific research traditions, as it is here in the comparison of Anglo-Saxon and German-language geographical landscape research. It becomes clear that Anglo-Saxon geographic landscape research was carried out much more continuously, whereas in the German-speaking world it was restricted for a long time to physical geography due to the Kiel Geographer's Day and came to a virtual standstill in human geography for more than three decades.

Power and Landscape: From Political Worldviews and Critical Landscape Research

5

If landscape is not simply understood as 'given', but as socially produced (on the level of the social, the individual as well as the material), then the question of the possibilities and limits of influencing these different levels becomes virulent. If the social power relations, on which the different possibilities and limits of influencing the landscape are based, are not unquestionably accepted, a critical attitude is created towards them. In contrast to philosophy, in which 'critique' is generally understood as a reflection on an "achievement or function" (Schweppenhäuser 2007, p. 27), the central element of critical landscape research lies in the (normatively) critical attitude towards social (power) relationships and their spatial (physical-spatial as well as social-spatial) manifestations. Since the basis of critique lies in different (political) worldviews, these—including their consequences in terms of interpretation and evaluation of landscape—are dealt with. Critical landscape research is 'transverse' to the theoretical approaches presented, i.e. it makes use of them to substantiate its criticism or to justify it normatively. The focus of the critique is an unequal distribution of power in society that is understood as unlegitimized, including consequences for the landscape and side effects as well as their safeguarding by educational institutions, which represent a part of systematic socialization (as education). In this respect, a brief outline of the connections between power and landscape is given first. This is followed by a presentation of the connection between (political) worldviews and landscape, before three critical approaches are presented: those of Critical Theory (for an overview, see: Dubiel 1992; Horkheimer 1977[1937]; Horkheimer and Adorno 1969; Agger 2006; Calhoun 1995; Horkheimer 1982; Morrow and Brown 1994), in Bourdieu tradition (Bourdieu 1989, 2000, 2016; Bourdieu, Calhoun et al. 1993; Harker et al. 1990). A central element of both critical approaches is the social conditionality and the social function of aesthetic judgements and finally the criticism of the lack of democratic legitimation of landscape policy through bureaucratization (Dahrendorf 1972, 1987) as the third critical approach.

© Springer Fachmedien Wiesbaden GmbH, part of Springer Nature 2019
O. Kühne, *Landscape Theories*, RaumFragen: Stadt – Region – Landschaft,
https://doi.org/10.1007/978-3-658-25491-9_5

5.1   Power and Landscape

The question of the connection between power (for this term, see Box 12) and land-scape has been increasingly addressed in spatial social sciences since the late 1990s. In general, the focus is on how social power processes inscribe themselves on physical space more than on how social landscape interpretations are dependent on power rela-tions. As a result of the omnipresence of power in social relations (Foucault 1977; Paris 2005; Popitz 1992) and the attachment of landscape to society, "landscapes are part of a process in which hierachies are reproduced and challenged" (Winchester, Kong and Dunn 2003, p. 5; some examples of power-related landscape research are: Gailing and Leibenath 2017; Kost and Schönwald 2015; Kühne 2008b; Leibenath 2015; Mitchell 2003, 2007; Mitchell 2002a, b; Olwig 2003; Schein 1997; Trudeau 2006; Wescoat 2009; Weber et al. 2017).

Box 12: Power

Power is an everyday and often unquestioned phenomenon. Power is also ambiv-alent: power can be associated on the one hand with freedom, the emancipation from nature, but on the other hand also with oppression. Heinrich Popitz (1992, p. 12) refers to the anthropogenic character of power relations; after all, they are "not God-given, they are not bound by myths, not necessary for nature, not sanc-tified by inviolable traditions. They are human work". Their reversibility results from this social bond of power (Popitz 1992), which in turn intensifies the strug-gle for power, whereby power struggles are a part of "the always-present negotia-tion of normality" (Paris 2005, p. 7). From a systems-theoretical perspective, more or less stable power relations can be described as an essential element of the sta-bility of society; after all, they meet the need for reliability and security (Parsons 1991[1951]; see also Anter 2012)—a view that Dahrendorf (1972) vehemently contradicts by referring to the social productivity of conflicts (arising from differ-ent distributions of power).

In his classical definition, Max Weber (1976[1922], p. 28) describes power as "any opportunity [German: 'Chance'] within a social relationship to assert one's own will against opposition, regardless of what this opportunity is based on". This definition formulates four criteria (Anter 2012):

1. The category of 'opportunity' that refers to the potentiality of power,
2. 'social relationship' referring to the personal character of power,
3. to the voluntaristic (the dominance of the will over the mind) element to which the 'own will' refers,
4. a potential resistance that opposes 'one's own will', to which the word 'resist' refers.

In contrast to power, domination is more specific: it does not contain absolute control over others, but is "always limited to certain contents and persons" (Dahrendorf 1972, p. 33; following Max Weber). Dahrendorf (1983) sees this stronger organization of (undifferentiated) power into domination as a central aspect of peaceful social development (as can be found, for example, in the representative democracy he favored). According to Max Weber (1976[1922]), the development from power to domination begins with the emergence of the modern state.

In addition to the genesis of different concepts (some of which are associated with the interpretation sovereignty), social development also brought with it an increasing possibility for humans to modify the physical foundations of appropriated physical landscapes according to their requirements. Both the genesis and discursive enforcement as well as the modification of physical spaces are connected with power. The modification of physical spaces are affected in numerous ways, in co-evolution with an increasing technical manageability as well as a systematization of economic appropriation (e.g. in the accumulation of sufficient economic capital for the construction of larger factory facilities) and legal regimentation, e.g. the enforcement of the construction of large infrastructures against the will of the local population, which formed a central element of the domestication of space (Engels 2010). The economic compulsion for efficient land management (especially in the wealthy countries of the world) forces a mechanization of agriculture (in the form of large fields and large stables), with the consequence that the physical foundations of appropriated physical landscapes corresponded less and less with the social landscape widespread (romantically shaped) ideas of appropriated physical landscape. Appropriated physical landscapes thus ultimately document an outdated state of power distribution. The enforceability of politically formulated landscape conditions also requires a systematic accumulation of power and transformation into domination.

The previous remarks illustrate the close interdependence of power and landscape. Thus, the physical foundations of appropriated physical landscape (in essential parts) can be described as the physical-spatially manifested consequences and side effects of social, power-mediated action. Yet with Max Weber (1976[1922]), action can be described as external or internal action, omission or tolerance with which the actor, or the actors, associates a sense. A neglected cultivation thus represents an act, as it were; after all, acting persons associate with the neglect the sense that a cultivation does not seem opportune because of certain considerations (see Kühne 2008b, 2018c). If the constitutive dimension of social landscape is included in the considerations of power and landscape, the emergence of an appropriated physical landscape can be described as being the result of the dictate of what is defined as economically necessary, modified by socially enforced (often aesthetic) norms and values, within the limits of political-administrative enforcement power, manifested in that which is legally permitted and forbidden under the aestheticizing construction of consciousness on the basis of social norm systems (Kühne 2012b, 2015c). The physical foundations of appropriated physical landscapes thus also become indicators for power distributions on a local, regional, national, continental to global scale under the influence of political, economic, social community, and cultural systemic logics (see Sect. 2.4.2 on autopoietic systems theory).

5.2   Political Worldviews and Their Landscape Implications

Physical spaces are also an expression of the political will of the world. Different ideas of how a society should be structured also give rise to ideas of how it should be organized spatially. Political worldviews do not become virulent in politics alone, they are also found in normative and moral ideas and implications of science in which socio-political preferences of authors mix (a striking example is the conflict between 'marxist' and 'bourgeois' social science). These often remain implicit and are sometimes expressed openly. As recent research has shown, this applies not only to social science studies, but also to those that see themselves as scientific, such as ecology (see e.g. Eisel 2009; Körner und Eisel 2006; Piechocki 2010).

The different political worldviews are very disparate "in their interpretations of historical change" (Berlin 1995[1969], p. 80). In connection with this, they have very different views regarding the question of "which are the elementary needs, interests and ideals of the people and who most likely represented these ideals, how comprehensively and over which periods of time" (Berlin 1995[1969], p. 80). Accordingly, the concepts of justice of the different political worldviews also differ considerably (Box 13) and (often implicitly) underlie the current discussions in the context of 'landscape and justice' (Ernston 2013; Mason and Milbourne 2014; Mitchell 2003, 2008). In scientific terms, binary distinctions are more common (e.g., enlightenment/counter-enlightenment positions as in Piechocki 2010, individualistic/communitarian positions as in Kühne 2015e), or three (as in Voigt 2009a, b) or four (as in Vicenzotti 2011a; cf. also Schwarzer 2014) political ideologies are distinguished. In the following, three political worldviews are to be characterized, which—to put it another way—can be understood as corners of a triangle into which other political worldviews can be classified: classical liberalism, conservatism, and socialism.

> **Box 13: The (in)equality of people: understandings of justice**
> The demand for 'justice' is pervading many political as well as scientific debates. In general, justice regulates interactions between people. What is meant by 'justice' is very different:
>
> 1. Egalitarianism (also known as the principle of equality or the pejorative 'watering can principle') assumes that everyone is entitled to the same quantity of a (scarce) good; regardless of the performance (however, it is defined) he performs.

Inequality is regarded as a situation that is contrary to the norm and must be eliminated (particularly through state intervention).

2. In accordance with the justice of performance, those who do much are also entitled to more goods. Inequality thus becomes an incentive to do more.

3. According to the communist principle, justice is achieved when everyone contributes according to his abilities and receives according to his needs. Here inequality is considered to be productive within limits, since people have different abilities.

4. Need-based justice is considered to have been established when everyone has met their basic needs (such as food, protection from disease, education that is sufficient to deal with the consequences of their own actions, etc.). Inequality is tolerated—beyond the basic needs that have been secured.

5. The sighthound principle (also known as 'first comes first serves') attributes scarce goods to them in the order in which they have registered their need. Here inequality is part of the incentive system to vigilantly pursue one's own interests.

6. With the random principle, everyone is given the same chance to receive a scarce good (e.g. distribution of a scarce good by lot). Inequality is accepted accordingly, since in the next raffle everyone again has the same chances of receiving a good.

7. The authoritarian principle grants the ruler the right to assign scarce goods to his subjects. Inequality is desirable because loyalty to the ruling system is rewarded.

8. The principle of procedural justice decouples the question of justice from the allocation of scarce goods. Justice is given when procedures for the distribution of scarce goods are carried out according to previously defined procedures, all participants in the process are subject to the same rules, and each participant has the right to participate in the distribution process. Inequality is considered unproblematic when the rules of procedure have been followed.

9. The principle of equal opportunities—independent of spatial, social, cultural, etc.—wants to be a principle of justice for all. Origin of the participants—giving everyone the same opportunities in life. Whether he makes use of these opportunities or not is then up to his personal responsibility. Inequality is regarded as unproblematic if it is due to individual and self-responsible decisions and is not due to unequal opportunities (e.g. due to family backgrounds).

Bohmeyer (2005), Kersting (2005) and Sen (2009, 2017) discuss in more detail the understandings of justice.

5.2.1   Liberalism, Conservatism and Socialism—Some Main Features

Liberal ideas are closely linked to the Enlightenment; they were essentially influenced by Thomas Hobbes, John Locke, Adam Smith, but also by Immanuel Kant. In the 20th and 21st century, it was associated with names such as Max Weber, Karl Popper, Ralf Dahrendorf, John Rawls, Armatya Sen and Martha Nussbaum. The central concept of liberalism (hence its name) is freedom. Ralf Dahrendorf (2007b, p. 26) understands freedom to mean first the "absence of coercion", more concretely people are "free to the extent that they can make their own decisions. In the state of freedom, we find conditions that reduce constraints to a minimum. The goal of liberalism or the policy of freedom is that there is a maximum of freedom under given restrictions" (Dahrendorf 2007b, p. 26). Amartya Sen (2009) sees freedom as a more precious value for two reasons: First, freedom gives us more opportunities to pursue our goals, the things we value collectively or individually. For example, freedom supports us in our decision to live the way we want. It supports us in the pursuit of the goals we seek to achieve. Secondly, however, we can attach importance to the actual decision-making process. Therefore, we do not want to be forced into a situation where others put pressure on us. Thus, liberalism's political context is linked to "the defence of certain individual rights and freedoms such as freedom of expression, non-discrimination on grounds of race, sex or nationality, procedural rights (e.g. the right to defence) and political rights to democratic participation and participation in elections" (López 1995, p. 17).

Liberalism is based on the axioms of a human being born free, endowed with equal rights, good by nature and gifted with reason as an individual (Leonhard 2001; Pennington 2002; Schaal and Heidenreich 2006; Bauer and Wall-Strasser 2016). At the centre of liberal ideas is the individual, who should be able to unfold as unhindered as possible from social constraints in personal responsibility (which also means the duty to earn one's own living). One should be able to freely choose an alternative according to one's own convictions, based on the largest possible number of options (political, economic, cultural, etc.). For liberalism, education is the basis for freedom, self-responsibility, and the maximization of life chances (see Box 14). According to liberalism an optimistic attitude towards the future is inherent, i.e. a 'better' future could be shaped by progress (Leonhard 2001), "Liberalism is necessarily a philosophy of change" (Dahrendorf 1979, p. 61). Accordingly, society is not subject to any superordinate order, nor does it develop teleologically towards a goal (Popper 2012[1945]). Rather, society's task is to offer individuals security in their quest for happiness and to open up opportunities in life for them. Karl Popper (2012[1945]) underlines the (liberal) demand for a society that is as open as possible: "In order to do this, we must maintain the conditions of rational, critical debate under which it remains possible to be of different views" (Dahrendorf 1980, p. 13). This means that not only in science but also in society in general there should be competition for the most suitable solutions to challenges and development opportunities. In scientific terms, this means that new perspectives (such as constructivism) are compatible with a liberal attitude if they do not pursue social or scientific teleologies (such as Marxism).

Box 14: Life chances
The concept of life chances represents (besides his contributions to role and conflict theory) a core of the sociology of Ralf Dahrendorf. Under life chances he understands "election chances, options. They demand two things, rights to participate and an offer of activities and goods to choose from" (Dahrendorf 2007a, p. 44). The election chances must be associated with a sense. Ralf Dahrendorf sees an opportunity in relation to Max Weber (1976[1922]) on the one hand a "structurally founded [...] probability of behaviour", and on the other hand he understands it "as something that the individual can have, something as an opportunity to satisfy interests" (Dahrendorf, 1979, p. 98). Figuratively speaking, Dahrendorf (1979, p. 50) understands life chances as "the baking forms of human life in society; they determine how far people can develop". Life chances in turn depend on social contexts, as Ralf Dahrendorf makes clear: "Life chances are possibilities of individual growth, the realization of abilities, desires and hopes, and these possibilities are provided by social conditions" (Dahrendorf 1979, p. 50). Life chances are determined by options and ligatures. While options represent "choices given in social structures, alternatives of action" (Dahrendorf 1979, p. 50), Dahrendorf defines ligatures as values, i.e. "deep bonds whose existence [gives] meaning to the chances of choice" (Dahrendorf 2007a, p. 45), they accordingly form the "foundations of action" (Dahrendorf 1979, p. 51). The reciprocal relationship between ligatures and options for the development of life chances can be succinctly formulated: "Ligatures without options mean oppression, while options without ties are meaningless" (Dahrendorf 1979, pp. 51–52). The relationship of the liberal Dahrendorf to ligatures is quite ambivalent, because on the one hand ligatures turn mere opportunities into "opportunities with meaning and meaning, i.e. life chances" (Dahrendorf 2004, p. 51), on the other hand they always have the tendency to produce obligations towards society that reduce the options of the individual.

Liberals have a split relationship with the state. On the one hand, the free person becomes a 'citizen' through the state, i.e. a person "who has sacrificed his freedom to the state, thus one who adapts" (Hank 2007, p. 150); on the other hand, the state enables man to overcome the "dull-animalist struggle for self-preservation" (Kersting 2009, p. 54) of the state of nature. Mises (1927, p. 33) briefly defines the tasks of a liberal state: "Protection of property, freedom and peace". This classical position of liberalism is peculiar to a critical attitude against further state activity (especially the state's social policy of redistributing wealth and income): "The salvation of the state lies not in happiness, but in law" (Krebs 2014, p. 66). The justice model represented here (see Box 13) is that of performance justice in the context of economic activity (cf. Opielka 2004), while in the context of fundamental rights egalitarianism and practical politics procedural justice is pursued.

In contrast to classical liberalism, a liberal basic position developed in the 20th century which can be described as 'liberalism of equal opportunities' (with different emphases here Ralf Dahrendorf, John Rawls, Amartya Sen, and Martha Nussbaum). The latter assumes that equal opportunities in life do not only arise formally through the guarantee of fundamental rights, but also substantially include "citizenship rights to be fulfilled […] social rights, such as the right to protection from need through no fault of one's own or the right to an adequate pension or education" (Dahrendorf 1983, p. 104). Whereby—here the core of the theory becomes clear as a liberal one—a primacy of freedom exists, because neither the increase of wealth or income nor a better distribution of economic resources can be regarded as reasons for the violation of freedoms to which all are entitled, as Sen (2009) emphasizes. This focus on equal opportunities means an expansion of the fundamental rights of egalitarianism in classical liberalism, and at the same time a restriction of its own (in the economic sense) principle of equal performance, because the fulfilment of 'social rights' is accompanied by a redistribution by the state, a process that is viewed critically—also by the representatives of 'Equal Opportunities Liberalism'—because redistribution produces 'bureaucracy' that on the one hand produces administrative costs, on the other hand generalizes individual emergencies and thus contributes to the humiliation of those affected (Dahrendorf 1987; Paris 2005). According to Dahrendorf (2007a, p. 86), the (economic) inequalities resulting from this approach are tolerable "if and as long as they do not enable the winners to prevent others from fully participating in society or, in the case of poverty, to prevent people from exercising their civil rights".

Early conservatism developed through critical examination of the French Revolution and its ideas (associated with the names Edmund Burke, Joseph de Maistre, and Karl Ludwig von Haller, among others). For conservatism (derived from the Latin 'conservare') tradition has a central function in the order of society. It forms the frame of orientation, order, and reference. As with liberalism, conservatism is also related to the ideas of rationality and enlightenment, not affirmative but negative (cf. Greiffenhagen 1971; Schoeps 1981; Lenk 1989). This creates a dilemma for conservatism; it is constitutively bound to that which it rejects (Greiffenhagen 1971; Trepl 2012). After all, it was only with the emergence of progressive, enlightened thought that the previously self-evident institutions such as religion, family, and people were subject to a pressure to justify and thus devise values of conservative thinking. Another dilemma for conservatism is to follow the logic of the Enlightenment in order to defend what it takes for granted: Conservatism saw itself forced to resort to reflective reason (Schoeps 1981; Lenk 1989). In contrast to liberalism, conservatism pursues a different normative understanding of human coexistence. It is not the 'society of independent individuals' that conservatism strives for, but a community in the sense of an organismic connection of people (Greiffenhagen 1971; Lenk 1989; Voigt 2009b; Trepl 2012). This connection means "that the individuals, like organs in the organism, serve the whole, and that in their respective places" (Trepl 2012, p. 141). This means an understanding of the relationship of the individual to society diametrically opposed to liberalism: the individual is not an individual endowed with equal rights vis-à-vis other people, but is part of a historically grown multiplicity, his position in society and even more in the community is determined by his function in the 'organism'. From the liberal position derives the right of the individual to be able to freely express his own opinion so that the most suitable argument may convince, while the conservative "does not argue with everyone about the right thing to convince him" (Trepl 2012, p. 145), rather he adopts "a paternalistic attitude against those who 'would not understand it after all' (Trepl 2012a, p. 145). The powerful man, because of his own position in the 'organism of community', takes a decisive position over the interests of the minority. The understanding of justice that dominates conservatism is correspondingly that of justice in need (Opielka 2004; cf. Schildberg 2010). The concept of freedom in conservatism is also different from that in liberalism: "Freedom in this conception means adaptation to the higher order of the whole" (Kötzle 1999, p. 23), not the maximization of individual life chances. If liberalism strives to regulate the influence of authorities, conservatism regards them as a guarantor for the structuring and preservation of the community. Authority relies (albeit in decreasing measure) on religion or tradition. The community normatively integrates itself 'harmoniously' into its social and natural environment (Eisel 2004; Lenk 1989; Voigt 2009b). Deviations from traditional social norms are rejected accordingly or are at least considered to require justification. With the core of conservative world interpretation of the idea of peculiarity or personality, the epistemological orientation of conservatism reveals a great affinity to essentialism; the search for the 'essence' of larger units (e.g. 'peoples' or 'landscapes') is one of the central objects of conservative research programs. Traditionality and historicity are then often used to derive a conservation norm, such as 'historically grown cultural landscapes' or 'traditional urban structures' in the spatial context (Eisel 1997; Piechocki 2010; Vicenzotti 2011a; Trepl 2012; Hauser 2012).

Eppler (1975) differentiated conservative positions by distinguishing between structural conservatism and value conservatism. While structural conservatism advocates the preservation of traditional privileges and power relations serving ultimately to represent a justification pattern for inequality of opportunity, value conservatism is directed towards the preservation of an environment worth living in, a society based on solidarity as well as the dignity of the individual. Such an interpretation of conservatism makes it connectable with the environmental movement, which has been growing since the 1970s, as well as with social democratic and trade union positions (Euchner, Stegmann et al. 2005). With such a shift in focus, he opened conservative thinking also to understand justice beyond needs-based justice, especially opportunity and procedural justice.

Socialism (from Latin 'socialis') originated in the continuation of the ideas of the French Revolution, and also in the rejection of liberal and conservative ideas in the 19th century (Bärsch 1981). The term 'socialism' is a summary of different theories and ideas, which are defined by the "primacy of 'society' respective of the 'societal'" (Bärsch 1981,

p. 170) over the individual (to whom, as shown, liberalism gives priority) as well as by the 'grown community' prioritized by conservatism. As a result of the prioritization of the 'social community', socialist currents reject the privileged status of individuals who have grown out of their pursuit of economic gain (Bärsch 1981). In this context, a distinction can be made between classical socialism, which prefers a collectivization of means of production, and communism, which "wants to transfer means of production as well as consumer goods into common property (distribution of goods)" (Bärsch 1981, p. 172; see also Fainstein 2010). The principles of justice of the socialist idea structure are the egalitarian or the communist. These are not realized in capitalism because of the self-interested actions of the people, so the fulfillment of the preferred standards of justice is shifted into the future. Regarding future orientation, there is a structural parallel to the idea of liberalism: both have an optimistic attitude towards the future, which distinguishes them from conservatism.

A structural parallel with conservatism is found in socialist world views in relation to the respective 'elites' (which, of course, are formed completely differently). Especially in revolutionary socialism, the masses are to be led to a 'just society' by a 'revolutionary elite': "What led them [the revolutionary elite] was the conviction that it was their task to free the exploited and oppressed" (Becker 2013, p. o.S.). Here, too, a paternalistic attitude becomes clear, which of course runs counter to the egalitarian basic idea of socialism. The 'outer leadership' by 'revolutionary elites' is to be replaced in egalitarian socialist societies by the 'inner leadership' of individuals in the sense of socialism, i.e. the individuals are to act out of their own conviction in the sense of the socialist community. Education is central to this process: Through educational processes the 'wrong' (self-interested) is to be replaced by a 'right' (solidary) consciousness (Bärsch 1981). Here, again, a structural parallel (with again a substantive contradiction) to the liberal educational approach becomes apparent: "The liberals want to stylise the citizen from the worker, to integrate him into the linguistic, political and spiritual traditions of the bourgeoisie, while the socialists seek to establish class solidarity and class consciousness, also politically, with the means of education" (Knoll 1981, p. 92).

Central for the socialist worldview is an objective to which state society should develop (teleology). Teleology becomes particularly clear in Marxism: As a result of the contradiction between production conditions and the productive forces, a sequence of social systems inevitably develops whose transitions are characterized by revolutions (Fig. 5.1). The sequence of social orders interpreted by Marxism as the law of development is called 'historical materialism'. Following the revolutionary paradigm, the 'self-destruction' of capitalism is assumed to be the term used to describe the control of society by market forces, according to which "the market economy always carries within itself the causes of its own downfall" (Herzog 2013, p. 109), since the industrial society of private property is immanent in the impoverishment of the working masses, which can only be lifted by a revolution borne by this (Bärsch 1981). Following this logic, even reformist socialist efforts (which, on the way to socialism, pursue reforms within the market economy system, e.g. for more participation in the workplace for workers, higher wages, etc.) will be understood as 'management and manipulation of the capitalist

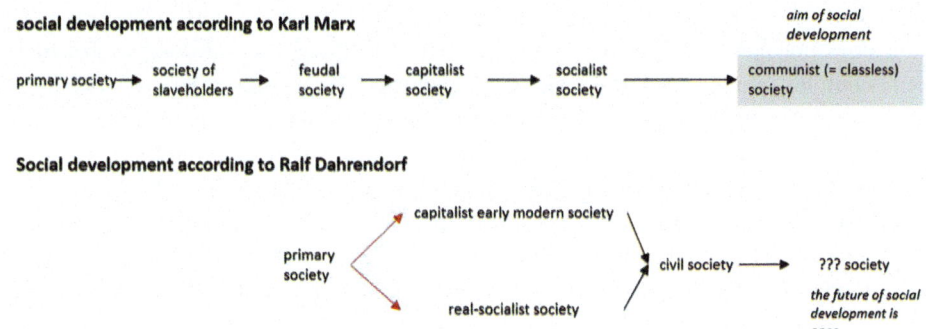

Fig. 5.1 The different stages of social development according to Marx and Dahrendorf. In Marx's case, history teleologically boils down to communist society; in Dahrendorf's case, on the other hand, the future of society is open (after Kühne 2017c)

crisis' (see e.g. Harvey 2005, 2008). The liberal democracy Marxist is also regarded as a 'hostage of capitalist interests', state institutions in liberal democracy are understood as instruments of economic elites (e.g. Agnoli 1968) and the liberal core idea of free will is interpreted as "an ideological 'fog formation' in the human brain" (Recki 2009, p. 29). The institutions of the liberal-democratic state, but also of the 'social market economy', are interpreted as instruments for pacifying the exploited masses with the aim of 'prolonging the death struggle of capitalism'. For Marxism, the driving force behind social development is the distribution of and control over economic goods, especially production technologies (see e.g. Daniels 1989; Harvey 2005; Henderson and Sheppard 2006). This reduction of social development, as well as the assumption of the predictability of social development similar to natural law, has led Marxism to be accused of arguing essentialistically at its core, since an 'essence' of social development is assumed here (e.g. Dahrendorf 1971; Kühne 2017c; Laclau and Mouffe 1985). For the liberal thinker Ralf Dahrendorf, on the other hand, real-socialism, alongside capitalist early modern society, is a path to liberal civil society, the more decisive difference being that the social future is open to him (and other liberal thinkers such as Karl Popper) and not predetermined (see Fig. 5.1; Dahrendorf 1972, 2007a; Popper 2012[1945]).

In the course of time, approaches developed in the context of socialism, liberalism, and conservatism, which led to (partial) new reflections and formulations. These are marked with the prefix 'Neo', whereby the individual designations can be understood in different ways (Box 15).

Box 15: The 'New Ismen': Neomarxism, neoconservatism and neoliberalism
Neomarxism
Neo-Marxism has developed increasingly since the Second World War. On the one hand, it sets itself apart (as 'Western Marxism') from the developments of real socialism in Eastern Central Europe and Eastern Europe; on the other hand,

it does not follow the idea of 'classical Marxism' that society develops through revolutions into the state of socialism/communism. The 'Frankfurt School' with its 'Critical Theory' had a special influence on neo-Marxism. Here the 'instrumental reason', i.e. the purpose-rational approach to the world that leads to the exploitation of man and nature, of capitalism but also of real socialism, is at the centre of critique (see Sect. 5.3). Neo-Marxism has had a considerable influence on sociological spatial research since the 1980s, especially through the writings of Henri Lefebreve (for further information see: Arato 2016; Gorman 1984).

Neoconservatism
Neoconservatism has been increasingly developed in the United States since the late 1960s. It shares in principle the values of 'classical conservatism', such as family, homeland, tradition, etc., but has a positive relationship to economic liberalism. Thus, the combination of democracy and market economy is regarded as the highest stage of social development, which must be defended against enemies from inside and outside by force of arms. Samuel Huntington's thesis of the 'Clash of Civilizations' (Huntington 2011), in which it is assumed that large-scale conflicts in the 21st century no longer arise between nations but between cultures, identities, and religions, provides an essential scientific basis for this. While political geography is intensively concerned with neoconservative ideas, their influence on landscape research remained rather subdued (see more detailed: Kristol 1995; Vaïsse 2010).

Neoliberalism
The word 'neoliberalism' has two completely different meanings (which, when used, should ultimately lead to the determination of the underlying understanding of use). First of all, the word 'neoliberalism' (1) describes a liberal movement that emerged in the 1930s (the so-called 'Freiburg School') whose core concern was the modernization of classical liberalism. They demanded a strong state, not subject to instrumentalization, combined with the goal of a clear competitive order to protect citizens and the market from its self-destructive effects (so-called Ordoliberalism). This reading of liberalism formed the 'social market economy' after the foundation of the Federal Republic of Germany. The word 'neoliberalism', however, (2) also describes a diagnosis (especially from a socialist world view) of contemporary society, which is characterized by deregulation of state tasks, economization of all areas of life, pressure to perform, globalization of all areas of life, and increasing polarization of society. It is precisely this significance of 'neoliberalism' that has gained considerable influence in social science spatial research in recent years (see, among others: Harvey 2005; Larner 2003; Meijer 1987).

5.2.2   Landscape and Political Worldviews: Understandings of City, Country, and Suburbia

If the spatial types 'wilderness', 'rural space', 'suburbium' and 'city' are judged from the perspective of the political systems of ideas of socialism, conservatism, and (classical) liberalism presented in the previous section, very different interpretations and evaluations result (for more details see Eisel 1982, 2009; Kirchhoff and Trepl 2009; Kühne 2015e; Vicenzotti 2006, 2011a; Voigt 2009a, b).

Liberal connotations of wilderness are quite contradictory, in one perspective as a symbol of the dangerous, pre-societal state of nature of struggle, in the other as a place of freedom in which the individual must prove himself (see also Pregill and Volkman 1999), through which it can "be valued as a means of overcoming itself" (Vicenzotti 2011a, p. 110). If it is viewed from an economic-liberal perspective, it can be regarded as a symbol for the unregulated self-control of the market, while wilderness as physical space is understood as an unproductive place (and thus ultimately as superfluous space). Conservatism, on the other hand, considers inner as well as outer wilderness to be "the sphere of the drive-bound. It is the temptation to resist that which is to be restrained and left behind" (Vicenzotti 2011a, p. 140; cf. also Kötzle 1999). In conservatism, however, wilderness can also be interpreted as a symbol of a paradisiacal origin or of 'innocent youth'. According to Marxist interpretation, 'wilderness' is symbolically connoted with the 'original state' of society, a social state that has been overcome.

From a conservative perspective, rural spaces, often interpreted as 'cultural landscapes', are "expressions, ideals and symbols of successful cultural development" (Vicenzotti 2011a, p. 147); here they represent the successful synthesis of 'land and people' into a 'superorganism' (Eisel 1982, 2004; Rodewald 2001; Vicenzotti 2011a); they are expressions of "perfection that corresponds both to the nature of the community (character of the people) and that of the living space" (Trepl 2012, p. 156). 'Historically grown cultural landscapes' are always interpreted from a conservative perspective as "historically grown products of traditional experience" (Vicenzotti 2011a, p. 154; similar to Muir 1998). They are also an expression of a conservative understanding of freedom, for here the "unadulterated and unaffected way of life is imagined, close to its origin and thus natural and precisely for this reason reasonable" (Vicenzotti 2011a, p. 160). Exactly these spaces represent for both liberalism and socialism "an advanced stage compared to the wilderness" but are "still below the stage of development of the city" (Vicenzotti 2011a, p. 116). Both associate rural life with political, social, and technical backwardness: Liberalism regards traditional rural communities as an expression of social control and a lack of education leading to inadequate life chances for the individual, as well as irrationally cultivated agricultural land that could only be used for tourism due to romantic ideas of landscape. Karl Marx also spoke of the 'idiocy of rural life' (Ipsen 1992), saying that traditional rural areas are considered obsolete by capitalism for socialism. As a result of the Marxist preference for urban settlements, as a place to live and work for the industrial workers who supported socialism, real socialism endeavoured to relocate the rural population to the cities or to urbanise rural areas, to industrialise rural land use, in order to implement socialist ideas in rural areas with the aim of creating solidarity between workers and 'working farmers' (Esser 1998; cf. Jaehne 1968; Domański 1997; Fierla 1999).

According to liberal ideas, the city is the symbolic place of the preferred social state, "the place where the state of nature has been overcome and the entry into civil society has taken place" (Vicenzotti 2011a, p. 121). The warlike natural state is not overcome by a feudal relationship of dependence; rather, it is a "place of the productive channelling of passions" (Vicenzotti 2011a, p. 122; cf. also Eisel 1982), in which the competition for life chances is not fought out by violence or its threat but is channeled into the economic. Conservatism considers the (big) city to be a place of seduction through buying pleasure, and the city itself is "imagined as a surrendering, opening, devouring female figure" (Löw 2008a, p. 198). Here, the modern metropolis is regarded as an expression of moral reprehensibility, unnaturalness, and artificiality, while the medieval city, written in guilds, is regarded as a symbol of human order (e.g. in Riehl 1925[1853] and Spengler 1950; critical on this in Häußermann and Siebel 2004). In the big city, the barbarity of the proletariat is opposed by the over-civilization of the bourgeoisie, both lacking roots in the concrete of the rural area (Vicenzotti 2011a; for the Anglo-Saxon area: Muir 1998).

The hybrid spaces between city and countryside, often referred to as 'suburban', are criticised from both conservative and socialist perspectives. The focus of socialist criticism is the striving for property, the dependence of the person financing his own home on the financial market and the withdrawal into the private home (e.g. Bourdieu 1998). Especially the emergence of gated communities and shopping malls, which goes hand in hand with the differentiation of 'city' and 'country', regarded as a symbol for a society that is individualizing or 'de-solidarizing' itself (among many: Soja 2007; Belina 2009), thereby developing contrary to the communitarian-egalitarian ideal. The criticism from conservative worldview is similar, although the normative comparative foil is not the urban-communitarian but the rural community. In particular, the loss of 'identity' of suburban settlements, their 'uniformity', and the influence of urban lifestyles are deplored (cf. Vicenzotti 2012; Hunt 2016). From a liberal worldview, on the other hand, there is a positive assessment, because life in the suburbium is valued for its pursuit of property and privacy as well as for its expression of individual spatial design.

This brief characterization of the different political and ideological basic attitudes—which often mutually refer to each other as 'ideological'—makes it clear that certain physical-spatial developments and structures are sometimes evaluated very differently, but sometimes also very similarly, albeit on a different normative basis. In addition, it becomes clear that the question of how a society should develop spatially is structured very differently from different political and ideological perspectives. This also serves to understand and assess concrete urban and spatial development policy: socialist policy will tend to promote urbanization in larger housing estates (preferably with common ownership), liberal policy will tend to promote urban and suburban areas, conservative policy will aim to strengthen rural areas.

5.3   Critical Landscape Research in the Tradition of Critical Theory

Critical theory is based on a 'philosophical-critical' view of science based on Hegel, Marx, and Freud. Their representatives are also referred to as the 'Frankfurt School' at the 'Institute for Social Research' (German: Institut für Sozialforschung) in Frankfurt (Main) because of their place of origin in the early 1930s. Members of the institute included Theodor W. Adorno, Herbert Marcuse, Erich Fromm, and Walter Benjamin. This 'old Frankfurt School' was followed by the 'new Frankfurt School', with representatives Jürgen Habermas and Oskar Negt. According to their view of science, the representatives of the 'Frankfurter Schule' are less concerned with describing, explaining, and typifying the world than with interpreting and (critically) evaluating it: "The facts that our senses bring us are socially preformed in two ways: by the historical character of the perceived object and by the historical character of the perceiving organ" (Horkheimer 1977[1937], p. 17), a thought that is also found in Daniels (1989) in relation to the 'duplicity of landscape': on the one hand as a power-determined idea, on the other hand through an equally power-determined physical landscape (with which he combines constructivist with positivist approaches and places it at the service of a Marxist-oriented critique of capitalist spatial production; cf. also Henderson and Sheppard 2006, Schein 1997). The subject of critical theory in a spatial context is the relationship between culture and nature or the aesthetics of nature and art (while landscape is more often dealt with from a Marxist perspective, e.g. Cosgrove 1984; Daniels 1989; Michaeli 2008; Michaelis et al. 1997; Wormbs 1996[1976]). The Marxist-oriented spatial and social sciences have their own claim not only to describe and analyse the world on their own, but also to change it (e.g. Samers, Bigger and Belcher 2015).

A central aspect of Critical Theory's examination of the relationship between culture and nature is the thesis put forward by Horkheimer and Adorno (1969), "that the history of man's liberation from overpowering powers has not led to a reasonable state of the world. By setting their emancipation in motion, an enterprise that consisted essentially in making themselves the masters and owners of nature, people have exposed themselves to a purely technical-instrumental rationality" (Lehmann 2009, p. 1). The use of reason is initially due to man's self-preservation (Horkheimer 1976): through his increasingly planning action he becomes more and more independent of the unpredictability of nature and can thus secure his survival ever more effectively. The subjugation of outer nature finds a connection with the mastery of the inner nature of man, which is reflected in a restriction of the freedom possibilities of the individual (Horkheimer 1977[1937]). With the contemplative distancing of man "in order to present it to himself as it is to be controlled" (Horkheimer and Adorno 1969, p. 36), also a "slander of nature in man" (Horkheimer and Adorno 1969, p. 61) goes along. According to Horkheimer and Adorno (1969, p. 37), this slander culminates in the "domination of man over himself" by developing and using reason in order on the one hand to direct external nature (physical foundations of appropriated physical landscape) towards his desires, and on the other hand to suppress his drives. Thus, reason becomes not only the form of man's dominion over his inner as well as outer nature, "but at the same time the form of man's dominion over other human natures" (Lehmann 2009, p. 1). According to Horkheimer and Adorno (1969, p. 15), the process of the rational allocation of power to the world is associated with alienation: "People pay for the increase in their power by alienating themselves from what they have power over. The Enlightenment relates to things like the dictator to people. He knows them as far as he can manipulate them. […] In transformation, the essence of things always reveals itself as the same, as the substrate of dominion". This domination usually remains unconscious because it is not questioned as normality; such an awareness of mechanisms of domination is one of the central self-imposed tasks of Critical Theory. The normalization and everyday occurence of power are carried out through socialization. Through socialization, the person to be socialized acquires an inseparable relationship with society, or as Horkheimer (1963, p. 8) puts it: "The individual for himself is an abstraction. It is intertwined with society; not only its fate but also its character depends in part on the particularities of the intertwining. Accordingly, landscape can be understood as the result of a threefold process of domination:

1. The development of the physical foundations of appropriated physical landscape into a "complex artifact" (Hugill 1995, p. 22) can be described as a physical manifestation of the emancipation process of man from a state of being at the mercy of nature's superiority to a civilization (apparently) dominating nature and enriching itself with it (similarly Kühne 2008b, 2015c; Popitz 1995).
2. The social foundations of appropriated physical landscapes have developed into an authority that culturally legitimizes the control of nature: The preference for a semi-open 'historically grown cultural landscape' has contributed to aesthetically exaggerating the inscriptions of unequal availability over land and thus to removing them from critical reflection. The sometimes sacralizing social constructions of 'historically grown cultural landscapes' thus form "a true cultural baggage" (Shepard 1967, p. 132; see also Duncan and Duncan 2001; Riley 1994; Fig. 5.2).
3. In the process of socialization, the patterns of interpretation and evaluation of (partial) social landscapes are transferred into individual landscape awareness (as an individually actualized social landscape). Any deviation from these standards would entail the loss of social recognition. Such negative sanctions complicate the development of alternative patterns of interpretation and evaluation, whereby "social actors are spontaneously prepared to do what society demands of them" (Wayand 1998, p. 226).

The 'ideological state apparatuses', formulates the French Marxist Louis Althusser (1977), such as the media and schools play a central role in the intergenerational perpetuation of patterns of interpretation and evaluation. After all, according to Althusser (1977, p. 122), "no ruling class can permanently hold state power without at the same time exercising its hegemony over and in the ideological state apparatuses". The school serves accordingly "the purposeful influencing", it is "aligned to the acquisition

Fig. 5.2 View of Medelsheim (Saarland, Germany) and surroundings. What from a conservative perspective represents a 'historically grown cultural landscape', whose Way of the Cross expresses the Catholic tradition that has lasted for centuries, can be understood completely differently from the point of view of Critical Landscape Research: The physical space can be interpreted as the result of an unequal distribution of power (e.g. by the different power of disposal over the surfaces); the Way of the Cross accordingly becomes an expression of normative religious unification. The aestheticization of the landscape in turn serves to conceal the power relations. This last interpretation is fundamentally shared from a liberal perspective, albeit for other reasons: from a liberal perspective, religion is not a public but a private matter. Also, it is not the ownership and ownership conditions that are the focus of criticism, but rather the bureaucratic 'shackles' that farmers are subjected to through state intervention in the management of their land (e.g. conditions for the conservation of fruit orchards, agricultural policy controlling land use, etc.; Photo: Kühne)

of socially desired knowledge, abilities and values" (Tillmann 2007, p. 114; cf. also Marcuse 1965[1937]). Although the power of the state has diminished, particularly as a result of globalization, it is still able to occupy central social power positions through its 'ideological state apparatuses' and "to assert dominant interests and control social relations based on clashes of interests" (Belina 2006, p. 13).

The modernization of society is also reflected—as shown—in the different dimensions of the landscape. Jürgen Habermas (1981) describes the rationalization of the lifeworld and the decoupling of system and lifeworld as an essential characteristic of modernity: For him, the lifeworld serves as a point of reference for situation definitions that are regarded as unproblematic by the persons involved (Habermas 1981, p. 107): "The lifeworld stores the preexisting interpretation work of preceding generations; it is the conservative counterweight against the risk of dissent that arises with every current process of communication". Habermas (1981, p. 248) describes the difference between lifeworld and system as follows: "While the aspect of understanding is the most relevant for the symbolic reproduction of the lifeworld in social action, the aspect of expediency is important for material reproduction. This takes place through the medium of targeted interventions in the objective world". With the rationalization of the lifeworld—Habermas follows on from Max Weber's concept of the disenchantment of the world—areas that were previously regulated in a traditional way are now subject to systematic investigation and rationalization. This rationalization also affects the thematic field of landscape: empirical methods are used to turn the physical foundations of the acquired physical landscape into an object of natural and social scientific positivist investigation, and later also the social and individually actualized foundations. Landscape is measured, delimited and classified, and subjected to a more or less normative (socially defined) system of legal regulations. In the course of rationalizing the world in which we live, physical space is subjected to individual rational economic and administrative action (Olwig 2008; similar to Gregory 1989; Michaeli 2008; Wormbs 1996[1976]). Wormbs summarizes the consequences of such handling of (materially understood) landscape (1996[1976], p. 244) as follows: "Since the worldwide expansion of the production of goods has also meant that the development of the earth has burst all the landscape reference frameworks of the past and created a dense network of industrial locations around the globe, irrationality and disorganization have become apparent in the overall technical instrument. They become known in the spatial and ecological incompatibility of all the individual parts, which are organised in a purely rational manner." Thus, the market-economy logic, which is based on individual profit, is linked to the fact that the costs of its production method, such as waste of raw materials, environmental pollution and damage to health, are transferred to social settlement (Wormbs 1996[1976]; Tilley 1997). The approaches of Critical Theory to the subject of nature presented in this section show essentialist traits as one aspect, as in relation to the 'nature' of man, and constructivist traits as another, as in the question of socialization or the question of the cultural conditionality of landscape understandings.

A major focus of Critical Theory is on how 'unjust' conditions are socially approved, how a culture of appropriateness can emerge. Herbert Marcuse (1965[1937], p. 63) understands such a culture as 'affirmative culture', which he appreciates as "those bourgeois epochs which, in the course of their own development, have led to the replacement of the spiritual-soul world as an independent realm of value and to its elevation through it. Their decisive move is the affirmation of a generally obliging, unconditionally affirmable, eternally better, more valuable world, which is substantially different from the actual world of the everyday struggle for existence. But which each individual 'from within' without changing any reality, can realize for himself". 'Affirmative culture' thus becomes a disciplinary system, "because culture swears the subjects to the existing—that is its affirmative character—and promises happiness, because it depicts a reality that contains utopian and liberal moments" (Cavalcanti 2004, p. 3). Yet culture—from the point of view of Critical Theory—in the form of artistic activity would be particularly suited to achieving a domination-free approach to reality (Adorno 1970). It is precisely the confrontation with nature that makes it an equal counterpart within the framework of a communicative action: "How clinging the beauty of nature and the beauty of art are proves itself in the experience that applies to them. It refers to nature only as appearance, never as material of work and reproduction of life. Like the experience of art, the aesthetic experience of nature is one of images. Nature as an apparent beauty is not perceived as an object of action. In the renunciation of the purposes of self-preservation, emphatic in art, the experience of nature is equally accomplished" (Adorno 1970, p. 112). For Adorno, aesthetics can thus be given an emancipatory character: An aesthetic experience of both nature and art makes it possible to experience a relationship between man and nature and other people that is not characterized by alienation. Through the emancipatory function of the aesthetic, Adorno also demands the representation of the ugly in order to denounce the world in the ugly (Adorno 1970, p. 79). With regard to the aesthetic experience of landscape, this should—according to the interpretation of Adorno (1970)—be carried out in the form of the domination-free appropriation of nature. The natural aesthetic fixation of the aesthetic landscape construction becomes clear in the following quote from Adorno (1970, p. 112): "As true as it is that anything in nature can be regarded as beautiful, so true is the judgment that the landscape of Tuscany is more beautiful than the surroundings of Gelsenkirchen" (Gelsenkirchen is an old industrial city in the Ruhr area, Germany). Hauser (2000) describes these remarks as antiquated; after all, today the surroundings of Gelsenkirchen can be addressed as a landscape, it has the unambiguous peculiarity of a distinct cultural landscape.

With the transition to mass production, for Adorno art has lost its emancipatory potential. The culture industry, with its omnipresence in the mass media, corrupts the sensuality of the subjects by making them believe in happiness and "what in them, how oppressed and neurotically atrophied, expresses itself as hope, once again subjugates it" (Schneider 2005, p. 195). For Adorno, the culture industry marked "a visible transition in which pure profit is superior to the work of art—culture is produced industrially and thus receives a transition from the quality of past art to the quantity of serial production" (Cavalcanti 2004, p. 5). Closely connected with the mass production of the art industry is kitsch for Adorno. In the course of mass reproduction, Romantic works, particularly Caspar David Friedrichs (Fig. 4.3), became for some critics 'the epitome of bad taste, since their works are exaggerated, unlikely, sought-after and arbitrary' (Illing 2006, p. 47). Besides this outer side—as Liessmann (2002) calls it—the cheap, mass production and the equally cheap and mass distribution, an inner side of kitsch can be formulated. This refers to the pretence of non-existent feelings and the pretence of art (Adorno 1970): "Where only the strikingly beautiful can be found, by pretending to shake, where only a false sentiment is created, by the illusion of deep emotionality, where only calculated tears flow" (Liessmann 2002, p. 9). Modern kitsch is thus also separated from the folk culture of the pre-modern era: Folk culture was authentic, while kitsch was fake (Adorno 1972; Greenberg 2007[1939]), whereby both are attributed with an essential essence. In this context, landscape can also be viewed under the mode of kitsch discourse (Gelfert 2000; Kühne 2008d): Thus, the current aestheticization of wilderness can be interpreted in the tradition of 'sublime kitsch', while the aestheticization of Arcadian landscape is related to "the lovely, Arcadian-paradisiacal nature [that] accompanies above all the kitsch of childlike innocence" (Gelfert 2000, p. 42). The 'historically grown cultural landscape' mostly represents a physical-spatial condition that no longer corresponds to current social, especially economic conditions. In the sense of Gelfert (2000) this state can be interpreted as 'fake art', contemporary appropriated physical landscape becomes a copy of an estimated original of a historically defined state of physical landscape. Thus, physical space, which was formerly marked by an 'authentic folk culture', is "transformed into kitsch in the present landscape view, because it is marketed as an expression of an authenticity that no longer exists" (Gelfert 2000, p. 15). When they are consumed, the observer becomes the epicure who enjoys himself (Gelfert 2000). Simplified programs and order pictures are thus appropriated with the effect of a distanceless sentimentalization as a "continuous flooding of experienced reality with one's own subjective feeling" (Gelfert 2000, p. 77).

The individual and social construction of landscape, in the reading of Critical Theory, can on the one hand have an emancipatory character if it succeeds without domination. On the other hand, it can also contribute to the stabilization of conditions described as unfair, because it can be shaped by kitsch as an expression of 'affirmative culture'. Central to the definition of landscape is the question of who is able to master discourses on landscape, how and when, and with what calculation (see in this context also Cosgrove 1984; Duncan and Duncan 2003, 2004). The extent to which people succeed in gaining the sovereignty to interpret what can be called landscape in social discourses and how different powers of disposal are reflected in physical-spatial structures is the subject of the following explanations.

5.4 Landscape as a Medium of Social Distinction and Power Processes: A Critical Approach Based on the Sociology of Pierre Bourdieu

Pierre Bourdieu (1930–2002) was a French sociologist and social philosopher who borrowed from Marx (e.g. in his class concept), but did not (consistently) argue Marxist, but rather oriented himself to Max Weber, Ernst Cassirer and Erwin Panofsky. He turned against 'schooling' in social science, as it was a major obstacle to progress in knowledge by preventing the overcoming of false antinomies. Instead, he pleaded for a "realpolitik of the concept" (Bourdieu 1992, p. 40), by preferring an orientation towards a theoretical structure, which he called a 'theoretical space', in order not to fall into a theoretical eclecticism (Jurt 2912), in this sense Bordieu could also be called a 'neopragmatist' from today's perspective.

The concept of the symbolic power of Bourdieu (e.g. 1982 and 1987[1979]; as well as Bourdieu and Passeron 1973) makes the struggle for the sovereignty of discourse (see Sect. 2.4.3 on discourse theory on the fundamentals) in a decentralized field of power comprehensible. Bourdieu and Passeron (1973, p. 12) define symbolic power (or symbolic violence) as "any power that succeeds in asserting meanings and asserting them as legitimate by obscuring the power relations underlying its power. Accordingly, power results from the socially differentiated access to symbolic capital, as those opportunities that are suitable for gaining and maintaining social recognition and social prestige in society as a whole or in individual social fields (Bourdieu 1987[1979]; see Box 16). With the development of the landscape view, landscape became a medium of social distinction (Kühne 2008b; cf. also Schenker 1994; in relation to architecture: Stevens 2002): The aestheticization of physical spaces into appropriated physical landscapes required the mastery of the landscape code; after all, only "those who know the code […] can generally understand the signs and continue to act" (Kastner 2002, p. 232). So anyone who had no training in the question of which elements of physical space in which constellation and using which vocabulary in which social context could be described as 'landscape' either did not have the right vocabulary or used it in an inappropriate way and thus unmasked an insufficiently developed taste (cf. Daniels and Cosgrove 1988; Ipsen 1992, 2006; Mitchell 2006; for the spatialization of codes see Lippuner 2008). The aesthetic attention of the world was accordingly highly exclusive: "aesthetic issues have been important only to a tiny minority of the population, whether artists, intellectuals, or the very rich whose contribution often seems restricted to the turning of works of art into mere commodities" (Porteous 2013, p. xvii).

Nevertheless, as if other cultural assets defined by the ruling class (see Box 16), the aestheticized access to landscape is taken over by the middle class. Thus, the romantic access to landscape was also imitated by the middle taste, whereby this popularization of the romantic-landscape code took place without the metaphorical depth of the Romanticists' landscape construction. In comparison to the poets, painters, and landscape writers of Romanticism (interpretable in the sense of a ruling class of intellectuals), the writings and images of the 'Homeland Security Movement' (as representatives of middle taste) seemed little inspired or original, even when they drew on romantic motifs. Another essential element of the trivialization of landscape was the emergence of low-cost modes of mass transport, first the railways, later the motor vehicle (cf. Clarke 1993; Green 2003; Vöckler 1998): "Landscape is no longer conceived in contemplation, but primarily as distraction" (Krysmanski 1996[1971], p. 224).

> **Box 16: Symbolic capital and social distinction according to Pierre Bourdieu**
> Symbolic capital occurs in the form of economic, social. and cultural capital, which share scarcity and desire (Bourdieu 1972, 1987[1979]). Economic capital is understood as material property that can be exchanged for money. Social capital "is described as a relational good inherent in social relations and presented as a resource of different social structures with different social reach for individuals and corporate actors or communities" (Maischatz 2010, p. 31). Cultural capital is divided into three subcapitals (Bourdieu 1983):
>
> 1. The objectified form comprises physical manifestations of human activity (books, technical equipment, works of art).

2. The incorporated form is directly linked to the physical existence of the acting person (education, cultural skills).
3. The institutionalised form represents the social representation of part of the incorporated cultural capital in educational titles (e.g. diplomas).

The different availability of symbolic capital is the basis for a vertical differentiation of society (and its parts). Bourdieu (1987[1979]) distinguishes between three basic classes:

1. The ruling class is composed of entrepreneurs (with much economic but little cultural capital) and intellectuals (with much cultural but little economic capital). It is the bearer of the legitimate taste, which is characterized by 'the sense of distinction', i.e. to imprint a taste that is (initially) not accessible to the other classes.
2. The middle class (also petty bourgeoisie) is the bearer of middle taste, which is characterized by 'educational zeal' and the constant attempt to imitate the taste of the ruling class.
3. The controlled class is the bearer of popular taste, which is oriented towards 'the decision for what is necessary'. It forms the rest of society.

This structure of society transcends "subjective intentions and individual or collective designs" (Bourdieu 1976, p. 179). The ruling class, but also the middle class, is striving to secure its symbolic capital against popularization. In the context of social capital, this stock protection takes place preferably through social closure (Maischatz 2010), i.e. unwanted persons are denied access to social networks.

The educated traveller of the Renaissance and still in Romanticism, for example, abstracted on his *Grand Tour*[1] a sequence of pictures based on different patterns of interpretation into a landscape impression and endured "extreme inconveniences of travelling with inner composure" (Lippard 2005[1999], p. 122). The tourist of the railway age expected a focused panorama, when possible in a pre-defined form through illustrated books and postcards, with the greatest possible travel and stay comfort (Burckhardt 2006; Lippard 2005[1999]; Vogel 1993). With the automobile, landscape becomes almost generally and everywhere publicly accessible (Lippard 2005[1999]) and

---

[1]The *Grand Tour* describes a journey of the sons of the European (at first especially English) nobility, later also of the bourgeoisie, to the sites of European culture in a special way ancient as well as through landscapes classified as worth seeing. The *Grand Tour* served to refine the skills acquired in education (e.g. in foreign languages or fencing) and at the same time to deepen knowledge of different regions of Europe (Dirlinger 2000; Brilli 2001; Löfgren 2002).

is experienced as a preselected "atmospheric picture, as a 'good view' consumed with the help of the Triple-A map" (Vöckler 1998, p. 278). In the second third of the 20th century, for Bourdieu (1987[1979], p. 108) "'kitschy' favourite motifs such as mountain landscapes, sunsets by the sea and forests" become an expression of the 'aesthetics' of the controlled class (cf. also Kühne 2008b; see also Box 17). Both the sublime, near-natural landscape, and the Arcadian landscape have thus been deprived of their ability to distinguish themselves for the legitimate taste (Kühne 2008b). With the transition from industrial to post-industrial society, however, the past three decades have once again seen the possibility of using landscape as a medium for distinctive aestheticization: Similar to the aestheticization of pre-industrial landscapes in the course of industrialization, physical manifestos of industrial society are now subjected to aestheticization that has a distinctive effect (see details; Kühne 2008b; cf. also Pütz 2007; see Box 7). People repeatedly oppose this distinctive aestheticization of the ruling class and the middle class by demonstratively developing and materializing their own aesthetic ideas, whether in the form of punk culture, carnival, or graffiti/murals (Bakhtin 1984; Cockcroft and Barnet-Sánchez 1993; Graham 1994, Fig. 5.3).

Fig. 5.3 Murals in Chicano Park in San Diego, California, as documents of an aesthetic resistance, on the one hand as a result of its design based on Aztec and Mexican symbolism, on the other hand as a result of the saying "Varrio SI, Yonkes NO" on the front mural. With this, the Hispanic inhabitants of the 'Barrio Logan' protested against the increased settlement of scrap yards at the end of the 1960s. The word 'Varrio' stands for Barrio, the 'V' was used as a sign for Victory, the word 'Yonkes' stands for Junkyards. In ignorance of this derivation, 'Yonkes' is often interpreted as 'Yankees', whereby the Mural is interpreted as a racist statement against Americans (Berestein 2007; Herzog 2004; Photo: Kühne)

Box 17: The exoticization of landscape: tourism

An essential expression of this "event society" (Schulze 1993) is the increasing importance of tourism, which—as Pott (2007, p. 49) notes—"is to be interpreted as a phenomenon of highly developed capitalist societies in which the time off from work and the high economic level make it possible to capitalise on the change of location in the form of goods as a holiday trip". The change of location brought about by the holiday trip is also accompanied by a change of role (Kreisel 2004, p. 75): "Change of location makes the spatial distance to everyday life possible, change of role permitted, at least temporarily distancing oneself from everyday and household duties". In addition, an substantial motive for travel lies in the need for prestige and distinction, which refer both to the personal social network at home (e.g. through reports on the journey in order to demonstrate the appropriation of cultural capital and the level of economic capital) and to the role played at the holiday resort by the person to be served (Böhm 1962; Hartmann 1967).

As regards the landscape reference of tourism, the concept of the 'tourist gaze' (Urry 2002[1990]) can be seen to have a special significance: "Places are chosen to be gazed upon because there is an anticipation. […] Such anticipation is constructed and sustained through a variety of non-tourist practices, such as film, newspapers, TV, magazines, records and videos which construct that gaze. […] what is then seen is interpreted in terms of these pre-given categories" (Urry 2002[1990], p. 3). The tourist's enjoyment of the landscape "is the feeling of the fulfilment of those images, those idioms that are built up in us in the course of our cultural history, through poetry and painting, but also through the sunken cultural assets, cover images of Threepenny novels, cinema, television and tourism advertising" (Burckhardt 2006, p. 70; cf. also Enzensberger 1962). According to Enzensberger (1962), tourism develops a dialectical relationship to the spaces and societies it visits: The tourist destroys by his presence the loneliness, but also the 'untouched' and 'undestroyed' nature (and culture) that he strives for. The journey is made in the expectation that such landscape stereotypes will be confirmed. Deviations from this are experienced as contrary to standards (cf. Bauman 1999). The stereotypical ideal state is again ascribed to the past, so that the taste judgement "Provence is no longer what it once was" is made (cf. detailed Aschenbrand 2016, 2017).

Richard Peet clarifies the connection between the social definition of (aesthetic) normative claims and power-specific inscriptions into physical space in such a pregnant way that this also justifies a longer literal quotation.: "In the social struggle to remake nature, the ideologies of male elites have prevailed as the hegemonic elements of landscapes, although we would find women, peasants, and workers remarkably successful in leaving signs of their counter-discourses were we truly to 'read' through a cladgender optic. Further, the discursive formations guiding the physical reconstruction of landscapes are aspects of the regulative powers of geo-historical formations; landscapes are the spatial surfaces of discursive/regulatory regimes, icons points of privileged access to regulative discourses" (Peet 1996, p. 97).

The explanations on landscape and power processes clearly show how significantly not only the physical foundations of landscape are subject to change, but also the social interpretation and evaluation of landscape. In this respect one can speak of a 'double landscape change' (Kühne 2018b), whereby the social and material dimensions are in close feedback with each other.

5.5   Criticism of the Loss of Participation in Landscape Processes

Criticism of the lack of democratic participation in landscape processes is expressed from different scientific and ideological directions. It is found in the tradition of 'critical theory', as already discussed in Sect. 5.3; it is uttered by Bourdieu and those who place themselves in his tradition, but it is led in particular by those who place themselves in the tradition of liberal thinkers (such as Dahrendorf, Popitz and Sofsky). These will be given special attention in the following, as the other approaches mentioned have already been assessed in the previous two sections.

Part of the modernization of society is its differentiation into different units (systems theory speaks here of systems, see Sect. 2.4.2, Bourdieu of fields), which are entrusted with the solution of specific problems. These units develop their own specific logics and discourses. The development of landscape-related expert systems (e.g. landscape architects and landscape planners, but also geographers, sociologists, cultural scientists, biologists, etc., with a reference to the landscape) can also be understood as an aspect of this development (cf. Alexander 1999; Burckhardt 2004; Craik 1972; Daniel 2001; Entrikin 1991; Howard 2011; Hülz and Kühne 2015; Hunziker et al. 2008; Kühne 2008b; Mitchell 2003; Morgan 1999; Stevens 2002; Dancer 2007; Trudeau 2006; Tewdwr-Jones 2002). This goes hand in hand with the "separation of people into those who are competent and those who are incompetent" (Bourdieu 2005[1977], p. 13). Scientifically legitimated experts have become representatives of a social system of problem-solving action that has become monopolized as a result of the social differentiation of society with independent functional logics in the sense of a radical constructivist access to landscape (cf. e.g. (Hilbig 2014; Kühne 2014a; Luhmann 1990; Matheis 2016; Tänzler 2007; Weingart 2003)). Zygmunt Bauman (2009a[1993], p. 294) critically paraphrases the result of this fragmentation: "In the course of expert guided empowerment, citizens of modernity internalize such a world completely with the fragmentation power of the experts, who are common and at the same time builders, administrators, and speakers of this world. According to Gerhard Hard (1973, p. 14), the development of a specific 'déformation professionelle' is based on the apparent certainty of having achieved "the coronation of a centuries, even millennia-long effort to create the same objects". Central to the expert transformation of power is the possibility of asserting one's own technical language as legitimate against the everyday language of the laity and the understanding of the landscape (Nassauer 1995): "The designer acquires definitory power if he succeeds in occupying the language. This turns into real power over living conditions when the measures that deprive people of their self-determined everyday life, free space, are enforced" (Lorberg 2006, p. 101). The discourses present in the professional world that struggle for hegemony (see Sect. 2.4.3) are certainly differentiated (see Box 18).

Box 18: Current expert discourses on landscape

However, the several generations of researchers who have been dealing with an object, in this case landscape, do not lead to a unification of views in the sense of convergence, but rather to different discourses with their own discourse sovereignty and logic (see Sect. 2.4.3 on the formation of landscape discourses in general). According to Kühne (2006a, 2008b; cf. also Groth and Wilson 2005[2003]; Hupke 2015; Jones and Daugstad 1997; Wojtkiewicz 2015; Wojtkiewicz and Heiland 2012), four discourses with specific logic of their own and landscape-related ideas can currently be traced in relation to landscape:

1. The discourse on the preservation and restoration of the physical foundations of appropriated physical landscapes pursues the goal of (re)establishing or maintaining a normatively defined ideal state, that of the classical paradigm of the 'historically grown cultural landscape' (see Sects. 2.2 and 2.5.1; cf. also Muir 1998).
2. The discourse of the successionist development of physical landscape is normatively characterized by a passive understanding of the structuring of the physical foundations of appropriated physical landscape as a side effect of ecological or social developments. In terms of science theory, a positivist approach is generally advocated (see Sect. 2.3).
3. The discourse of the reflexive design of the physical foundations of appropriated physical landscapes is shaped by the view that alternative evaluations of the construction of social landscapes can be produced through targeted changes in the elements of physical space. This discourse is usually based on a social constructivist understanding of the world (see Sect. 2.4.1; Fig. 5.4).
4. The discourse of the reinterpretation of the social landscape is normatively shaped by the fact that the construction (especially as regards its evaluative elements) of appropriated physical landscapes is to be carried out as far as possible without interfering with the physical foundations, but by reinterpreting the social and individually actualized social landscape. This discourse is based on constructivist approaches (see Sect. 2.4).

Fig. 5.4 The landmark 'Tiger and Turtle' on the Heinrich-Hildebrand-Höhe in the Angerpark in Duisburg-Angerhausen (Ruhr Region, Germany), based on a pattern of a roller coaster, can be interpreted as an expression of the 'discourse of the reflexive design of the physical foundations of landscape'; after all, it is an element of the effort of the old industrial region Ruhrgebiet (Ruhr Region) to create a new image of itself. (Photo: Kühne)

Particularly in conflict situations, however, the discursive claims to interpretive sovereignty over alternative discourses are appropriated (cf. also Schultheiss 2007). The own discourse is socially secured against alternative discourses by generating especially social, often also cultural, capital among other things in the form of the mutual granting of recognition and respect—through reciprocal quotations, reciprocal invitations to lecture events or positive mentions to third parties (cf. Bourdieu 2005[1983]; Kühne 2008b). However, these third parties are not chosen arbitrarily, they are the 'reference group'. The term reference group "denotes the fact that an individual orients his behaviour towards the consent or rejection of groups" (Dahrendorf 1971[1958], p. 45), i.e. such groups "to which his positions necessarily relate him" (Dahrendorf 1971[1958], p. 45). The relationship of authority between experts (especially within a discourse) is based on a double recognition process (Popitz 1992, p. 29): "On the recognition of the superiority of others than the authoritative, the authoritative and on the aspiration to be recognised by these authoritative, to receive signs of probation", whereby the authoritative then form the reference group. Here the relations of recognition are mostly asymmetrical and reciprocal at the same time: "We want to be especially recognized by those whom we especially recognize" (Popitz 1992, p. 115). What the landscape experts have in common is the distinctive demarcation from the laity that manifests itself through the availability of institutionalized cultural capital, namely the possession of legitimizing diplomas (cf. also Bourdieu 2004). In the pursuit of recognition by colleagues (Schneider 1989), landscape experts often find themselves in strict contradiction "to the propagated emotional neutrality of the scientist, which he calls objectivity, and to that of the artist, who has given his desire the name 'divine inspiration', and to that of the protector, who speaks of the object of protection 'per se'" (Schneider 1989, p. 128).

This striving for recognition takes place in a social context of classical representative democratic institutions, in one sense through greater participation (ultimately by parts) of the population, and in another through the general gain in importance of expertise, as noted by Beyme (2013, p. 13; similar to Michelsen and Walter 2013)—both within and outside the state bureaucracy: "The decline of the classes and the rise of the experts seem to decisively weaken the democratic parties. Factual competence has often replaced the enthusiasm of amateurs". The result is a "scientification of politics" (Jörke 2010, p. 275), which has led to "experts and planners [...] having pushed the classical intellectual off the stage as it were" (Michelsen and Walter 2013, p. 365). This process is associated with the consequence of an ever-stronger focus on social challenges, i.e. the loss of placing administrative and especially political action in context, and the assessment of implications and side effects. This abstract statement can be substantiated using the example of nature conservation (Hupke 2015, p. 150): "Nature conservation makes [...], one follows its self-understanding, rare species more frequently, but also frequent species should not become rarer. Nature conservation basically needs a 'growing planet'".

A central element of Weber's understanding of the relationship between politics and administration is its strict separation (Weber 1976[1922]): while the politician is concerned with generating majorities for his politics, the civil servant must carry out what is decided in the political process. If, however, the civil servant assumes political responsibility (e.g. by refusing to make political decisions), he transfers the logic of administration to politics, whereby politics is carried out in the form of an administrative practice that breaks down processes (cf. Hahn 2014; Michelsen and Walter 2013; Van Assche and Verschraegen 2008; see also Fig. 4). The result is a shift of power from parliaments to administrations: Thus, bills usually come from the ministerial bureaucracy and not from the parliaments (which would be responsible for this according to the principle of the separation of powers), but rather from administrations, which in turn later monitor compliance (Anter 2012; Kühne 2008b; with regard to nature conservation and bureaucracy see also Hampicke 2013). It is in the interest of the administrations to suggest to outsiders that power is concentrated at the top of the administration, since this corresponds to social expectations (including democratic legitimacy; Luhmann 2000) and—as discussed earlier—power can develop its potential especially when it is not obvious. The relationship between the 'quality' of the government and the degree of autonomy of the administration is sharpened by Fukuyama (2013) in a u-shaped graph: If the administration is bound by strict political guidelines, it is deprived of its discretion, factual issues become political issues, and it becomes inefficient, since every decision is taken from the top of the hierarchy. In the other extreme, complete autonomy, the actions of the bureaucracy are only insufficiently politically legitimized; it follows its own logic (as described above; see Sect. 2.4.2 for specific system logics). If the political guidelines are lacking, this calls "non-political administrative action onto the agenda, which is rising in the favor of the output-oriented citizenry in view of the decreasing problem-solving ability of political institutions" (Michelsen and Walter 2013, p. 109; cf. also: Pennington 2002). To put it exaggeratedly: government action does not have to be democratically legitimized, it should above all be efficient (= inexpensive). But in this context Sofsky comes to a very sobering balance of state action: The state "does not save from material

Fig. 5.5 The relationship between the scope and autonomy of the administration and the quality of government (after: Fukuyama 2013)

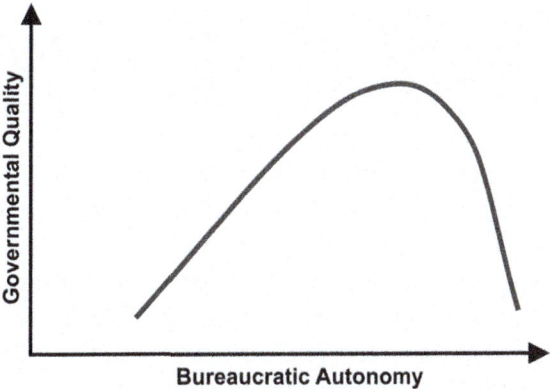

hardship, is unable to create work or economic growth, lets traffic routes and education rot in many places" (Sofsky 2007, p. 104), while the "growth of state administration and parastatal control centers" (Sofsky 2007, p. 104) continues. The approach presented to examine the power orientation of landscape discourses is based on a constructivist understanding of reality: power discourses are socially generated and make use of the reference to physical objects (Fig. 5.5).

The criticism expressed by the approaches discussed in this chapter (Box 19 summarizes essential aspects once again), especially the criticism of the deficit of democratic participation, had the effect that efforts were made to involve the population more intensively in questions of landscape development, which are discussed in more detail in Sect. 6.2.

Box 19: Power and landscape: from political worldviews, critical landscape research and a differentiated history of discipleship—a brief summary

According to Max Weber, power offers the possibility to enforce one's own will against resistance. Power, which is particularly present in the political system, is used in different political worldviews to achieve different social goals, whereby spatial arrangements are also interpreted differently (conservatism prefers rural spaces, socialism urban ones, which unites it with liberalism, which, however, also values suburban spaces positively). The approaches to critical landscape research presented in this chapter are united by the rejection of current social power relations. What they have in common is a critical attitude towards the state, albeit from different backgrounds. Critical theory sees in it the vicarious agents of economic interests, by means of state organs (especially schools) social structures (i.e. the dependence of the human being on the economy) are to be perpetuated. Bourdieu expands the basis of critique by not only evaluating economic interests as drivers of an educational system that maintains power relations, but also including other components of 'symbolic capital'. Liberal approaches, on the other hand, criticize the educational system's function of suppressing alternative interpretations of the world by forming discourse sovereignties and thus restricting individual freedoms. Accordingly, the discursive hegemonialization of 'expert special knowledge' (see Chap. 4) is criticized here, as are the bureaucratic inscriptions into physical space (such as subsidies), which in turn are conveyed as 'beautiful landscapes' in education. From Bourdieu's perspective, the question of how landscape becomes a medium of social distinction in order to secure the symbolic power of the 'ruling class' is in the foreground. From the point of view of 'critical theory', the question of how to prepare physical space for economic interests and its social landscape's aesthetic charge is specifically focused.

Current Issues in Social Science Landscape Research: Theoretical Classifications

This chapter is dedicated to current topics of landscape research and its theoretical framing. These current developments challenge traditional views of landscape and have therefore contributed to the updating of the theme of 'landscape' in science, politics, and public discussion. In this respect they can also be interpreted as phenomena of a 'landscape crisis' (Berleant 1997), in the spirit of raising awareness of a previous 'natural attitude' sense of unconscious interpretation of the world (Nassauer 1995). The theories presented in the previous chapters are related to questions of the moralization of landscape, conflicts over changes in the physical foundations of landscape (in particular the expansion of facilities for the production of renewable energies), but also to the question of hybridization tendencies, formerly dichotomously conceived spatial categories (such as city and country). First, the theoretical approaches already mentioned will be used: The discussion of the 'moralization of landscape' is primarily carried out from the perspective of Niklas Luhmann's autopoietic systems theory (see Sect. 2.4.2), whereby results from research on social constructivism and discourse theory are also used (Sects. 2.4.1 and 2.4.3). The treatment of conflicts over changes in landscape is specifically based on the sociology of Ralf Dahrendorf already mentioned in Sect. 5.5. The discussion of postmodernization processes of landscape, which are addressed in various ways (particularly in Sect. 3.6), in turn draws on different positivist and constructivist, but also critical perspectives. It can therefore also be understood as a 'neopragmatic' (see Sect. 2.6) combination of different theoretical approaches.

6.1 The Moralization of Landscape

The scientific examination of the connection between morality and landscape has been taking place increasingly since the 1970s. A central aspect of the thematicization of this connection was 'the normative relationship between space and behaviour' (Cresswell

© Springer Fachmedien Wiesbaden GmbH, part of Springer Nature 2019

O. Kühne, *Landscape Theories*, RaumFragen: Stadt – Region – Landschaft,
https://doi.org/10.1007/978-3-658-25491-9_6

2003, p. 279), connected with the question of how a 'good' life could be designed in an aesthetically pleasant environment, but also how moral ideas inscribe themselves upon physical spaces (cf. Tuan 1989). In the following, we will focus more on the question (from a constructivist perspective) of the social consequences of the moralization of spaces interpreted as landscapes.

The moralization of landscape has a long tradition. At the latest, the (romantic) critical examination of the physical-spatial manifestations of enlightenment, rationalization, and industrialization has brought with it not only an aesthetic but also a moral assessment of the spaces interpreted as landscapes (Kirchhoff and Trepl 2009; Kühne 2013c; Trepl 2012). Landscape, interpreted as a physical object, thus became a medium of critique of modernization, a pattern of interpretation that is still updated today when the physical foundations of landscape are subjected to changes (Aschenbrand et al. 2017a; Kühne et al. 2016, 2017). By 'morality' can be understood a system of normative rules (roles, norms) and values that determine the actions of people as a result of social conventional-ization processes. As Berleant (1997) points out, it also resembles the aesthetic approach to landscape, both arise in cultural contexts, both have individual parts, and both refer to social conventions. Conventions in general, on the other hand, arise through commu-nication (with communication also obeying conventions), which in turn means that they do show a certain degree of variability (Berr 2014, 2017). With Niklas Luhmann (2017), communication can be understood as the only original social action on which society is ultimately based. Communication manifests itself in a threefold selection: information, notification, and understanding (Luhmann 2017). The following discussion of the morali-zation of landscape is based on Luhmann's systems theory presented in Sect. 2.4.2.

In early modernity, moral concepts were mostly based on religion and, with their determination of normality and anormality, produced "a scheme of generalization trans-verse to the type of situation and behavior" (Luhmann 2017, p. 126). The functional differentiation of society into different social subsystems with exclusive tasks for soci-ety (e.g. the economy for the supply of goods and services, science for the production of socially binding knowledge, etc.; see Kühne 2019) was not only associated with an increase in society's "conflict potential and conflict ability" (Luhmann 2017, p. 220). Rather, there was also a differentiation of moral ideas that competed with religiously defined morality and replaced it in large parts of society. At the same time, the impor-tance of moral communication through the mass media grew (Luhmann 1996). With the increasing differentiation of society, the complexity of the relations between different parts of society, as well as the references of society to its non-social environment, also increased. The differentiation of the logics of the individual social subsystems in dealing with one another and with the social environment was decomplexed by the expansion of the mode of moral communication, which means that economic questions are not judged economically (for example, with regard to the efficiency of resource use), political ques-tions are not judged politically (i.e., with regard to the question of generating or secur-ing power), but morally (for example, with regard to lump-sumization, money/politics spoil character; Luhmann 1993). This also means, "if there are already starting points for conflicts", moralization tends to "generalize the substance of the conflict" (Luhmann 2017, p. 128). Individual cases are understood as generally valid and then stigmatized as 'typical'. Grau (2017, p. 12) goes so far as to understand moral communication as a constitutive feature of modern democratic societies; they "can hardly communicate factual issues in any other way than in the mode of excitement and indignation". Morality is hierarchically placed above the specific logics of the social subsystems and in social communication to the effect that "disputes are created, arise from disputes and then intensify the dispute" (Luhmann 1989, p. 370). Far-reaching moral communication proves to be socially quite dysfunctional; after all, moralizations are difficult to take back (cf. Bogner 2005) and they aim at generating social disregard. This is oriented towards a disciplining effect (with regard to adherence to social norms; Haus 2003; Luhmann 1993), whereby—as mentioned above—social norms become more diverse as a result of social differentiation and their binding nature diminishes, which is often associated with the consequence that the disciplining effect fails to materialise because the focused person follows different moral concepts (a more detailed introduction to Luhmann's sociology is provided by Kneer and Nassehi 1997).

The theme of landscape seems to be particularly suitable for moral communication: First, its everyday significance is high (whether during walks, in feature films and documentaries, in paintings, etc.; cf. e.g. Kühne 2018d). Secondly, what is called 'landscape' is occupied emotionally, for instance in the form of 'Heimat' (Hüppauf 2007; Kühne et al. 2016; Kühne and Spellerberg 2010; Schlink 2000). Thirdly, aestheticization takes place along social stereotypes, which in turn experience normative-moral validation (Burckhardt 2006; Kühne 2012c, 2013b; Linke 2017b). Fourthly, the processes of what can be understood as 'landscape' are very complex (which applies to both individual and social construction processes; among many): Bourassa 1991; Bruns 2016; Bruns and Kühne 2013; Kühne 2015d). And fifthly, the processes of the emergence of the physical structures known as 'landscape' are also complex (e.g. Küster 2013[1995]; Poschlod 2017; Schenk 2011).

In both non-expert and expert communication, an essentialist or positivist understanding of landscape dominates. Accordingly, changes (aimed for) in the material world become in a special way the subject of conflicts in which the conflict parties make use of the mode of moral communication. The (planned) construction of wind power plants, for example, is moralised accordingly as 'destruction of the historical cultural landscape that has grown up' or 'destruction of the home', while the other conflict party brands 'destruction of the climate' or 'irresponsibility towards future generations' (among many: Kühne and Schönwald 2013; Weber et al. 2017). Here, the above-mentioned pattern of moral generalization becomes clear: it is no longer the individual wind turbine in the context of a specific section of space and its inhabitants that is the subject of discussion, but rather nothing less than 'the salvation of the world', not only for the people living today, but also for future generations (see Spaniards 2006; Fig. 6.1). The result of moralization is a radical decomplexation of landscape-related communication: instead of a comprehension of the complexity of economic, scientific, planning or political system

Fig. 6.1 The use of wind power has a centuries-old tradition in Europe (see windmill in the province of Limburg in the Netherlands, left). While windmills have a nostalgic-positive connotation, modern wind turbines (here in Saarland, Germany, specifically by conservatives, suburbanites, older people, and men; see Kühne 2018d) are characterized as 'ugly'. In addition to the aesthetic attribution, they become the subject of moral communication, which stretches between 'future-oriented' and 'sustainable' on the one hand, and 'homeland-destroying' on the other. (Photos: Kühne)

logics or of the complex relationship between society and its environment, here also of different aesthetic approaches to the social environment, a moral discrediting of alternative worldviews, not an acceptance of 'alternative, but quite legitimate interpretations of the world' (Dahrendorf 1969c). Instead of the objective discussion about the individual case (wind power plant/wind farm/bypass road/railway station/gravel pit …) with regard to economic efficiency, 'spatial compatibility', political feasibility etc., there is a morally, aesthetically, and even ontologically complete reduction of the 'other side', up to the point of denying the right to act as an equal partner in discourse, because "the ideological opponent becomes a pathological case. And one does not discuss with patients, one must heal patients" (Grau 2017, p. 47). In such a way a paternalistic attitude develops: Since the other side is 'sick', it has lost its decision-making authority over landscape issues.

This type of morally based landscape communication in turn becomes particularly explosive with the increasing differentiation of social morals (this also applies to aesthetics) and thus also the differentiation of social ideas, which are regarded as a 'good' (and also a 'beautiful') landscape: as a result of different regional, social, cultural, etc., the social and social morals of the landscape become more and more differentiated. This also applies to persons with academic landscape expertise (here, for example, the attitudes of 'cultural landscape holders' and 'successionists' differ considerably; e.g. Kühne

2008b). The diversity of socially produced landscape morals is increasing, which means that more and more alternatives must be dominated in the quest for hegemony of one's own landscape morals.

According to the previous remarks, a moralization of communication (in general, here in relation to landscape) means not least a sclerotization of society. Alternative interpretations are no longer sayable and are made conceivable at last. However, they also mean the loss of the advantages of a functionally differentiated society: the construction of landscape is no longer differentiated, economic, political, or scientific, but predominantly (or even exclusively) against the background of a special morality, with the result that landscape contingencies are less and less accepted. This loss of contingency refers on the one hand to the diversity of accepted landscape concepts and on the other hand to the physical foundations of landscape. The moral claim of a comprehensive restoration of a 'historically grown cultural landscape' does not represent, for example, the diversity of current social demands on physical spaces; for example, economic and social demands on physical spaces (such as food security or the desire to live in modern buildings) are suppressed.

A rising moral level—often based on different political worldviews (see Sect. 5.2)—may lead to the desired success in the short term (e.g. however, social dysfunctionalities dominate when regarding the consequences of moral communication (here of landscape). It leads—in Luhmann's sense—to sclerotization by de-differentiating social communication. This is associated with a reduced adaptability of society to changing environmental conditions, since it leads to a restriction of what can be said and, ultimately, of what is conceivable, to a reduction in alternative interpretations. The variety of alternative interpretations, in turn, is a prerequisite for competition for suitable ideas of landscape development. Luhmann (1989, p. 370) succinctly formulates the danger of the moral closure of patterns of interpretation: "Morality is a risky undertaking. Those who moralise take a risk and, if they resist, will easily find themselves in a position to have to look for stronger means or lose self-respect". The specific logic of value, which favors a 'radicalization of morality' in the form of moralizations, can be illuminated in ethical reflection and differentiated and criticized according to possible manifestations. This concerns concealed or hidden normative premises in (incomplete) moral arguments, the question of the meaning of 'good', the need to distinguish between questions of 'good life' and 'justice', and the examination of the generalizability of moral maxims and 'hypermorals'. Here, ethics can contribute to the clarification of 'moralizing' ways of thinking and argumentation mechanisms.

6.2   Conflicts Over Changes in the Physical Foundations of Landscape

The conflicts over landscape are increasing in number and scope, whether with regard to the energy turnaround with the increasing presence of wind power and photovoltaic plants (see e.g. Kühne 2011a; Leibenath and Otto 2013; Selman 2010; Stremke 2010;

Weber et al. 2017), the associated expansion of electricity grids (Kühne and Weber 2015; Weber et al. 2016), increasing the attractiveness of urban living close to cities (e.g. Gebhardt and Wiegandt 2014; Kühne 2016a; Redfern 2003), deindustrialization (Hauser 2001, 2004; Kühne 2007; Vicenzotti 2006), the expansion of transport infrastructures (e.g. Brettschneider 2015; Reuter 2001), also the transition to near-natural forestry (Kühne 2015b), and much more. The question to whom landscape (usually understood as a physical object or appropriated physical landscape) belongs is frequently appropriated, as Berleant (1997, p. 21) explains: "Conflict between aesthetic and economic values often results in the separation of individual property interests from the broader social context and public interests". An approach to understanding the complexity of the conflict field of changes in the physical foundations of landscape lies in differentiated claims as general and private goods. Landscape is generally regarded as a public good, in contrast (at least in market economies) to most individual areas, buildings, trees, etc., which represent the physical foundations of their construction. This difference establishes a tension relationship in principle, which, however, is not subject to reflection, since the individual availability of the compartments is not interpreted critically in principle, nor is the reference to the common good of the synopsis (cf. Apolinarski et al. 2006; Gailing et al. 2006; Schneider 2016; Walker and Fortmann 2003). According to Olwig (2002), the valuation of landscape as a common good refers once again to the medieval origins of the concept of landscape in the Germanic linguistic area in the sense of a territory in which certain norms of a community apply, beyond domination. If landscape is regarded as a common good, the significant modification of its physical foundations for the purpose of making individual profits is valued as an illegitimate encroachment on the rights of the general public.

This section now addresses the question of whether and under what conditions landscape conflicts can be regarded as productive. Conversely, it is also concerned with the question of the conditions under which they can be considered socially dysfunctional. The following explanations are based on the conflict theory of Ralf Dahrendorf (see also Sect. 5.5), which, among other things, proceeds from the normality of social conflicts on the one hand, and from a function (under certain conditions) of conflicts which serves productivity, i.e. social progress, on the other (Dahrendorf 1957, 1969b, 1969b, 1972, 1992; see also: Gratzel 1990; Kühne 2017c, 2018a; Matys and Brüsemeister 2012; Niedenzu 2001). In terms of landscape theory, the following explanations are based on social constructivist landscape theory (Sect. 2.4.1).

Ralf Dahrendorf develops his conflict theory in distinction to both the structural functionalism of Talcott Parsons (who, as shown in Sect. 2.4.2, was a major source of ideas for Niklas Luhmann) and to Marx's interpretation of conflicts (see also Sect. 5.3 on Critical Theory). Structural functionalism is based on the division of society into subsystems which fulfil specific tasks for the whole of society, i.e. "a relatively stable system of parts whose function is determined in relation to the system" (Dahrendorf 1968b, p. 239; see also Staubmann and Wenzel 2000). Dahrendorf (1968b, p. 238) sees the dilemma of this theory in "how the element of movement, conflict and change can be reintroduced into its models at the level of analytical abstraction, i.e. how theoretical analysis can do justice to the essentially processual character of social reality". He follows Karl Marx in his view that conflicts are in principle to be understood as socially productive, but he fundamentally criticizes the idea of society and the form of the conflicts understood by Marx as productive (Dahrendorf 1952, 1961, 1968b, 1969c, 1972): The path to communism takes place as a "work of natural forces or of divine foresight" (Dahrendorf 1952, p. 13) in the form of (bloody) revolutions (see Fig. 5.1). As a liberal he rejects both, communism, because it (as a classless society) lacks the conflict to further develop society (and the individuals), and the view that fundamental social conflicts must be resolved by revolutions claims too many lives. Accordingly, he considers conflicts to be productive only when they run without bloodshed.

Dahrendorf's conflict theory does not refer to individual conflicts, but to social conflicts, namely those that can be traced back to differences in social rank. Dahrendorf sees the main cause of social conflicts in the antagonism between the forces of persistence and those of progression (Bonacker 2009; Dahrendorf 1957; Kühne 2017c). According to Dahrendorf (e.g. 1957, 1972), social conflicts always involve both the striving for and the obstruction of life chances, which Dahrendorf (2007a, p. 44) "initially [as] election chances, options. They demand two things, rights to participate and an offer of activities and goods to choose from".

Social conflicts vary according to 'intensity' and 'violence' (Dahrendorf 1972), whereby 'intensity' refers to social relevance: "It is high if much depends on it for the participants, i.e. if the costs of defeat are high" (Dahrendorf 1972, p. 38; similar Dahrendorf 1965). The 'violence' of social conflicts ranges from non-binding discussions to revolutions and World Wars. Dahrendorf (1972) describes particularly intensively and violently those conflicts that are developed in several dimensions, for example, when economic, political, cultural/religious, education-specific, etc., are involved. Aspects culminate (such as relative poverty with political disadvantage, a different religion from that of the majority society, barriers to participation in the (higher) education system; the classic example of Dahrendorf was the conflict in Northern Ireland; even today many other similar conflicts can be found in the context of the relationships between majority and minority societies).

Social conflicts have a history, they do not arise suddenly, as Dahrendorf (1972) states. He divides their genesis into three phases:

1. Dahrendorf uses the term 'structural starting position' to describe the emergence of 'quasi-groups' of societal subsets. These are characterised by the fact that they each have—in certain contexts—the same interests.
2. In the phase of 'becoming aware of latent interests', the conflict parties emerge by the 'quasi-groups' becoming aware of their interests.
3. In the 'phase of trained interests', the degree of organization of the conflict parties 'with their own visible identity' increases (Dahrendorf 1972, p. 36). In this phase of dichotomizing the conflict, different interests are transformed into internal conflicts within the individual conflict parties (Dahrendorf 1972).

With regard to dealing with conflicts, Dahrendorf (1972) sees three principal possibilities, of which he considers only one to be productive. He rejects the *suppression of conflicts,* since neither the object of the conflict nor the cause of the conflict is eliminated here. Rather, obstructing the formation and manifestation of conflict groups means an increased virulence of the conflict, which in turn increases the danger of a violent eruption. At the same time, he rejects a *resolution of conflicts,* which is connected with the removal of the social contradictions underlying the conflict. However, this was neither feasible, since there was no society without superior and subordinate relationships, nor was it desirable, since—as mentioned above—society thus lost its dynamism. Dahrendorf favours the third form of dealing with conflicts: their *regulation,* which is characterised by four aspects:

1. Like social conflicts in general, the conflict must be recognised as normal, and not as a situation that is contrary to norms.
2. The regulation refers to the forms of the conflict, not to its causes.
3. A high degree of organization of the conflict parties has a positive effect on the efficiency of the regulation.
4. The success of conflict regulation depends on compliance with certain rules. The recognition of the equivalence of the conflict parties is just as central as the recognition of the principled justification of the worldview of the other conflict party.

Dahrendorf considers conflict regulation "the rational taming of social conflicts" to be "one of the central tasks of politics" (Dahrendorf 1972, p. 44). This 'taming' can take place on two levels, one is on the political level itself, when political conflicts in the democratic constitutional state do not lead to revolutions, but are regulated by peaceful changes of government through elections, and the other being on the societal level, when politics creates the framework for the non-political regulation of conflicts (Dahrendorf 1972, 1990, 1992; for more on Ralf Dahrendorf's conflict theory see e.g. Bonacker 1996; Kühne 2017c; Lamla 2008; Niedenzu 2001).

This possibility of contributing to conflict regulation by defining framework conditions is based on domination. The specificity of domination over more general power (Dahrendorf follows Weber's concept of power, power as an opportunity to assert one's will even against resistance; see Sect. 5.1) lies in "an institutionalized permanent relationship of the exercise of power by a superordinate person or group of persons over subordinate groups understood, which would not be possible without a minimum of recognition and obedience […]" (Imbusch 2002, p. 172; Dahrendorf 1972). In addition, the superiors are expected to control the behaviour of the subordinate part of society. This control also includes the negative sanction of norm deviations, because "a legal system (or a system of quasi-legal norms) watches over the effectiveness of rule" (Dahrendorf 1972, p. 33). In the transformation from power to rule, Dahrendorf recognizes an advantage of liberal democracy, in which the exercise of power is regulated by the control of powers and legitimized by free, equal, and secret elections (Dahrendorf 1980, 1987, 2003): "Power is never good […]. But it is all the more bearable the clearer it is where the sources of the initiative and where the sources of control lie" (Kreuzer et al. 1983, p. 69). In the following, these fundamental considerations on conflict, including also power and domination, are related to the conflicts over landscape.

Social differentiation increases the number of potential conflicts, as the number of specific logics, interpretations, and evaluation patterns multiplies (Luhmann 2017). With this development, not only the demands on the use of physical spaces are multiplying, but also the socially existing patterns of landscape interpretation and evaluation. An increasing global cultural exchange also means a (at least potential) multiplication of patterns of interpretation and evaluation applied to specific physical spaces (Bruns 2013, 2016; Bruns and Kühne 2015).

The internalized social landscape assessment and interpretation patterns are applied in the process of socialization (see Sect. 4.2; for more details see e.g. Kühne 2008a, 2017a; Lyons 1983; Nissen 1998; Proshansky et al. 1983; Stotten 2013). The normative content of 'native regular landscape' is directed towards familiarity, that of 'stereotypical landscape' towards adherence to social aesthetic norms. If an object constellation is evaluated in the mode of the 'native regular landscape', any change in this constellation that is interpreted as essential is described as contrary to the norm, whereas in the construction mode of the 'stereotyped landscape', on the other hand, this change is only described as contrary to stereotypical social expectations (i.e. is generally interpreted as 'ugly'; Fig. 6.2). To illustrate this with an example: If the construction of a wind farm is interpreted on the basis of the 'native regular landscape', a negative attitude is adopted, since the physical foundations of landscape are subject to a change that is generally considered to be a clear one. The assessment on the basis of 'stereotypical landscape' is carried out in large parts of the Central European population as 'ugly', but can also refer to the aesthetic assessment pattern of 'sublimity' or cognitively to 'modern' (Kühne 2018d; for the aesthetic interpretation patterns in this context see in particular Sects. 3.2, 3.3 and 3.4). As essentially interpreted changes in the physical foundations of landscape, which also contradict the social notions of 'attractiveness', they form an essential basis for landscape conflicts between companies, spatial planning, politics as well as population groups interpreted as affected (in different conflict constellations). Here, too, we can see that landscape conflicts also have their basis in the contrast between the forces of perseverance and those of change. The changes, both on the levels of the social landscape and the physical space, can show a varying degree of intensity and brutality. Depending on how large the part of a population that is considered to be affected is, what possibilities exist for influencing decision-making processes, how actors are networked, etc., the following factors should be taken into consideration. This means that the conflict can range from a technical dispute over landscape understanding (see e.g. Hokema 2013; Vicenzotti 2011b) to a trigger for bloody disputes. The positions taken by the conflict parties can vary considerably (according to: Hofinger 2001; Kühne 2018f; Weber et al. 2016, 2018):

1. Active hostility (combat, even beyond what is legally permissible),
2. active opposition (participation or organization of the resistance),

Fig. 6.2 "Energy is renewable, 'Heimat' is not", whereby the picture of the firewood does not lack a certain irony. The poster shown here illustrates the importance of a 'native home landscape' in the conflict over the construction of wind turbines. This emotional occupation of 'landscape' is difficult to model and can be reduced in the planning process. A conflict develops that is largely disordered and characterised by mutual distrust between those affected and the operators/planning/politics. Because of the strong political push for energy system transformation in Germany, the political system has no longer become an independent body for the weighing of interests, but a party to the conflict. In addition to the high degree of moralization of the conflict, this contributes to an increase in 'disenchantment with the state'. (Eichenauer et al. 2018; Photo: Kühne)

3. rejection (expression of verbal or non-verbal criticism),
4. conflict (there is a dispute, but without a clear fixation of one's own opinion),
5. indifference (there is no active discussion),
6. tolerance (acceptance takes place in submission to social power relations),
7. conditional acceptance (based on rational considerations, a project is accepted under certain conditions, such as monetary compensation),
8. consent (positive evaluation from own conviction),
9. active involvement (participation or organization of support),
10. active promotion (support, even beyond what is legally permissible).

In the course of conflicts, here landscape conflicts, there is usually a shift in the positions taken by those involved (Fig. 6.3). While in the initial situation the largest number of people involved occupy a neutral position and only a small number of supporters are involved in the project, and the number of opponents is small, depending on the course of the conflict, there is sometimes extreme polarization (until the legal framework is exceeded) or a party to the conflict succeeds in binding the 'neutral' people involved (other distributions than those described can also be found in practice).

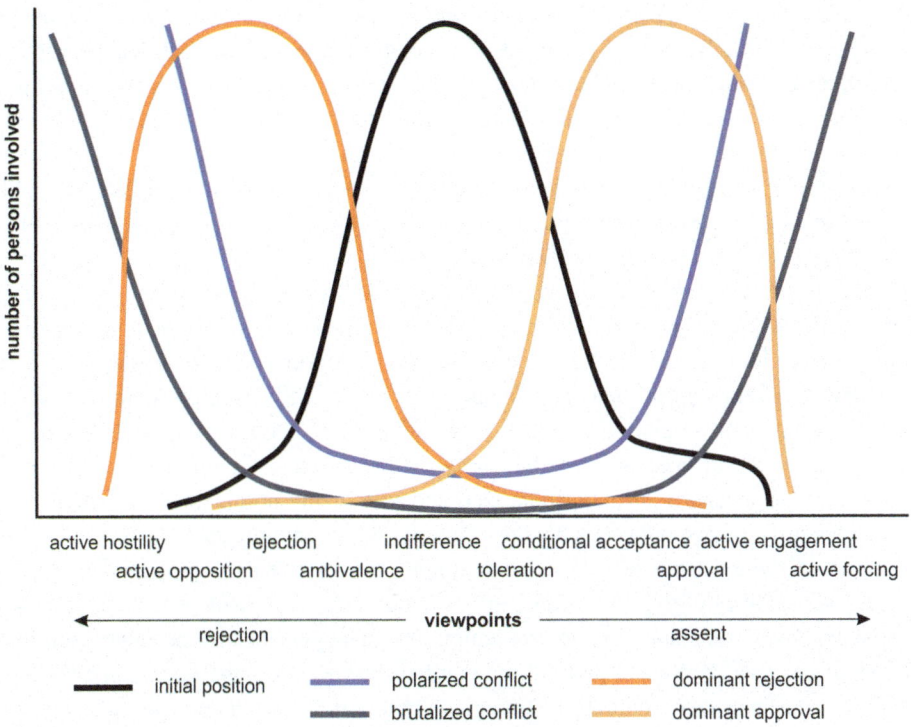

Fig. 6.3 Idealized examples of the distribution of positions taken by those involved in landscape conflicts. (Own design)

In democratic states, it seems difficult to suppress (permanently) landscape conflicts, since the participation of different actors is legally prescribed (in Germany only by the counter-current principle of spatial planning). An attempt to solve landscape conflicts, i.e. to eliminate their social causes, would be to maintain a social status quo, since changes in landscape and its physical foundations are based on changes in society. This also meant limiting a maximization of life chances. Another strategy is to avoid landscape conflicts by changing the physical foundations of landscapes below the 'perceptional threshold' or by removing them from perception through 'camouflage' (an extreme example of this is the County Jail in downtown Los Angeles, whose design is adapted to its surroundings in such a way that it could also be an office complex, a shopping mall, or a multi-storey car park; for more details see Kühne 2012b, 2013b; Weber 2017a). The regulation, which cannot, however, do without certain foundations, is regarded as the ultimately appropriate way for democratic societies to deal with landlocked conflicts: 1) the organization of the parties to the conflict, 2) the mutual recognition of each other's position as a legitimate expression of (landscape) needs, 3) compliance with certain procedural rules, and 4) the existence of an independent authority capable of enforcing the regulations found, as well as 5) the imputability of responsibility for decisions. In liberal democracy, the latter specifically includes the regular review of the satisfaction of the electorate with the balance of power of the elected representatives (Dahrendorf 1969a). According to Dahrendorf (1994, p. 69), "the autonomy of the many organizations and institutions" is essential for a successful regulation of landscape conflicts, whereby autonomy is understood to mean independence "from a centre of power" (Dahrendorf 1994, p. 69). For example, that citizens' initiatives do not serve as a mouthpiece for polit- ical parties. Dealing with each other, but also within the conflict parties, requires polite- ness, tolerance, and non-violence (Dahrendorf 1994).

Dealing with current landscape conflicts shows (at least in Germany, but also in other parts of the world) a more or less great distance to these necessities: 1) The organiza- tion of the conflict parties in spatial conflicts is often rather diffuse in the process of negotiation, actors step in, others withdraw. 2) It is precisely the representatives of cit- izens' interests (e.g. organised in citizens' initiatives) who see themselves challenged to be recognised as an organised conflict party. In the struggle for this recognition, they often resort to means of strongly polarized and moralizing argumentation, which 3) is not necessarily in accordance with the rules of fair communication. 4) According to Dahrendorf, the existence of an independent authority to monitor compliance with rules is the responsibility of the state. However, in numerous current landscape conflicts (such as the expansion of plants for the production and management of renewable energies), the latter has itself become a party to the conflict. Furthermore, the legal framework for dealing with landscape conflicts is ambiguous and can be interpreted in contradictory ways. What can hardly be operationalised in a generally binding manner as a result of a social differentiation under landscape 'beauty' (whose preservation is demanded in the Federal Nature Conservation Act (Bundesnaturschutzgesetz); which is also documented by the large number of 'landscape assessment procedures'; e.g. Roth and Bruns 2016). 5) As a result of the diffuse conflict situation, both on the part of the original conflict parties, e.g. entrepreneurs vs. citizens' initiatives in the extraction of raw materials, then with the expansion of nature conservation associations, sports clubs etc., and political and administrative influence, it is more difficult to attribute decisions or to external- ise them to the courts. Thus the question of a changed use of space is transformed not only into an administrative, but also into an aesthetic, moral, and political question, and then ultimately into a binding jurisprudence (cf. among many Aschenbrand et al. 2017a, 2017b; Brettschneider and Schuster 2013; Federal Government 2014; Gailing 2015b; Hoeft et al. 2017; Hook 2018; Kühne and Weber 2018[online first 2017]; Walter et al. 2013; Weber and Kühne 2016).

Although the high degree of organizational capacity of the conflict parties as a result of the expansion of education since the late 1960s (Dahrendorf 1968a) potentially con- tributes to an orderly settlement of conflicts, the increasing differentiation of the individ- ual interests (from species protection to geotope protection, landscape aesthetic issues, use interests for dog owners, hang-gliders, geocachers, people interested in bathing, etc.) counteracts the formation and organization of conflict interests.

The attempts to solve or suppress landscape conflicts appear to be only slightly in keeping with a democratic-plural society. The solution of landscape conflicts intended to eliminate their social causes, but these lie in the plural and differentiated society, whose parts on the one hand have different demands on landscape and its physical foundations, yet on the other hand are becoming more and more diverse in terms of landscape interpretations and evaluations. Thus, the solution of landscape conflicts would mean a unification of society. The suppression of landscape conflicts meant a disregard of landscape needs, interpretations and evaluations of citizens, which would be enforced by mechanisms of domination and could ultimately be broken up by eruptive social events alone. In this respect, in a democratically constituted society the way of regulating landscape conflicts seems the appropriate one (see also Antrop 2000; Hülz and Kühne 2015; Kamlage et al. 2014).

However, the main obstacles in the regulation of landscape conflicts are often the low degree of organization of the conflict parties combined with high moralization (see Sect. 6.1): instead of recognizing the positions of the 'other side' as legitimate, the actors of the 'other side' are morally discredited (Berr 2018; Kühne 2008d; Spanier 2006). Thus, 'destroyers of homeland and landscape' meet 'destroyers of the future of mankind' (cf. Kühne and Weber 2015; Renn 2012). The low specificity of the conflict object also does not facilitate the settlement of landscape conflicts, to which the current legal situation in Germany also contributes: There is no legal regulation as to what is to be understood by landscape or even its 'beauty'. Thus, 'masked' arguments (often related to species protection, as it is regarded as a 'sharp sword') come to the fore against the motives of preserving the physical foundations of 'native regular landscape' or 'stereotypical landscape'. The fact that in current landscape conflicts the state also assumes the dual function of conflict party and 'neutral authority' makes conflict regulation even more difficult.

The hoped-for increase in legitimacy through the inclusion of additional actors in participation processes, which Harris (2002) calls the 'new paradigm' of planning, results from the increase in perspectives (here on landscape) in an increasingly differentiated society (Healey 1997), as it is ultimately produced by the 'expansion of education' (Dahrendorf 1968a; Hadjar and Becker 2009; Hoffmann-Lange 2000). A participation of the population that increases the legitimacy of planning in comparison with alternative procedures, such as that provided for by the European Landscape Convention (Council of Europe 2000; cf. also Olwig 2007; see Box 20), is thus dependent on certain conditions that can be derived from the principles of fairness of opportunity and procedure (see Box 13): All sections of the population must be empowered to participate in the procedures. This concerns cultural, economic, and social capital as well (i.e. care must be taken to ensure that certain sections of the population that would otherwise not participate can contribute to the planning process). The planning process and the possibilities for influencing it must be clearly explained, agreements on procedures must be adhered to, and transparency created (Roe 2018; for more detailed information on landscape and justice, see Setten, Brown and Rørtveit 2018). If such criteria are not met, the massive loss of legitimacy threatens not only the concrete planning, but also the loss of trust in the democratic organization of the state (cf. Kühne 2018b).

Box 20: The European Landscape Convention

The European Landscape Convention (ELC) can be described as a framework for action that takes into account the physical foundations on the one hand and the social foundations of appropriated physical landscapes on the other. The European Landscape Convention is intended to promote protection, development, and intergovernmental cooperation on these issues. The Convention, which was initiated by the Council of Europe in 2000 and entered into force in 2004, has so far been ratified by 29 states and signed by two states without ratification (Iceland and Malta). It was neither ratified nor signed by nine states (including Germany and Austria), which—according to Hunziker (2010, p. 33) "currently the most relevant definition of landscape, that of the European Landscape Convention" defines landscape as follows: "'Landscape' means an area, as perceived by people, whose character is the result of the action and interaction of natural and/or human factors" (Council of Europe 2000, Article 1, paragraph 1). The scientific-theoretical classification of the definition is not clear, because landscape is interpreted both constructivist ('perceived by people') and, in the second part of the definition, representational. The 'character' points to a rather essentialist reference, while the word 'factors' refers to a more positivist approach to the obligations to capture landscape, as set out later in the Convention, whereby the classic conceptual separation between cultural and natural landscape is dispensed with (Antrop 2006). This theoretical attitude can be interpreted as 'postmodern eclecticist' (on postmodern spatial references, see Sect. 6.3) or, in view of the extensive tasks required by the Convention for the recording, evaluation, and development of landscapes with public participation, as 'neo-pragmatic' (see Sect. 2.6).

The European Landscape Convention is associated with far-reaching demands for the integration of the public into landscape development: after all, "the perceptions and views of all members of civil society in the broadest sense are relevant, not only the views of a political or academic elite (and certainly not only their idea of the landscape)" (Bruns 2010, p. 34; see also Jones et al. 2007). The goal is a democratization of the evaluation and planning process that goes far beyond informing the public, as in classical planning processes (Mitchell 2003; Jones et al. 2007). Landscape-related interpretations of the population are to be included in every phase of the development (especially the physical foundations) of appropriated physical landscapes (Bruns 2010): in the inventory, in the analysis (e.g. the change of the physical foundations from appropriated physical landscapes), in the discussion and adoption of landscape quality objectives, in the assessment of appropriated physical landscapes, as well as in the influence on decisions relating to the development of landscapes.

In the scientific context, broadening the understanding of landscape, but also dealing with the physical foundations of landscape, requires an increasingly inter-disciplinary and transdisciplinary scientific perspective (Naranjo 2006; Pedroli and Van Mansvelt 2006; Jones et al. 2007; Selman 2010): On the one hand, different disciplines must be involved in landscape research (not only natural sciences, but also humanities and social sciences); on the other hand, the dialogue between sci-ence and practice becomes the basis for successful landscape policy.

Landscape conflicts can in principle be recognised as productive for society under cer-tain specified conditions. However, the basic principle for this is the acknowledgement that landscape conflicts are not to be understood as a condition contrary to norms, as a deviation from the construct of a 'general social consensus'. Instead, landscape conflicts should be understood as an element of a developing and generating life chances in soci-ety. The negotiation of landscape conflicts should be given an institutional framework that enables the parties to the conflict to negotiate in an organized manner with clear negotiating rules, e.g. on the development of concrete areas designated as landscapes. In view of a pluralizing society (with increasingly diverse demands, interpretations, and evaluations of landscape), attempts to suppress landscape conflicts with the help of standardized 'landscape assessment procedures', as is common in landscape planning, for example, can be described as at best inadequate, if not dysfunctional.

6.3   Landscape and Postmodernism: From Appreciation of Historical Hybridization and Pastiche Formations

For more than three decades, postmodern developments have been discussed in the social as well as spatial sciences (among many: Antrop 2000; Basten 2005; Clarke 2006; Dear and Flusty 1998; Ellin 1999; Harvey 1989; Klotz 1985; Scott and Soja 1996; Soja 1989; Wood 2003). Reflections have also found increased expression in landscape research (Bätzing 2000; Cosgrove 1997; Fontaine 2017b; Kühne 2006a; Weber 2016a; Zukin 1992) and planning sciences (Allmendinger 2000; Hartz and Kühne 2007; Lanz 1996). In the investigation of postmodern spatial developments, it is central how the differenti-ation, polarization, aestheticization, but also economization of society affects the design of physical spaces as well as social constructions of space. Especially in the early years of postmodern space research, urban fragmentation processes (e.g. in the form of gated communities, shopping malls, edge cities, etc.) were often interpreted as the dissolution of an ordered settlement structure, were in the foreground of interest, and were often referred to as 'neoliberalization' (Castree 2008; see Box 15). These analyses supple-mented and reinterpreted research on suburbanization (among many academies for spa-tial research and regional planning 1975; Brake et al. 2001; Burdack and Hesse 2006;

Donzelot 2004; Hayden 2004; Hesse and Siedentop 2018; Masotti and Hadden 1974). Almost all attempts to "characterize the new, postmodern structure of the city" ended in a recourse "to the image of a grid or net, whereby, however, this does not mean the figure of a spider's web, but that of a goal net or even that of a catch fence" (Basten 2005, p. 57). The different compartments no longer follow a universal development scheme, as was characteristic of modernity, but become increasingly dependent on individual developments (cf. e.g. Degen 2008), with which they blatantly contradict the ideas in modern urban planning of "creating a uniform cityscape" (Löw 2010, p. 154; Cosgrove 2006; Sieverts 1998[1997]). This development is driven economically by the change from the Fordist to the post-Fordist accumulation regime (Box 21).

Box 21: Regulation theory

Regulation theory refers to fundamental social change since the beginning of industrialization. It assumes different accumulation regimes. Accumulation regime is a synthetic view of the organization of production and capital flows. The mode of remuneration, value added generation and distribution, the state quota and its flexibility are examined. Three different successive accumulation regimes can be distinguished: extensive accumulation, the accumulation form of Fordism and that of post-Fordism. This phase is reached differently in national economies, but also in regions (Aglietta 1976; Hirsch and Roth 1986; Ipsen 2006; Moulaert and Swyngedouw 1989; Swyngedouw et al. 2002).

The phase of extensive accumulation, which can also be described as the first phase of economic modernity, began in Central and Western Europe in the middle of the 19th century and ended after the First World War. The phase is characterised by low productivity: Production can only be increased if the input of labour, land, and capital is increased approximately proportionally to the increase in production. The state intervenes only to a small extent in regulating production; it merely defines the political framework of economic activity.

The accumulation regime of Fordism (after: Henry Ford, who introduced large-scale assembly line production into automobile production) laid the foundation for the development of the mass consumer society. In Central and Western Europe, the Fordist accumulation regime—gradually and clearly differentiated regionally—prevailed from the 1920s to the 1950s. As regards work organization, Fordism was based on the scientific management approach of Taylorism named after Frederick Winslow Taylor (exact determination of the time and place of service provision, top-down communication within the company, extreme disassembly of the individual work tasks, etc.; Grap 1992). The introduction of assembly lines achieved considerable increases in productivity, which, however, were at the expense of the "polarization of qualifications and responsibilities between planners and executors" (Lipietz 1991, p. 132). The result is standardized but inexpensive mass consumer goods (Volkswagen, fast food, mass tourism hotels). Economies of scale were achieved as a result of large batch sizes (i.e. the cost per unit was reduced by mass production). Fordism was also associated with the creation of mass purchasing power, since a clientele was needed for the mass-produced goods: Wage increases anticipated productivity gains, while working hours were reduced. Fordist modernity is linked to the development of the welfare state: It intervenes in the economic, social, and cultural activities of people. Its aim is to prevent a strong polarization of society through social assistance and income transfers.

The post-Fordist accumulation regime (from the 1970s onwards) can be interpreted as a consequence of the change in social values in the affluent societies of North America, Europe, East Asia, and Oceania. In the context of the transition to postfordism, the demand for standardized, industrially manufactured products is declining. Rather, consumers strive to shape their individual image by selecting and combining individually designed goods. Compared to Fordism, production in small, flexible batch sizes based on computer-aided production processes is gaining in importance. There is a shift in production from large enterprises to small and medium-sized flexible enterprises, often through outsourcing of production stages from large enterprises. Industrial production is shifting from heavy industrial production to high-tech production, and industrial production is increasingly being shifted to third countries (especially emerging markets) (see also Krätke 1996, Schnur 2015).

A central element of postmodern development is the appreciation of both the historical and the local (see among others: Crang and Tolia-Kelly 2010; Harvey 2001; Harvey and Wilkinson 2018; Herring 2018; Kühne 2006a, 2007). Because of globalization, people are disembedded, i.e. they are lifted out of the traditional and local context (e.g. the village community, the modern mining settlement). At the same time, a longing for re-embedding in the local context develops (Giddens 1990). Robertson (1995) characterizes this simultaneity of the global and the local with the expression 'glocalization', which describes a "simultaneous increase of processes of generalization and specialization" (Ahrens 2001, p. 14). Postmodern man is anxious to compensate for the increase in contingencies caused by globalization: Home, familiarity, and cosiness are again filled with meaning, 'cultural landscape' is understood as a carrier of specific and positively evaluated regional peculiarity (Olwig 2011; also: Kühne 2009b; Kühne and Hernik 2015). This longing for historical and local or regional localization is also expressed in architecture: "While modernity sought to liberate itself from all history" (Klotz 1985, p. 423), postmodern architecture and landscape architecture (Hoesterey 2001) endeavor to address regional, ethnic, and historical aspects. As a rule, however, this approach does not represent a simple preservation or copy; the historical is additionally related to the new: "History as a regained perspective no longer allows us to gain stimuli from the interest in pure forms, but instead to engage in the spirit of irony" (Klotz 1985, p. 423).

The postmodern reference to the historical always remains a staging: historical formal languages are oriented towards contemporary needs, they become the backdrop that is supposed to create a pleasant atmosphere, or as Prigge and Herterich (1988, p. 315) express: "The ornamental, the tendency towards historicism, the inclination towards the monumental and the appearance of craftsmanship simulate the edifying, rootedness and stability of values, while all this is in reality deeply questioned". Urban redevelopment as well as village renewal endeavour to replace the fordist-modern transformation of buildings and settlements with a state oriented towards the pre-functionalist formal language in order to transform them into an (idealized) initial state. There are almost continuous decouplings between form and function: a historicizing form that suggests a historical use (e.g. as a farmhouse) contains a nonhistorical or only partially historically founded function (e.g. as a residential building). Even the historical formal language is sometimes achieved through the use of current materials and techniques (double glazing instead of cassette windows). Such an "aesthetic re-enchantment" of the world is constitutive for postmodernism, which rejects the functional concept of modernism, whereby postmodernism can be interpreted as a "sign of the reconnection to Romanticism" (Pohl 1993, p. 29; similar to Safranski 2007). Where in modernity the (as pure as possible) model of enlightenment and reason was valid, postmodernism aestheticizes. In this context, it becomes clear that historical heritage is hybridized with contemporary uses and claims (cf. Harvey and Wilkinson 2018), a process that will be examined in more detail below.

The conceptual version of the two words 'hybrid' and 'hybridity' (see Hein 2006; Kraidy 2005) has changed considerably over the past two centuries: In the 19th century 'hybridity' was understood as a biological crossing (Hein 2006). In this context, hybridizations meant "the development of new combinations by grafting one plant or fruit onto another" (Niederveen Pieterse 2005, p. 401). In contrast, in the last decades of the 20th century the concept of hybridity experienced the expansion of a "cultural strategy of mixing and negotiating differences" (Hein 2006, p. 55). The extension takes place in the context of the postmodern discussion: instead of the modern striving for purity, dichotomy, and unambiguity in which the mixed, the blended, and the impure is "something inappropriate that should remain outside for fear of endangering the basic order of things" (Bauman 2009[1993], p. 241), postmodernism turns more to contradictions and diversity, to ambiguities, which it not only accepts but values (Kühne 2012b, c). In this context, the connotations of 'hybridity' also changed: While originally primarily "infertility, decomposition, dissolution, degradation and degeneration" (Zapf 2002, p. 40) was associated with it, in the context of postmodernization "the re-focusing from physiological to cultural phenomena also leads to a reevaluation" (Zapf 2002, p. 40), no longer hybridity is connotated with unproductivity, but purity (Zapf 2002). The hybridization concept thus makes it possible to turn away from (conceptual) dichotomous confrontations, such as "'white' and 'black', 'master' and slave', 'self' and 'other' in favor of a third, hybrid category" (Ackermann 2004, p. 148). Other modern dichotomies are also: ugly—beautiful (see detailed chapter 3), good—bad, man—woman, intellect—emotion, city—country, culture—nature (among many: Fuller 1992; Kühne 2012c; Holzinger 2004; Mölders et al. 2016; Riley 1994; Spirn 1988).

Hybridizations take place especially in linguistic contexts. For Michail Bachtin (e.g. 1985), linguistic hybridity concept is based on the assumption that language is "not only a linguistic system, but a historically and socially specific way of speaking and seeing, which was connected with a certain belief system and consciousness" (Hein 2006, p. 55). According to Bakhtin's approach it is possible through language "to let two opposing voices speak within one and the same movement, which ironize and unmask each other" (Ackermann 2004, p. 148). From a systems theory perspective, Jung (2009, p. 129) emphasizes that hybridization is not a communication event and is not an "oscillation between 'one's own' and 'foreign' relevance and validity criteria"; rather, hybridization is understood "as a stabilized reference context of a communication structure". Following Bakhtin, a distinction can be made between unintentional organic hybridization and intentional hybridization (see Grimm 1997; Wirth 2012; Hein 2006). An organic hybridization accordingly refers to a latent overlapping and mixing of different 'languages'. Thus, the existence of homogeneous cultures with fixed 'sense boundaries' will not "be regarded as the normal case of cultural development" (Reckwitz 2001, p. 189). 'Intended hybridization', on the other hand, is a conscious, artistic-dialogical confrontation of different languages and meanings (Grimm 1997; Hein 2006). By means of 'intended hybridization', the speaker can succeed in "liberating himself from the power of language and the direct word [editor's note], since he recognizes and simultaneously destroys the separateness of a social language. Thus, he can develop a certain distance to the various social discourses and use a language to unmask the others" (Hein 2006, p. 56). Intended hybridization can accordingly be understood with Homi Bhabha as a "model of resistance and cultural politics in general" (Grimm 1997, p. 4).

Homi Bhaba (2012) sees the spaces created by hybridization as 'third spaces'. These spaces are characterized by the fact that differences are not hierarchically ordered (Bhabha 2000a, b). Bhabha (2012, pp. 68–69) describes this space as one of "continuous crossing [...] rather than a journey whose destination one knows". The negotiations conducted in this liminality phase recognize that the "levels of conflict or antagonism are indeed very close, not simply polarized, but much closer and much more chaotic" (Bhabha 2012, pp. 71–72). Bipolar power structures are replaced by net-like authority structures (Bhabha 2012; Foucault 1983[1976]). A 'third space' "belongs to all inhabitants equally, regardless of their origin, culture, religion" (de Toro 2007, p. 379).[1]

---

[1]The word 'Thirdspace'—compared to Homi Bhaba—is filled with a different meaning by the postmodernist theorist Edward Soja (1996, 2003): Soya's (2003, p. 273) Thirdspace concept can be interpreted as an attempt "to understand how the fundamental triangle of historicity, sociality and spatiality can be brought back into balance". It thus aims at a change of perspective that wants to break up the duality of perceived space (Firstspace), the "world of direct, immediate spatial experience of empirically measurable and cartographically comprehensible phenomena" and mental space (Secondspace), which focuses on "cognitive, constructed and symbolic 'worlds'" (Soja 2003, pp. 274–275).

The concept of hybridity is subject to a critique from different perspectives: First, the concept, as a result of the ongoing emphasis on difference, "conceals losing sight of what unites" (Ackermann 2004, p. 152). Secondly, the concept is assumed to promote hidden essentialisms; finally, hybridity implies a previous purity (Rademacher 1999). Third, if the starting points for the formation of hybridities are not assumed to be essentialist cultures, the concept of tautology is assumed, since cultures would already be assumed to be hybrid in themselves, for then, according to Ackermann (2004, p. 153), "globalization […] would be nothing other than a hybrid formation of already hybrid cultures". In this context, Hall 1996 (w.p.) "therefore speaks of a slow, gradual transition between a hybridity as a characteristic of the marginal contact zones and a much more general hybridity encompassing all cultures, without assuming autonomous units. But one cannot escape the logical trap entirely, which is why I use hybridity rather as a polemical metaphor, as an 'impure' concept, and not as an analytical concept". Fourthly, Ha (2005) criticises the commercialization of hybridity, which on the one hand is successful, because "hybridity sells well because it is considered sexy" (Ha 2006, w.p.), but in the end (in essentialist reading) is nothing more than a "postmodern new edition of an outdated multiculturalism" (Ha 2006, w.p.) and accordingly has not (completely) departed from the modernist idea of a society in the form of a nation state. However, this criticism is countered by the fact that hybrid persons are feared specifically because they elude the known classification possibilities and their "multiple affiliation threatens the principle of order" (Mecheril 2009, p. 21) and are accused of disloyalty and little trust (Mecheril 2009).

In comparison to related approaches such as *mestizaje,* creolization, or syncretism, 'hybridity' does not describe a "homogenising fusion" in its understanding of mixing (Zapf 2002, p. 40), but rather a "linking of disparate elements such as in collages, bricolages or in 'deconstructive' pop-cultural techniques such as scratching, sampling and cut'n'mix" (Zapf 2002, pp. 40–41). This makes the concept especially suitable for spatial processes, since different forms of hybridization "contain the one in the other" (Tschernokoshewa 2005, p. 15). Bhabha (2012, p. 67) also understands hybridity as a "doubling" that "always opens the way to a thinking of the iterative and the contingent," whereby this formation of iteratives and contingencies is always to be understood as a process (Bhabha 2012) that is spatially and temporally contextualized.

The emergence of spatial hybridizations takes place both on the level of material objects, the physical-spatial structuring of uses, and also on the level of social (aesthetic) landscape understandings and in particular their individual actualization. In the context of increasing social and spatial mobility, one's own (home-normal landscape and especially stereotypical) landscape interpretation and evaluation patterns are confronted with physical-spatial contexts that only rudimentarily correspond to one's own ideas. Rather, these patterns of interpretation and evaluation also experience changes through the confrontation with people having other patterns of interpretation and evaluation (cf. in this context: Hofmeister and Kühne 2016; Kühne 2017b; Whatmore 2002, 2017). Not only in relation to the individually actualized social landscape do hybridizations occur through confrontation with different cultural landscape interpretations and evaluations, these also flow into social landscape interpretations.

In the context of the delimitation of aesthetic access to the world (see Sect. 3.6), which is no longer limited to artistic engagement with the world, the delimitation of the moral as a result of the delimitation of the mass media, etc. (see Sect. 6.1), in the context of the increasing importance of communication in virtual social networks (Berr 2017; Grau 2017; Kühne 2019) and, additionally, of the competition of scientific expertise with alternative ontological statements (such as 'alternative facts'; among others Nowotny 2005; Weingart 2001, 2003; Weingart et al. 2008), postmodernism also hybridizes the judgments of the aesthetic, the moral, and the ontological. In such hybrid judgments determining morality, ontology, and aesthetics, that which is morally defined as 'good' is judged to be 'true', and only this can be considered 'beautiful'. Thus 'beautiful' is a space defined as landscape if it is understood as 'true' (often in the sense of essentialist interpretation as its 'essence') and is used as 'morally' desired (for the moralization of landscape, see Sect. 6.1). For example—from the perspective of people involved in citizens' initiatives against the extraction of mineral resources—a lake is described as 'beautiful' if it is of 'natural' origin and not a consequence of the extraction of mineral resources, which is understood as 'morally reprehensible' (Weber et al. 2018; more generally: Kühne 2008b).

The example of the 'dredging lake' directs the view from the social hybridization processes as regards the (aesthetic) interpretation and evaluation of landscape to the hybridizations in physical spaces (Fig. 6.4). The 'dredging lake', for example, illustrates the emergence of cultural natural hybrids: It is neither clearly attributable to a sphere of the 'cultural' nor clearly to that of the 'natural'. Are anthropogenically produced habitats of animal and plant species whose development is beyond the direct control of humans? This in turn leads to the question of whether and to what extent pure

Fig. 6.4 A dredging lake on the Lower Rhine (Germany). It illustrates the dilemma of dichotomous construction of nature and culture, even if its material equipment is optimised regarding the creation of 'valuable' habitats; it remains the result of economic processes. Its aesthetic evaluation is certainly burdened by its economic past: Lakes are often conditionally attributed to 'beauty' when they are 'natural' waters, whereas the aesthetic evaluation of dredging lakes often includes a moral judgment that leads to an aesthetic devaluation (Weber et al. 2018). This means that a hybridization to an aesthetic-moral judgment also arises at the level of evaluation. (Photo: Kühne)

naturalness or pure culturalness can exist at all on the level of the objects relevant for the construction of landscape. In view of the anthropogenic enrichment of the atmosphere with carbon dioxide on the one hand, and the ultimately natural origins of the materials with which humans restructure physical spaces on the other, 'naturalness' and 'culturalness' can ultimately only be understood as ideally typified poles of a scale of hybridities (for more details see e.g. Haber 2001; Heiland 2006; Kühne 2012c, 2018g; Zierhofer 2003). According to this perspective, material spaces can only be described as cultural nature hybrids, whereby the degree of hybridity varies (constructs such as the dichotomy from 'natural landscape' to 'cultural landscape' thus lose importance). In addition to the hybridization of natural culture, postmodern spatial development is also leading to an increasing 'urban land hybridization'. However, not (necessarily) in the form of a gradient, but through diverse compartments (Kühne 2012b; continuing: Kühne 2016a; Kühne and Schönwald 2015; Kühne et al. 2017; Weber 2017a) of varying degrees of urbanity and rurality. The term 'urbanruralhybrid' describes an intensifying differentiation, fragmentation, and complexity between the poles of urban and rural. This differentiation becomes clear in different dimensions; see also the basis Fig. 4.1):

1. structural, e.g. in terms of development, infrastructure,
2. functional, e.g. centrally located,
3. lifeworld, so to reasonably form and develop the elements of life such as residing, working, looking after oneself, recovering, etc., in view of the economic, administrative, and family situation,
4. emotionally, such as in relation to a local connection,
5. aesthetic, the interpretation of spaces according to the interpretation patterns beauty/ugliness/hastiness/picturesqueness/kitsch, as well as,
6. cognitive, e.g. in the form of space description and understanding.

Processes of social urban rural hybridization mean the penetration of formerly rural, suburban, and urban lifestyles (cf. Gailing 2015a; Kropp 2015; Kühne 2005b; Mölders et al. 2016). The differentiation and hybridization of the world of life and work, for example, in the dissolution of boundaries between work and leisure, the spread of home office and e-learning, leisure activities at the workplace, serve to create new spaces or recode existing physical spaces. Co-working spaces are created, cafés and parks are used as places of work, offices also serve as places for communal evening arrangements, temporary living is gaining in importance, etc.).

Hybrid spaces are not limited to different 'cultural' or 'natural' phenomena but can also be identified in relation to the interplay of different 'natural' phenomena, such as coasts, lakeshores, and rivershores, transitional spaces between vegetations and climates, which are not subject to the ordering and dichotomizing systematics of modern order. It is precisely these spaces—due to their reduced adjustability—that also favour social spaces that are exempt from the rules of everyday life (e.g. Fiske 2011). These research questions can be classified within the framework of hybrid geographies (Whatmore 2002, p. 1), which, in addition to the above-mentioned distinctive differences, also call into question those "between human and non-human; social and material; subjects and objects" and can thus be framed by the actor network theory or the assemblage theory (see Sects. 2.5.2 and 2.5.3).

With postmodernization, two further communication elements developed alongside irony (Hoppmann 2000): intertextuality and polysemy/polyvalence. Intertextuality and polysemy/polyvalence refer to changed forms of formation and reception of 'texts'. 'Text' is not limited to the written or spoken word. Images, human bodies, material objects, and object constellations, etc., can also be understood as 'text', but also landscapes (see Box 3), since they are or can be objects of symbolic communication, i.e. capable of interpretation and accordingly open to different interpretations (cf. Butler 1993; Foucault 1977, 2001; Strüver et al. 2000).

Intertextuality refers to the reference of texts to other texts. In the material structuring of the world, the architecture of postmodern buildings refers to historical stylistic quotations, floor plans, and the design of open spaces in settlements show reminiscences of historical models. Even smaller, the 'shabby vintage' style of furniture simulates past design practices as well as patina; here, following the hybridity-sensitive terminology, one could also speak of 'hybridization of the past and present'. This intertextuality is not only temporal, but also spatial, when, for example, architectural styles that are considered 'regionally typical' in other parts of the world are quoted and combined with other styles that can also be understood as 'hybridizations of architectural styles'. Intertextuality also arises, however, when buildings or open spaces are overshadowed in a form that refers to new residents or uses. The hybridizations that arise in this way can also be termed 'subsequent use hybridizations'. Such intertextualities can also be read as hybridizations, for example in relation to the penetration of current technology with historical design or the mixture of the representation of different social or cultural contexts. Through video games and simulation programs, but also Internet videos, it is in principle possible to "combine time and place in any way" (Vester 1991, p. 55), so that intertextuality is increasingly created virtually (in detail in the context landscape: Fontaine 2017a, b).

Polysemy/polyvalence refers to the multiplicity of statements in texts. As substancial means of expression of polysemy/polyvalence of texts the metaphor, the transfer of a concrete concept to an abstract one, and the allegory as the representation of an abstract concept by an image can be grasped (Hoppmann 2000). Following Kühne (2006a), the concept of polysemy/polyvalence can be transferred to the use of physical spaces, whereby here, due to the greater connectivity of the term in the social and spatial sciences, the term 'polyvalence' following Vester (1993) is followed:

- 'Polyvalent spaces' can be used to identify physical spaces that are subject to different usages/assignments. The 'simple polyvalence' describes a physical space that is determined by multiple use by a social subsystem (in the field of economy, for example, by the combination of agriculture and energy use by wind turbines). 'Complex polyvalence' can be defined as the use of land by at least two social subsystems (e.g. agriculture and recreation). When a special symbolic charge is applied to a physical space, such as the Hollywood sign or the Rütli meadow, one can speak of 'hyper-polyvalence of the first degree'. One can speak of a 'second-degree hyper-polyvalence' when physical spaces are adapted to their symbolic connotations, mostly stereotypical notions.

- Physical spaces can be described as 'monovalent', but they are exclusively subject to use (such as agricultural use).
- The term 'nonvalent spaces' refers to those physical spaces that are not subject to any direct use (e.g. as settlement land, agricultural land, forestry land, etc.) or to any specific symbolic requirement. These include areas that have never been used, such as desert areas, or areas whose use has been abandoned (such as brownfields), as well as 'residual areas' between other uses, each of which has not been symbolically charged.

Whereas in Fordist Modernism the desire to create monovalent spaces dominated, in Postfordist Postmodernism—also in the context of spatial structures and functions—the 'modernist striving for purity' (Fayet 2003), the acceptance to desirability of polyvalent structures, but also in relation to a mixture of surfaces of different valences and last but not least degrees of hybridity, gives way to the 'modernist striving for purity' (Fayet 2003). Among other things, the consequence of this new structuring and functionalization of the valencing of spaces can be described with the 'postmodern space pastiche' to be addressed in the following (the concept of the pastiche for space research is made available, among others, in Aitken and Zonn 1994; Gottdiener 2000; Hetheringtion 1998).

The word 'pastiche' is used to describe "not simply de-differentiation", it "requires difference formation in order to lead to hybrid crossings, recombinations, reintegrations" (Vester 1993, p. 29; for more on the concept of pastiche, see e.g. Hoesterey 2001). Difference means "not only a relative difference, i.e. a difference related to something in common" (Scherle 2016, p. 61), but also a difference "which is (no longer) held together by a uniform foundation and which breaks open the classical question of the relation of the one and the many, the general and the specific" (Scherle 2016, p. 61; see also: Bhaba 2000). For spaces, both in their material as well as socially and individually constructed level, this means: The term 'spatial pastiche' describes the dissolution of functional separations as well as predefined spatial structures, i.e. a spatial organization as preferred by modern spatial planning. Pastiches are characterized by functional mixing and spatial structural changes, such as tasks of use, new uses, restructuring of uses, new connections of functions, as well as symbolic charges and stagings etc. of different degrees of valence (Fig. 6.5). Postmodern space pastiches are formed from compartments of varying degrees of hybridity. This hybridity can be very different: it spans between the polarities of urban and rural ('urbanruralhybrids'), refers to different forms of design (e.g. quoting past architectural styles), merges into previously separate spheres of life (e.g. leisure and working in cafés), mixes the previously normatively separate spheres of culture and nature, global and local coexist or interpenetrate each other (Bowring 2013; Fig. 6.6), in between there are spatial residuals of a modern structuring and functionalization of

Fig. 6.5 After the beginning of the systems transformation, a postmodern space pastiche emerged in Warsaw (Poland)—also due to the extensive renunciation of administrative requirements for the use of space. This is characterised by the physical co-presence of pre-socialist (bottom left), socialist (top left and bottom right), and post-socialist elements. The postmodern staging (here by light) is even given to the Palace of Culture and Science, which was unpopular in Poland at the time as a symbol of Soviet influence (bottom right). The gain in significance of the economic becomes particularly clear in the large-format advertising, which—ironically enough—is carried by the buildings of socialist functionalism due to their straight-line architecture. (Czepczyński 2008; Czesak et al. 2015; Koch 2010; Kühne 2016b; Photos: Kühne)

spaces and their side effects aesthetics, since these ultimately represent—in the sense of hybridity-related thinking—an approach to a pole of hybridity (Kühne 2012a; for the emerging structures and functions, see for example: Hofmeister 2008; Kühne 2006a, 2012b, 2017b; Kühne and Schönwald 2015; Schönwald 2017; Zierhofer 2003), but it can also be directed in the sense of a transfer of the aesthetic design of a theme park to the design of housing estates, the so-called 'Disneyfication', etc. (Sorkin 1992; Warren 1994). The formation of space pastiches is taking place with greatest intensity in those

Fig. 6.6 Document of a multiple hybridization in space pastiche: The 'Preußische Bergwerks-direktion' (Prussian Mining Directorate) in Saarbrücken (Germany), transformed into the Shopping Mall, today 'Europagalerie' (Gallery of Europe; here during the reconstruction in August 2009). In addition to the hybridization of old and new (including architectural), there is the hybridization of global and local. (Branches of international chains in a building linked to local or regional history; Photo: Kühne)

parts of the world that are characterized by a low state administrative influence on the (especially flat) spatial structure (such as in the United States and Poland; cf. Gawroński 2015; Kühne 2012b, 2016b).

The term 'space pastiche' is characterised by a special openness: It comprises different intensities of hybrid formation of the different compartments of the pastiche. Besides the already mentioned (fordistic) modern residual stocks, he is also able to integrate the persistent structures of the developments of the 'grid' postmodernism. Despite the conceptual framing of modern compartments, as well as compartments attributable to 'grid postmodernism', into the concept of 'space pastiche', the focus of the structural and functional developments described under 'space pastiche' lies constitutively on those emergences that are not characterized by distinct demarcation, but by connection and graduality, i.e. hybridity, such as the Edgeless Cities and 'urbanizing former suburbs' (URFSURBS; Kühne 2016a, 2017b; Kühne and Schönwald 2015; Kühne et al. 2016, 2017; Weber and Kühne 2017).

An example of processes that can be understood as 'space pastiche formation' can be associated with the emergence of 'Edgeless Cities' (Lang 2003). The emergence of Edge Cities (Garreau 1992; Henderson and Mitra 1996; Teaford and Harris 1997) was already associated with a functional and structural differentiation process characterized by the concentration of service activities in convenient locations (such as major airports or freeway intersections). The emergence of the Edgeless Cities can be associated with a further spatial differentiation process: 'Edgeless Cities' emerge in different forms, sizes, and densities, and can also be found in a variety of arrangements (Lang et al. 2013, p. 727). Since they are not clearly defined, they lack an unambiguously definable 'outside', which makes their 'inside' difficult to grasp unambiguously. Correspondingly, only a small amount of their own 'identity' is ascribed to them, which is why "they are not perceived as a place" (Lang et al. 2013, p. 732). They are specially shaped along busy roads and can take on considerable dimensions (several hundred square kilometres) (see also: Bingham et al. 1997). They can be interpreted as the expression of a hybridization of centrality and non-centrality, as well as the transition from central-local point-like compression to a linear and planar expression of variable centrality intensities.

Another form of urbanruralhybridization can be defined by the term 'urbanizing former suburbs' (URFSURBS; Kühne 2016a, 2017b; Kühne and Schönwald 2015; Kühne et al. 2016, 2017; Fig. 6.7). This allows the extension of 1) 'urban' lifestyles, 2) inner-city functions (e.g. working in 'upper grade' of service occupations, facilities for hybrid work-leisure arrangements) and 3) structures (e.g. in the form of certain 'typical inner-city buildings' such as (high-rise) office buildings or apartment buildings) in suburban spaces close to the city centre, often together in combination (cf. Kühne 2016a, 2017b; Kühne and Schönwald 2015; Kühne et al. 2016, 2017; Weber and Kühne 2017). The development of URFSURBS is the result of societal changes that result in a loss of the attractiveness of suburban housing. They range from the increase in the importance of life beyond the classic modern two-generation family and the gain in importance of the cultural and creative industries to the rise in energy prices (Gallagher 2013; Hanlon 2008, 2010; Hesse 2008, 2010; see Fig. 6.8 for summary). Different intensities of URFSURBanization can be determined (Kühne and Schönwald 2015; Kühne et al. 2016, 2017; Kühne and Schönwald 2018):

1. A rather low intensity of change can be found where existing physical structures persist while maintaining the existing use (usually housing). However, the buildings were renovated and used for residential purposes by people with a higher level of 'symbolic capital' (Bourdieu 1989).
2. A higher intensity of change can be found in neighbourhoods in which a change of use is carried out while (largely) retaining the physical structures (empty shops are converted into cafés, old industrial buildings converted into apartments, etc.).
3. The change becomes much more intense and sensory impressive when physical structures are revised, although the type of use is largely retained (for example, the replacement of several single-family houses by apartment houses on their pooled properties).
4. The greatest intensity of change occurs where both physical structures and their use are subject to revision, for example in the construction of residential and office buildings with shops, on previously industrially used areas.

Fig. 6.7 The formation of URFSURBs in San Diego, California. Expression of the gain in importance of the downtown area, combined with the normative affirmation of this (top left picture). A restrained intensity of change is found where physical structures are preserved (upside right). The other photos document a higher intensity of change in physical structures towards an urban building structure. (Photos: Kühne)

Both Edgeless Cities and URFSURBS map current processes of hybridization of uses and structures between modernity and postmodernity, as well as between 'grid' postmodernism and 'pastiche' postmodernism. Like the conflicts over the transformation of energy systems and the conflicts over moralization, the topicality of theoretical reflection on landscape developments becomes clear, which is summarised once again in Box 22.

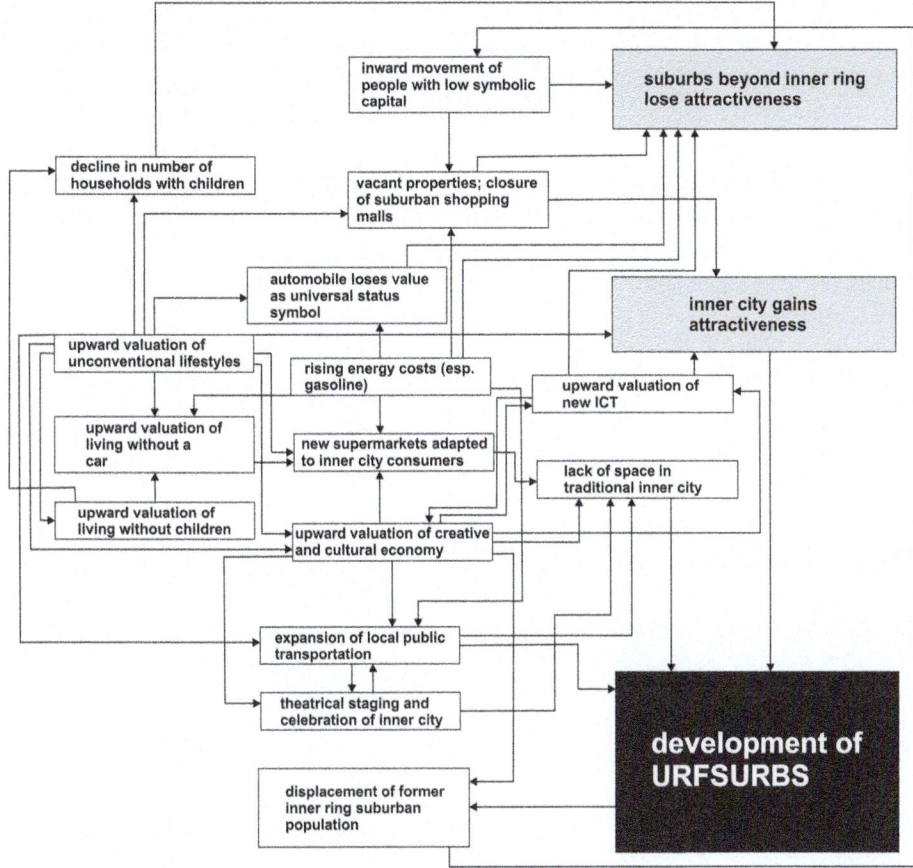

Fig. 6.8 The development of URFSURBS in feedback with social, economic, and other spatial processes. (Kühne 2016a)

moral, 'Heimat', etc.—the assessments are made is a first step towards conflict regulation, because it is an essential precondition for recognising alternative world interpretations. A greater tolerance towards 'ambiguous' and 'hybrid' spatial developments seems quite opportune in view of postmodern spatial developments. With the diversity of lifestyles, cultural mixes, the interpenetration of work and leisure, etc., the differentiation of spatial demands is also increasing. To pursue a restrictive and unambiguous spatial development strategy for administrative purposes seems unlikely to be successful.

Conclusion

7

The multiperspectivity of landscape-theoretical research can be made clear by means of the photo series shown in the Fig. 1.1. The depicted physical space can be interpreted essentialistically as a landscape that has undergone intensive anthropogenic transformation with the development of specific survival strategies since Roman times, at the most recent. Positivistically, it can be understood as an object in which the proportions of land uses, geological units or preference rates can be quantified. Constructivist can be asked, based on which social conventions we describe the depicted with the attribute 'picturesque' or 'beautiful' or also which elements are described as 'ugly'. Objects described as contrary to the norm, whether regarding stereotypical, native-regular, or professional ideas, can trigger resistance (such as the unrecognizable wind turbines). Here, landscape-related conflict research can determine conflict intensities—for example, based on a discourse analysis—but can also provide practical information on conflict regulation. With the help of autopoietic landscape theory, it can be understood which different logics different social subsystems apply to 'landscape' or the change of physical basis of landscape in order to be able to analyse conflicts, but possibly also to promote the mutual acceptance of arguments of the respective other conflict party within the framework of conflict regulation without resorting to moralizations. Nevertheless, it can also be asked based on critical landscape research who was able to assert his interests here and in what way, and how this assertion could come to be regarded as 'normal'. This, in turn, can be linked to 'inverse landscapes': What interests could not manifest themselves here, from whatever constellations of power, although this would be quite possible (such as buildings or meadows)? However, it can also be asked to what extent political worldviews influence the evaluation of spaces interpreted as landscapes, such as whether the suburban settlement in the back of the photographer is interpreted as an expression of enabling individual opportunities for life (in the liberal sense), as undermining the traditional community (conservatism), or as an expression of social de-solidarization (socialism). Beyond these cognitive considerations, however, the depicted 'landscape' can also

© Springer Fachmedien Wiesbaden GmbH, part of Springer Nature 2019
O. Kühne, *Landscape Theories*, RaumFragen: Stadt – Region – Landschaft,
https://doi.org/10.1007/978-3-658-25491-9_7

be approached atmospherically phenomenologically, for example how different olfactory or tactile stimuli (e. g. in the form of wind pressure, temperature) affect the experiencing individual. The space depicted in the photographs can also be examined with the actor network theory to see how animate and inanimate actants relate to each other and—even more—how they developed from historical networks. The added value of a theoretical multi-perspective approach to a research object, here landscape, is illustrated in Fig. 7.1.

Landscape theory means thinking about landscape, its development, its construction, its evaluation, its symbolic meaning, its connection to lifeworld practice, its aesthetic interpretation, etc., abstracted from the individual case. Landscape theory deals with the three basic dimensions of the social, the individual, and the material as well as their mutual references, which is why essential concepts (Fig. 7.2), theories, and world views (Fig. 7.3) presented in this book can be assigned to this triangle. The different references can be assigned differently in the 'tripole' of the individual, the social, and the material. What is striking here is the lack of a theoretically and ideologically 'purely' individual approach to landscape, while the theoretical and ideological contributions deal primarily with the relationship between the dimension of the material and the social (specifically in relation to the social landscape). This seems hardly possible due to the dependence of

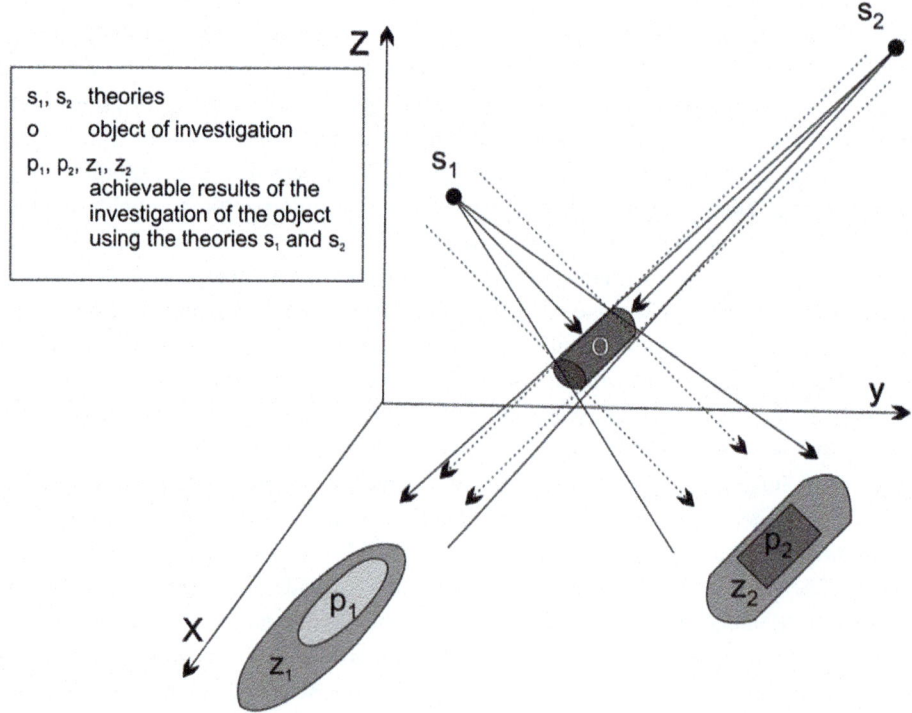

Fig. 7.1 Visualization of the necessity of theoretical pluralism (after: Hügin 1996)

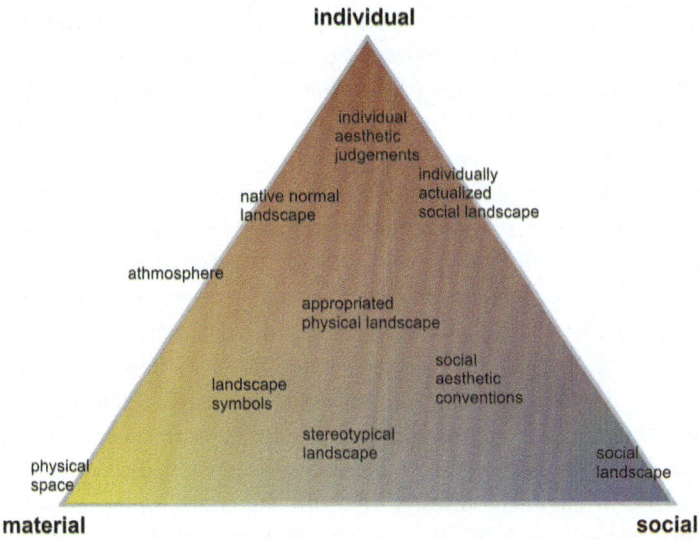

Fig. 7.2 The references of the social, the individual, and the material in relation to depicted land-scape-related concepts, in extension of Fig. 2.1. (Own design)

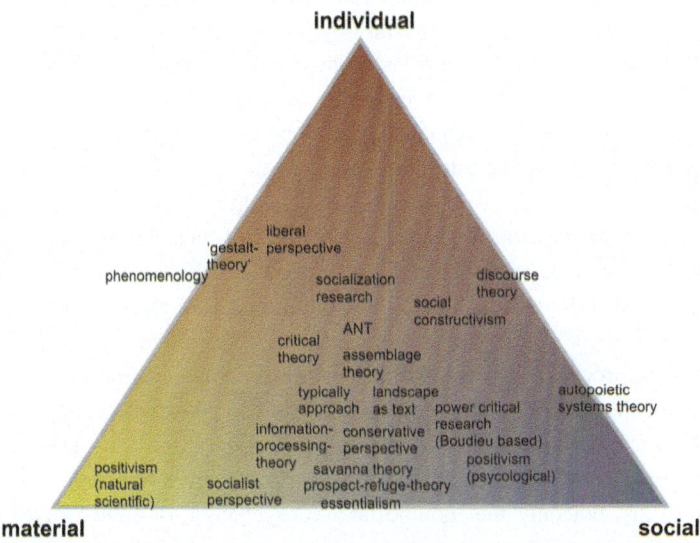

Fig. 7.3 The references of the social, the individual, and the material in relation to presented landscape-related theories and worldviews, in extension of Fig. 2.1. (Own design)

the complex concept of landscape on social concepts of landscape through the process of socialization. The conceptual attention, on the other hand, shows that the different individual, social, and material references can be grasped conceptually. In view of this discrepancy, a 'gap' can certainly be assumed especially in the theoretical examination of landscape in relation to individual processes of appropriation. The theoretical as well as conceptual diversity of the attention paid to landscape also means that normative judgements on the subject of landscape are difficult to substantiate in general terms (see also Berleant 1997), so normative approaches are individual, social (e. g. with regard to age and gender), culturally and not least theoretically very differentiated.

But not only a general norm in relation to landscape development seems questionable: The explanations in this book have also shown the diversity of aesthetic and moral landscape constructs; even ontological references are not produced on a uniform basis within societies and certainly not globally. As a result of the feedback relationship between social interpretations, evaluations, and their research—a socialization of scientists, not only in relation to 'normal native landscapes' and 'stereotypical landscapes', but also in relation to culturally bound 'expert special knowledge stocks', the attempt to create globally valid theories (e. g. on landscape preferences) seems at least worthy of supplementation. Especially in landscape research it seems important to understand national and partly regional particularities of landscape research as a resource for the international concern with landscape. The same can be said for the diversity of theoretical approaches to landscape (Box 23): The theoretical approaches presented formulate specific perspectives on the research object 'landscape', their explanatory capacities and demands are limited in each case (for example, social constructivist theory is not suitable for formulating concrete design norms for material objects, and the phenomenological approach will contribute little to the discursive striving for hegemony of competing landscape interpretations). In this respect, the question of whether a theory is 'new' or 'old' should not be used as an indicator of its quality when dealing theoretically with landscape, but rather as its ability to contribute to knowledge on the subject of landscape. As well as aesthetic processes, processes of socialization, development of power, etc. (cf. Berleant 1997), there is also a need to take into account the fact that the research processes also follow their own dynamics. This should—in the sense of Karl Popper (2005[1934]) and Ralf Dahrendorf (1980)—not be limited by excluding certain perspectives as 'not opportune' in advance.

In view of the process of differentiation up to the individualization of moral concepts, aesthetic approaches as well as ontological questions in relation to landscape, a stronger focus of landscape-theoretical (but also empirical) concern on the individual construction or individual landscape experience—in the respective variability—seems to be a challenge. Thus, not only the 'double landscape change' of social interpretation and evaluation on the one hand and the material foundations of landscape on the other hand is considered, but the third, and so far neglected component of the investigation of the change of landscape is delineated as 'triple landscape change' (Fig. 7.4).

Fig. 7.4 The topicality of landscape is decreasing rather than increasing in the course of intensive social transformation processes. Even if essential patterns of their appropriation (see Fig. 4.3) remain valid, their form has certainly changed. For example, the importance of technology is increasing, especially of smartphones (images above left, Death Valley National Park, California, above right, San Francisco, California, and center right, Seattle, Washington), with which impressions are preserved and shared (thus reinforcing conventions of perception, but also creating new patterns of interpretation). Access to the experience of landscape was also subject to a technical change: the impression of landscape often no longer requires the laborious ascent up or over mountains and dunes but can often be gained comfortably from the car (photo below right, Ocean Shores, Washington). Postmodern irony allows the speculation that the untechnical enjoyment of wild nature is now reserved for animals (photo below right, Crater Lake, Oregon). The transformation processes and persistent patterns documented in the photographs illustrate the need for an abstract, theoretical approach to landscape. For landscape theory can also arouse curiosity about knowledge, but also about new experiences, about the interpretation of experiences, about the interplay of individual approaches, the socially mediated, and the materialities of physical space

Box 23: The diversity of approaches to landscape

What landscape is cannot be answered unambiguously from the perspective of theoretical landscape research. Depending on which theoretical position is taken, landscape is…

…a being (or its expression) or a 'superorganism', from the synthesis of culture and nature (essentialism),

…an objectively given object that can be captured with empirical methods of measuring, weighing, and counting (positivism),

…a social construct that is the result of socialization and negotiation processes (social constructivism),

…a text which, when read, reveals the power structures inscribed upon physical space (landscape as text),

…a construct formed from the differentiated logics of economic, political, social community, moral, etc., communication (radical constructivism),

…an object of discourse for the purpose of attaining hegemonic interpretations (discourse theory),

…a lived space that is individually experienced and charged with meanings (phenomenology),

…an object and medium of social power processes (critical landscape research),

…a palimpsest in which historical cultural developments are inscribed (Berkeley School),

…a way to see the world (new cultural geography),

…a medium of social conflicts (conflict-theoretical landscape research),

…a medium of participative processes (governance perspective)

…and other things.

Literature

Ackermann, A. (2004). Das Eigene und das Fremde: Hybridität, Vielfalt und Kulturtransfers. In F. Jaeger & J. Rüsen (Eds.), *Handbuch der Kulturwissenschaften: Vol. 3. Themen und Tendenzen* (pp. 139–154). Stuttgart: Metzler.

Adorno, T. W. (1970). *Ästhetische Theorie. Gesammelte Schriften* (Vol. 7). Frankfurt a. M.: Suhrkamp.

Adorno, T. W. (1972). Theorie der Halbbildung. In T. W. Adorno (Ed.), *Gesammelte Schriften: Vol. 8. Soziologische Schriften 1.* (pp. 93–121). Frankfurt a. M.: Suhrkamp.

Agger, B. (2006). *Critical social theories*. Boulder: Paradigm.

Aglietta, M. (1976). *Régulation et crises du capitalisme. L'expérience des Etats-Unis* (Perspectives de l'economique). Paris: Calmann-Lévy.

Agnoli, J. (1968). *Die Transformation der Demokratie*. Hamburg: Europäische Verlaganstalt.

Ahrens, D. (2001). *Grenzen der Enträumlichung. Weltstädte, Cyberspace und transnationale Räume in der globalisierten Moderne: Vol. 127 Forschung Soziologie*. Opladen: Leske + Budrich.

Aitken, S. C., & Zonn, L. (1994). *Re*-presenting the place pastiche. In S. C. Aitken & L. Zonn (Eds.), *Place, power, situation, and spectacle. A geography of film* (pp. 3–25). Lanham: Rowman & Littlefield.

Akademie für Raumforschung und Landesplanung. (Ed.). (1975). *Beiträge zum Problem der Suburbanisierung: Vol. 102. Forschungs- und Sitzungsberichte*. Hannover: Selbstverlag.

Albert, G. (2005). *Hermeneutischer Positivismus und dialektischer Essentialismus Vilfredo Paretos*. Wiesbaden: VS Verlag.

Alexander, E. R. (1999). Response to commentaries: Planning theory and practice—Mixing them or minding the gap. *Environment and Planning B: Planning and Design, 26*(1), 1–4.

Allmendinger, P. (2000). *Planning in postmodern times*. London: Routledge.

Althusser, L. (1977). *Ideologie und ideologische Staatsapparate. Aufsätze zur marxistischen Theorie: Vol. 3. Positionen*. Hamburg: VSA Verlag für das Studium der Arbeiterbewegung.

Anter, A. (2012). *Theorien der Macht zur Einführung*. Hamburg: Junius.

Antrop, M. (1997). The concept of traditional landscapes as a base for landscape evaluation and planning. The example of Flanders Region. *Landscape and Urban Planning, 38*(1–2), 105–117.

Antrop, M. (2000). Background concepts for integrated landscape analysis. *Agriculture, Ecosystems & Environment, 77*(1–2), 17–28.

Antrop, M. (2006). Sustainable landscapes: Contradiction, fiction or utopia? *Landscape and Urban Planning, 75*(3–4), 187–197.

© Springer Fachmedien Wiesbaden GmbH, part of Springer Nature 2019
O. Kühne, *Landscape Theories,* RaumFragen: Stadt – Region – Landschaft,
https://doi.org/10.1007/978-3-658-25491-9

Antrop, M. (2018). A brief history of landscape research. In P. Howard, I. H. Thompson, E. Waterton, & M. Atha (Eds.), *The Routledge companion to landscape studies* (2nd ed., pp. 1–16). Abingdon: Routledge.

Antrop, M., & van Eetvelde, V. (2000).Holistic aspects of suburban landscapes: Visual image interpretation and landscape metrics. *Landscape and Urban Planning, 50*(1–3), 43–58.

Apolinarski, I., Gailing, L., & Röhring, A. (2006). Kulturlandschaft als regionales Gemeinschaftsgut. Vom Kulturlandschaftsdilemma zum Kulturlandschaftsmanagement. In U. Matthiesen, R. Danielzyk, S. Heiland, & S. Tzschaschel (Eds.), *Kulturlandschaften als Herausforderung für die Raumplanung. Verständnisse—Erfahrungen—Perspektiven: Vol. 228. Forschungs- und Sitzungsberichte* (pp. 81–98). Hannover: Selbstverlag.

Appleton, J. (1975). *The experience of landscape*. London: Wiley.

Appleton, J. (1984). Prospects and refuges re-visited. *Landscape Journal, 3*(2), 91–103.

Arato, A. (2016). *From Neo-Marxism to democratic theory: Essays on the critical theory of soviet-type societies*. London: Routledge.

Areopagita, P.-D. (1988 [um 500]). *Über die göttlichen Namen*. Stuttgart: BGL.

Arnreiter, G., & Weichhart, P. (1998). Rivalisierende Paradigmen im Fach Geographie. In G. Schurz & P. Weingartner (Eds.), *Koexistenz rivalisierender Paradigmen. Eine post-kuhnsche Bestandsaufnahme zur Struktur gegenwärtiger Wissenschaft* (pp. 53–85). Opladen: Westdeutscher Verlag.

Aschenbrand, E. (2016). Einsamkeit im Paradies. Touristische Distinktionspraktiken bei der Aneignung von Landschaft. *Berichte. Geographie und Landeskunde, 90*(3), 219–234.

Aschenbrand, E. (2017). *Die Landschaft des Tourismus. Wie Landschaft von Reiseveranstaltern inszeniert und von Touristen konsumiert wird*. Wiesbaden: Springer VS.

Aschenbrand, E., Kühne, O., & Weber, F. (2017a). Rohstoffgewinnung in Deutschland: Auseinandersetzungen und Konflikte. Eine Analyse aus sozialkonstruktivistischer Perspektive. *UmweltWirtschaftsForum* (online first).

Aschenbrand, E., Kühne, O., & Weber, F. (2017b). Steinharter Widerstand? Bürgerinitiativen und die Akzeptanz der Rohstoffgewinnung. *GesteinsPerspektiven, 2017*(2), 8–12. http://webkiosk. stein-verlaggmbh.de/gp-02-17/57998424. Accessed 20 Feb 2018.

Augenstein, I. (2002). *Die Ästhetik der Landschaft. Ein Bewertungsverfahren für die planerische Umweltvorsorge: Vol. 3. Berliner Beiträge zur Ökologie*. Berlin: Weißensee.

Augustinus, A. (1962 [390]). *Theologische Frühschriften* (Die Bibliothek der alten Welt: Reihe Antike und Christentum). Zürich: Artemis (Vom freien Willen [De libero arbitrio] und Von der wahren Religion [De vera religione]).

Bachtin, M. (1985). *Literatur und Karneval. Zur Romantheorie und Lachkultur*. Berlin: Ullstein.

Bakhtin, M. M. (1984). *Rabelais and his world*. Bloomington: Indiana University Press.

Banham, R. (2009 [1971]). *Los Angeles. The architecture of four ecologies*. Berkeley: University of California Press.

Barnett, C. (2015). Postcolonialism: Powers of representation. In S. C. Aitken & G. Valentine (Eds.), *Approaches to human geography. Philosophies, theories, people and practices* (2nd ed., pp. 163–180). Los Angeles: Sage.

Barrett, J. C., & Ko, I. (2009). A phenomenology of landscape: A crisis in British landscape archeology? *Journal of Social Archaeology, 9*(3), 275–294.

Bärsch, C.-E. (1981). Sozialismus. In J. H. Schoeps, J. H. Knoll, & C.-E. Bärsch (Eds.), *Konservativismus, Liberalismus, Sozialismus. Einführung, Texte, Bibliographien: Vol. 1032. Uni-Taschenbücher Politologie, Neuere Geschichte, Soziologie* (pp. 140–249). München: Fink.

Bartels, K. (1989). Über das Technisch-Erhabene. In C. Pries (Ed.), *Das Erhabene. Zwischen Grenzerfahrung und Größenwahn* (pp. 295–318). Weinheim: VCH Acta Humaniora.

Basten, L. (2005). *Postmoderner Urbanismus. Gestaltung in der städtischen Peripherie: Vol. 1. Schriften des Arbeitskreises Stadtzukünfte der Deutschen Gesellschaft für Geographie.* Münster: LIT.

Bataille, G. (1985). *Visions of excess. Selected writings, 1927–1939: Vol. 14. Theory and history of literature.* Manchester: Manchester University Press.

Bätzing, W. (2000). Postmoderne Ästhetisierung von Natur versus „schöne Landschaft" als Ganzheitserfahrung—Von der Kompensation der „Einheit der Natur" zur Inszenierung von Natur als Erlebnis. In A. Arndt, K. Bal, & H. Ottmann (Eds.), *Hegels Ästhetik. Die Kunst der Politik—Die Politik der Kunst.* Zweiter Teil (pp. 196–202). Berlin: Akademie.

Bauer, L., & Wall-Strasser, S. (2016). *Liberalismus/Neoliberalismus.* Wien: Verlag des ÖGB.

Bauman, Z. (1999). *Unbehagen in der Postmoderne.* Hamburg: Hamburger Edition.

Bauman, Z. (2009 [1993]). *Postmoderne Ethik.* Hamburg: Hamburger Edition.

Baumgarten, A. G. (2009 [1750–1758]). *Ästhetik* (Philosophische Bibliothek, 572a/b, 2 vols.). Hamburg: Meiner.

Bauriedl, S., Fleischmann, K., Strüver, A., & Wucherpfennig, C. (2000). Verkörperte Räume— „Verräumte" Körper. Zu einem feministisch-poststrukturalistischen Verständnis der Wechselwirkungen von Körper und Raum. *Geographica Helvetica, 55*(2), 130–137.

Becker, W. (2013). *Macht ohne Maß und kein Ende? Katholizismus, Kapitalismus (Imperialismus) und Kommunismus.* Leipzig: Engelsdorfer.

Belina, B. (2006). *Raum, Überwachung, Kontrolle. Vom staatlichen Zugriff auf städtische Bevölkerung.* Münster: Westfälisches Dampfboot.

Belina, B. (2009). Kriminalitätskartierung—Produkt und Mittel neoliberalen Regierens, oder: Wenn falsche Abstraktionen durch die Macht der Karte praktisch wahr gemacht werden. *Geographische Zeitschrift, 97*(4), 192–212.

Bell, D. (1999 [1973]). *The coming of post-industrial society. A venture in social forecasting.* New York: Basic Books.

Bender, B. (2002). Time and landscape. *Current Anthropology, 43*(S4), S103–S112.

Berger, P. L., & Luckmann, T. (1966). *The social construction of reality. A treatise in the sociology of knowledge.* New York: Anchor books.

Berleant, A. (1997). *Living in the landscape. Toward an aesthetics of environment.* Lawrence: University Press of Kansas.

Berlin, I. (1995 [1969]). *Freiheit. Vier Versuche.* Frankfurt a. M.: Fischer.

Bermingham, A. (1989). *Landscape and ideology. The english rustic tradition 1740–1860.* Oakland: University of California Press.

Berr, K. (2008). Carus und Hegel über Landschaftsmalerei. Landschaftsästhetik nach dem „Ende" der Landschaftsmalerei. In A. Gethmann-Siefert & B. Collenberg-Plotnikov (Eds.), *Zwischen Philosophie und Kunstgeschichte. Beiträge zur Begründung der Kunstgeschichtsforschung bei Hegel und im Hegelianismus* (pp. 243–256). München: Fink.

Berr, K. (2014). Zum ethischen Gehalt des Gebauten und Gestalteten. *Ausdruck und Gebrauch, 2014*(12), 30–56.

Berr, K. (2017). Zur Moral des Bauens, Wohnens und Gebauten. In K. Berr (Ed.), *Architektur- und Planungsethik. Zugänge, Perspektiven, Standpunkte* (pp. 111–138). Wiesbaden: Springer VS.

Berr, K. (2018). Ethische Aspekte der Energiewende. In O. Kühne & F. Weber (Eds.), *Bausteine der Energiewende* (pp. 57–74). Wiesbaden: Springer VS.

Beyme, K. v. (2013). *Von der Postdemokratie zur Neodemokratie.* Wiesbaden: Springer VS.

Bhabha, H. K. (2000a). *Die Verortung der Kultur: Vol. 5. Stauffenburg discussion.* Tübingen: Stauffenburg.

Bhabha, H. K. (2000b). How newness enters the world: Postmodern space, postcolonial times, and the trials of cultural translation. In J. Procter (Ed.), *Writing black Britain, 1948–1998. An interdisciplinary anthology* (pp. 300–306). Manchester: Manchester University Press.

Bhabha, H. K. (2012). Über kulturelle Hybridität: Tradition und Übersetzung. In A. Babka & G. Posselt (Eds.), *Über kulturelle Hybridität. Tradition und Übersetzung* (pp. 17–57). Wien: Turia + Kant.

Bischoff, W. (2005). *Nicht-visuelle Dimensionen des Städtischen: Olfaktorische Wahrnehmung in Frankfurt am Main, dargestellt an zwei Einzelstudien zum Frankfurter Westend und Ostend.* Dissertation, Johann Wolfgang Goethe-Universität, Frankfurt a. M.

Bloemers, T., Kars, H., van der Valk, A., & Wijnen, M. (Eds.). (2010). *The cultural landscape & heritage paradox. Protection and development of the Dutch archaeological-historical landscape and its European dimension.* Amsterdam: Amsterdam University Press.

Blotevogel, H. H. (1996). Aufgaben und Probleme der Regionalen Geographie heute. Überlegungen zur Theorie der Landes- und Länderkunde anläßlich des Gründungskonzepts des Instituts für Länderkunde, Leipzig. *Berichte zur deutschen Landeskunde, 70*(1), 11–40.

Blumer, H. (1969). *Symbolic interactionism.* London: University of California Press.

Blumer, H. (1973). Der methodologische Standort des symbolischen Interaktionismus. In Arbeitsgruppe Bielefelder Soziologen (Ed.), *Alltagswissen, Interaktion und gesellschaftliche Wirklichkeit* (Vol. 1, pp. 80–146). Reinbek bei Hamburg: Rowohlt.

Bogner, A. (2005). Moralische Expertise? Zur Produktionsweise von Kommissionsethik. In A. Bogner & H. Torgersen (Eds.), *Wozu Experten? Ambivalenzen der Beziehung von Wissenschaft und Politik* (pp. 172–193). Wiesbaden: VS Verlag.

Böhm, W. (1962). Zur Motivation junger Auslandsreisender. Ein Bericht über eine empirische Studie. In Deutsche Gesellschaft für Internationalen Jugendaustausch (Ed.), *Jahrbuch für Jugendreisen und internationalen Jugendaustausch* (pp. 111–122). Bonn: Jugendforum-Verlag.

Böhme, G. (1995). *Atmosphäre. Essays zur neuen Ästhetik* (Edition Suhrkamp). Frankfurt a. M.: Suhrkamp.

Bohmeyer, A. (2005). Der Begriff „Gerechtigkeit"—Eine philosophische Einführung. https://library.fes.de/pdf-files/akademie/online/03579.pdf. Accessed 17 Nov 2018.

Bonacker, T. (1996). *Konflikttheorien. Eine sozialwissenschaftliche Einführung mit Quellen: Vol. 2. Friedens- und Konfliktforschung.* Opladen: Leske + Budrich.

Bonacker, T. (2009). Konflikttheorien. In G. Kneer & M. Schroer (Eds.), *Handbuch Soziologische Theorien* (pp. 179–197). Wiesbaden: VS Verlag.

Borgeest, C. (1977). *Das sogenannte Schoene. Ästhetische Sozialschranken.* Frankfurt a. M.: Fischer.

Born, M. (1977). *Geographie der ländlichen Siedlungen: Vol. 1. Die Genese der Siedlungsformen in Mitteleuropa.* Stuttgart: Teubner.

Bosch, A. (2018). Die Schönheit der Welt als Lebensfrage. In A. Bosch & H. Pfütze (Eds.), *Ästhetischer Widerstand gegen Zerstörung und Selbstzerstörung* (Kunst und Gesellschaft, pp. 25–35). Wiesbaden: Springer VS.

Bosco, F. J. (2015). Actor-network theory, networks, and relational geographies. In S. C. Aitken & G. Valentine (Eds.), *Approaches to human geography. Philosophies, theories, people and practices* (2nd ed., pp. 150–162). Los Angeles: Sage.

Bourassa, S. C. (1990). A paradigm for landscape aesthetics. *Environment and Behavior, 22*(6), 787–812.

Bourassa, S. C. (1991). *The aesthetics of landscape.* London: Belhaven.

Bourdieu, P. (1979 [frz. Original 1972]). *Entwurf einer Theorie der Praxis auf der ethnologischen Grundlage der kabylischen Gesellschaft.* Frankfurt a. M.: Suhrkamp.

Bourdieu, P. (1982). *Leçon sur la leçon.* Paris: Les Éditions de Minuit.

Bourdieu, P. (1987 [1979]). *Die feinen Unterschiede. Kritik der gesellschaftlichen Urteilskraft.* Frankfurt a. M.: Suhrkamp.

Bourdieu, P. (1989). Social space and symbolic power. *Sociological Theory, 7*(1), 14–25.

Bourdieu, P. (1991). Physischer, sozialer und angeeigneter physischer Raum. In M. Wentz (Ed.), *Stadt-Räume* (pp. 25–34). Frankfurt: Campus.

Bourdieu, P. (1992). *Rede und Antwort: Vol. 547. Edition Suhrkamp.* Frankfurt a. M.: Suhrkamp.

Bourdieu, P. (1998). *Der Einzige und sein Eigenheim.* Hamburg: VSA-Verlag.

Bourdieu, P. (2000). *Les structures sociales de l'économie* (Collection Liber). Paris: Seuil.

Bourdieu, P. (2016). *La distinction: Critique sociale du jugement* (Le sens commun). Paris: Editions de Minuit.

Bourdieu, P., & Passeron, J.-C. (1973). *Grundlagen einer Theorie der symbolischen Gewalt.* Frankfurt a. M.: Suhrkamp.

Bourdieu, P., Calhoun, C. J., LiPuma, E., & Postone, M. (Eds.). (1993). *Bourdieu: Critical perspectives.* Chicago: University of Chicago Press.

Bowring, J. (2013). Navigating the global, the regional and the local: Researching globalization and landscape. In E. Waterton, I. Thompson, & P. Howard (Eds.), *The Routledge companion to landscape studies* (pp. 281–289). New York: Routledge.

Brady, E. (2003). *Aesthetics of the natural environment.* Edinburgh: Edinburgh UniversityPress.

Brake, K., Dangschat, J. S., & Herfert, G. (Eds.). (2001). *Suburbanisierung in Deutschland. Aktuelle Tendenzen.* Opladen: Leske + Budrich.

Brettschneider, F. (2015). Richtig kommunizieren. „Stuttgart 21" und die Lehren für die Kommunikation bei Infrastruktur- und Bauprojekten. In G. Bentele, R. Bohse, U. Hitschfeld, & F. Krebber (Eds.), *Akzeptanz in der Medien- und Protestgesellschaft. Zur Debatte um Legitimation, öffentliches Vertrauen, Transparenz und Partizipation* (pp. 281–299). Wiesbaden: Springer VS.

Brettschneider, F., & Schuster, W. (Eds.). (2013). *Stuttgart 21. Ein Großprojekt zwischen Protest und Akzeptanz.* Wiesbaden: Springer VS.

Brilli, A. (2001). *Als Reisen eine Kunst war. Vom Beginn des modernen Tourismus: Die „Grand Tour"* (Vol. 274). Berlin: Wagenbach.

Brook, I. (2018). Aesthetic appreciation of landscape. In P. Howard, I. H. Thompson, E. Waterton, & M. Atha (Eds.), *The Routledge companion to landscape studies* (Routledge companions, 2nd ed., pp. 71–82). Abingdon: Routledge.

Bruns, D. (2010). Die Europäische Landschaftskonvention—Eine Aufforderung zu mehr Landschafts-Governance. *Garten + Landschaft, 120*(2), 33–35.

Bruns, D. (2013). Landschaft—Ein internationaler Begriff? In D. Bruns & O. Kühne (Eds.), *Landschaften: Theorie, Praxis und internationale Bezüge* (pp. 153–168). Schwerin: Oceano.

Bruns, D. (2016). Kulturell diverse Raumaneignung. In F. Weber & O. Kühne (Eds.), *Fraktale Metropolen. Stadtentwicklung zwischen Devianz, Polarisierung und Hybridisierung* (pp. 231–240). Wiesbaden: Springer VS.

Bruns, D., & Kühne, O. (2013). Landschaft im Diskurs. Konstruktivistische Landschaftstheorie als Perspektive für künftigen Umgang mit Landschaft. *Naturschutz und Landschaftsplanung, 45*(3), 83–88.

Bruns, D., & Kühne, O. (2015). Zur kulturell differenzierten Konstruktion von Räumen und Landschaften als Herausforderungen für die räumliche Planung im Kontext von Globalisierung. In B. Nienaber & U. Roos (Eds.), *Internationalisierung der Gesellschaft und die Auswirkungen auf die Raumentwicklung. Beispiele aus Hessen, Rheinland-Pfalz und dem Saarland: Vol. 13. Arbeitsberichte der ARL* (pp. 18–29). Hannover: Selbstverlag. https://shop.arl-net.de/media/direct/pdf/ab/ab_013/ab_013_02.pdf. Accessed 26 Nov 2018.

Bruns, D., & Münderlein, D. (2017). Kulturell diverse Landschaftswertschätzung und Visuelle Kommunikation. In O. Kühne, H. Megerle, & F. Weber (Eds.), *Landschaftsästhetik und Landschaftswandel* (pp. 303–318). Wiesbaden: Springer VS.

Bruns, D., & Paech, F. (2015). „Interkulturell_real" in der räumlichen Entwicklung. Beispiele studentischer Arbeiten zur Wertschätzung städtischer Freiräume in Kassel. In B. Nienaber & U. Roos (Eds.), *Internationalisierung der Gesellschaft und die Auswirkungen auf die Raumentwicklung. Beispiele aus Hessen, Rheinland-Pfalz und dem Saarland: Vol. 13. Arbeitsberichte der ARL* (pp. 54–71). Hannover: Selbstverlag. https://shop.arl-net.de/media/direct/pdf/ab_013/ab_013_05.pdf. Accessed 26 Nov 2018.

Bundesregierung. (2014). Neue Trassen für die Energiewende. http://www.bundesregierung.de/Content/DE/Artikel/2014/11/2014-11-10-keine-energiewende-ohne-trassen.html. Accessed 8 Dec 2014.

Burckhardt, L. (2004). *Wer plant die Planung? Architektur, Politik und Mensch.* Berlin: Martin Schmitz.

Burckhardt, L. (2006). *Warum ist Landschaft schön? Die Spaziergangswissenschaft.* Kassel: Martin Schmitz.

Burdack, J., & Hesse, M. (2006). Reife, Stagnation oder Wende? Perspektiven zu Suburbanisierung, Post-Suburbia und Zwischenstadt: Ein Überblick zum Stand der Forschung. *Berichte zur Deutschen Landeskunde, 80*(4), 381–399.

Burke, E. (1989 [1757]). *Philosophische Untersuchung über den Ursprung unserer Ideen vom Erhabenen und Schönen: Vol. 324. Philosophische Bibliothek* (2nd ed.). Hamburg: Meiner.

Burr, V. (2005). *Social constructivism.* London: Routledge.

Butler, J. (1993). Körper von Gewicht. Über die diskursiven Grenzen des ‚Körpergeschlechts'. *Neue Rundschau., 104*(4), 57–70.

Buttimer, A. (1980). Home reach and the sense of place. In A. Buttimer & D. Seamon (Eds.), *The human experience of space and place* (pp. 166–187). London: Croom Helm.

Buttimer, A., & Seamon, D. (Eds.). (2015). *The human experience of space and place.* Abingdon: Routledge.

Büttner, N. (2006). *Geschichte der Landschaftsmalerei.* München: Hirmer.

Calhoun, C. J. (1995). *Critical social theory: Culture, history, and the challenge of difference.* Oxford: Wiley-Blackwell.

Carlson, A. (2009). *Nature and landscape. An introduction to environmental aesthetics.* New York: Columbia University Press.

Carol, H. (1973). Grundsätzliches zum Landschaftsbegriff (1957). In K. Paffen (Ed.), *Das Wesen der Landschaft: Vol. 39. Wege der Forschung* (pp. 142–155). Darmstadt: WBG.

Castree, N. (2002). False antitheses? Marxism, nature and actor-networks. *Antipode, 34*(1), 111–146.

Castree, N. (2008). Neoliberalising nature: The logics of deregulation and reregulation. *Environment and Planning A, 40*(1), 131–152.

Cavalcanti, S. O. (2004). Kultur Medien Macht. Kulturindustrie als Massenbetrug zwischen Manipulation und rückwirkendem Bedürfnis—Zur Entstehungsgeschichte der Kulturtheorie der kritischen Theorie. http://www.sopos.org/aufsaetze/41bee2e9c632c/1.phtml. Accessed 20 Nov 2018.

Chalmers, A. F. (2013). *What is this thing called science?* (4th ed.). Indianapolis: Hackett.

Chemero, A. (2003). An outline of a theory of affordances. *Ecological Psychology, 15*(2), 181–195.

Chilla, T. (2005). Stadt und Natur—Dichotomie, Kontinuum, soziale Konstruktion? *Raumforschung und Raumordnung, 63*(3), 179–188.

Chilla, T., Kühne, O., Weber, F., & Weber, F. (2015). „Neopragmatische" Argumente zur Vereinbarkeit von konzeptioneller Diskussion und Praxis der Regionalentwicklung. In O. Kühne & F. Weber (Eds.), *Bausteine der Regionalentwicklung* (pp. 13–24). Wiesbaden: Springer VS.

Chilla, T., Kühne, O., & Neufeld, M. (2016). *Regionalentwicklung.* Stuttgart: Ulmer.

Clarke, D. (2006). Postmodern geographies and the ruins of modernity. In S. C. Aitken & G. Valentine (Eds.), *Approaches to human geography* (pp. 107–121). London: Sage.

Clarke, G. (1993).Introduction. A critical and historical overview. In G. Clarke (Ed.), *The American landscape. Literary sources & documents* (pp. 3–51). Mountfield: Helm Information.

Corner, J., & Balfour, A. (Eds.). (1999). *Recovering landscape: Essays in contemporary landscape theory.* New York: Princeton Architectural Press.

Cosgrove, D. E. (1984). *Social formation and symbolic landscape.* London: University of Wisconsin Press.

Cosgrove, D. E. (1985). Prospect, perspective and the evolution of the landscape idea. *Transactions of the Institute of British Geographers, 10*(1), 45–62.

Cosgrove, D. E. (1989). A terrain of metaphor: Cultural geography 1988–1989. *Progress in Human Geography, 13*(4), 566–575.

Cosgrove, D. E. (1993). *The Palladian landscape. Geographical change and its cultural representations in sixteenth-century Italy.* University Park: Pennsylvania State University Press.

Cosgrove, D. E. (1997). Spectacle and society: Landscape as theater in premodern and postmodern cities. In P. E. Groth & T. W. Bressi (Eds.), *Understanding ordinary landscapes* (pp. 99–110). New Haven: Yale University Press.

Cosgrove, D. E. (1998). *Social formation and symbolic landscape.* Wisconsin: University of Wisconsin Press.

Cosgrove, D. E. (2004). Landscape and Landschaft. *German Historical Institute Bulletin, 35*(Fall), 57–71.

Cosgrove, D. E. (2006). Modernity, community and the landscape idea. *Journal of material culture, 11*(1–2), 49–66.

Cosgrove, D. E., & Daniels, S. (Eds.). (1988). *The iconography of landscape. Essays on the symbolic representation, design and use of past environments: Vol. 9. Cambridge studies in historical geography.* Cambridge: Cambridge University Press.

Cosgrove, D. E., & Jackson, P. (1987). New directions in cultural geography. *Area, 19*(2), 95–101.

Council of Europe. (2000). *European landscape convention.* European treaty series: 176. Accessed 17 Jan 2017.

Craik, K. H. (1972). Appraising the objectivity of landscape dimensions. In J. V. Krutilla (Ed.), *Natural environments. Studies in theoretical and applied analysis* (pp. 255–266). Baltimore: Johns Hopkins University Press.

Crang, M., & Tolia-Kelly, D. P. (2010). Nation, race, and affect: Senses and sensibilities at national heritage sites. *Environment and Planning A, 42*(10), 2315–2331.

Cresswell, T. (2003). Landscape and the obliteration of practice. In K. Anderson, M. Domosh, S. Pile, & N. Thrift (Eds.), *Handbook of cultural geography* (pp. 269–282). London: Sage.

Croce, B. (1930). *Aesthetik als Wissenschaft vom Ausdruck und allgemeine Sprachwissenschaft, Theorie und Geschichte.* Tübingen: Mohr.

Czepczyński, M. (2008). *Cultural landscapes of post-socialist cities. Representation of powers and needs.* Hampshire: Ashgate.

Czesak, B., Pazdan, M., & Różycka-Czas, R. (2015). Die städtische Landschaft in der Transformation: Krakau und Warschau. In O. Kühne, K. Gawroński, & J. Hernik (Eds.), *Transformation und Landschaft. Die Folgen sozialer Wandlungsprozesse auf Landschaft* (pp. 165–181). Wiesbaden: Springer VS.

Dahrendorf, R. (1952). *Marx in Perspektive. Die Idee des Gerechten im Denken von Karl Marx.* Hannover: Dietz.

Dahrendorf, R. (1957). *Soziale Klassen und Klassenkonflikt in der industriellen Gesellschaft.* Stuttgart: Enke.

Dahrendorf, R. (1961). *Gesellschaft und Freiheit. Zur soziologischen Analyse der Gegenwart.* München: Piper.

Dahrendorf, R. (1965). *Industrie- und Betriebssoziologie.* Berlin: De Gruyter.

Dahrendorf, R. (1968a). *Bildung ist Bürgerrecht. Plädoyer für eine aktive Bildungspolitik.* Hamburg: Christian Wegner.

Dahrendorf, R. (1968b). *Pfade aus Utopia. Arbeiten zur Theorie und Methode der Soziologie.* München: Piper.

Dahrendorf, R. (1969a). Aktive und passive Öffentlichkeit. Über Teilnahme und Initiative im politischen Prozeß moderner Gesellschaften. In M. Löffler (Ed.), *Das Publikum* (pp. 1–12). München: Beck.

Dahrendorf, R. (1969b). Sozialer Konflikt. In W. Bernsdorf (Ed.), *Wörterbuch der Soziologie* (pp. 1006–1009). Stuttgart: Enke.

Dahrendorf, R. (1969c). Zu einer Theorie des sozialen Konflikts [1958 erstveröffentlicht]. In W. Zapf (Ed.), *Theorien des sozialen Wandels* (pp. 108–123). Köln: Kiepenheuer & Witsch.

Dahrendorf, R. (1971a). *Die Idee des Gerechten im Denken von Karl Marx.* Hannover: Verlag für Literatur und Zeitgeschehen.

Dahrendorf, R. (1971b [1958]). *Homo sociologicus. Ein Versuch zur Geschichte, Bedeutung und Kritik der Kategorie der sozialen Rolle.* Opladen: Westdeutscher Verlag.

Dahrendorf, R. (1972). *Konflikt und Freiheit. Auf dem Weg zur Dienstklassengesellschaft.* München: Piper.

Dahrendorf, R. (1979). *Lebenschancen. Anläufe zur sozialen und politischen Theorie: Vol. 559. Suhrkamp-Taschenbuch.* Frankfurt a. M.: Suhrkamp.

Dahrendorf, R. (1980). *Die neue Freiheit. Überleben und Gerechtigkeit in einer veränderten Welt.* Frankfurt a. M.: Suhrkamp.

Dahrendorf, R. (1983). *Die Chancen der Krise. Über die Zukunft des Liberalismus.* Stuttgart: Deutsche Verlags-Anstalt.

Dahrendorf, R. (1987). *Fragmente eines neuen Liberalismus.* Stuttgart: Deutsche Verlags-Anstalt.

Dahrendorf, R. (1990). *Betrachtungen über die Revolution in Europa in einem Brief, der an einen Herrn in Warschau gerichtet ist.* Stuttgart: Deutsche Verlags-Anstalt.

Dahrendorf, R. (1992). *Der moderne soziale Konflikt. Essay zur Politik der Freiheit.* Stuttgart: Deutsche Verlags-Anstalt.

Dahrendorf, R. (1994). *Der moderne soziale Konflikt. Essay zur Politik der Freiheit.* München: Deutscher Taschenbuch Verlag.

Dahrendorf, R. (2003). *Die Krisen der Demokratie. Ein Gespräch mit Antonio Polito.* München: Beck.

Dahrendorf, R. (2004). *Der Wiederbeginn der Geschichte. Vom Fall der Mauer zum Krieg im Irak.* München: Beck.

Dahrendorf, R. (2007a). *Auf der Suche nach einer neuen Ordnung. Vorlesungen zur Politik der Freiheit im 21. Jahrhundert.* München: Beck.

Dahrendorf, R. (2007b). Freiheit—Eine Definition. In U. Ackermann (Ed.), *Welche Freiheit. Plädoyers für eine offene Gesellschaft* (Vol. 5, pp. 26–39). Berlin: Matthes & Seitz.

Daniel, T. C. (2001). Whither scenic beauty? Visual landscape quality assessment in the 21st century. *Landscape and Urban Planning, 54*(1–4), 267–281.

Daniels, S. (1989). Marxism, culture, and the duplicity of landscape. In R. Peet & N. Thrift (Eds.), *New models in geography: Vol. 2. The political-economy perspective* (pp. 196–220). London: Unwin Hyman.

Daniels, S., & Cosgrove, D. (1988). Introduction: Iconography and landscape. In D. Cosgrove & S. Daniels (Eds.), *The iconography of landscape. Essays on the symbolic representation, design and use of past environments: Vol. 9. Cambridge studies in historical geography* (pp. 1–10). Cambridge: Cambridge University Press.

Danto, A. C. (1981). *The transfiguration of the commonplace. A philosophy of art.* Cambridge: Harward University Press.

de Landa, M. (2006). *A new philosophy of society. Assemblage theory and social complexity.* London: continuum.

De Visscher, S., & Bouverne-De Bie, M. (2008). Recognizing urban public space as a co-educator: Children's socialization in ghent. *International Journal of Urban and Regional Research, 32*(3), 604–616.

Dear, M., & Flusty, S. (1998). Postmodern urbanism. *Annals of the Association of American Geographers, 88*(1), 50–72.

Degen, M. M. (2008). *Sensing cities. Regenerating public life in Barcelona and Manchester.* London: Routledge.

DeLue, R. Z., & Elkins, J. (Eds.). (2008 [2001]). *Landscape theory.* New York: Routledge.

DeMarrais, E., Gosden, C., & Renfrew, C. (Eds.). (2004). *Rethinking materiality. The engagement of mind with the material world.* Cambridge: McDonald Institute for Archaeological Research.

Dettmar, J. (2003). Brachflächen in der Zwischenstadt: Bausteine einer postindustriellen Landschaft. Erfahrungen aus dem Ruhrgebiet. In G. Arlt, I. Kowarik, J. Mathey, & F. Rebele (Eds.), *Urbane Innenentwicklung in Ökologie und Planung: Vol. 39. IÖR-Schriften* (pp. 23–32). Dresden: Selbstverlag.

Dettmar, J. (2004). Ökologische und ästhetische Aspekte der Sukzession auf Industriebrachen. In H. Strelow & V. David (Eds.), *Ökologische Ästhetik. Theorie und Praxis künstlerischer Umweltgestaltung* (pp. 128–161). Basel: Birkhäuser.

Dewey, J. (1958). *Experience and nature.* New York: Dover.

Dewey, J. (1988 [1934]). *Kunst als Erfahrung: Vol. 703. Suhrkamp Taschenbuch Wissenschaft* (1st ed.). Frankfurt a. M.: Suhrkamp.

Dickie, G. (1973). Aesthetics. An introduction. *Journal of Philosophy, 70*(10), 303–307.

Dickie, G. (1997). *Introduction to aesthetics. An analytic approach.* Oxford: Oxford University Press.

Dirlinger, H. (2000). *Bergbilder. Die Wahrnehmung alpiner Wildnis am Beispiel der englischen Gesellschaft 1700–1850: Vol. 10. Historisch-anthropologische Studien.* Frankfurt a. M.: Lang.

Donzelot, J. (2004). La ville à trois vitesses—Relégation, périurbanisation, gentrification. In Esprit (Ed.), *La ville à trois vitesses: Gentrification, relégation, périurbanisation* (pp. 14–39). Paris: Esprit.

Dorschel, A. (2003). *Gestaltung. Zur Ästhetik des Brauchbaren* (2nd ed.). Heidelberg: Winter.

Drexler, D. (2009a). Kulturelle Differenzen der Landschaftswahrnehmung in England, Frankreich, Deutschland und Ungarn. In T. Kirchhoff & L. Trepl (Eds.), *Vieldeutige Natur. Landschaft, Wildnis und Ökosystem als kulturgeschichtliche Phänomene* (Sozialtheorie, pp. 119–136). Bielefeld: Transcript.

Drexler, D. (2009b). *Landschaft und Landschaftswahrnehmung: Untersuchung des kulturhistorischen Bedeutungswandels von Landschaft anhand eines Vergleichs von England, Frankreich, Deutschland und Ungarn.* Dissertation, Technische Universität München, München. https://mediatum.ub.tum.de/doc/738822/738822.pdf. Accessed 16 March 2017.

Drexler, D. (2013). Die Wahrnehmung der Landschaft—Ein Blick auf das englische, französische und ungarische Landschaftsverständnis. In D. Bruns & O. Kühne (Eds.), *Landschaften: Theorie, Praxis und internationale Bezüge* (pp. 37–54). Schwerin: Oceano.

Dubiel, H. (1992). *Kritische Theorie der Gesellschaft. Eine einführende Rekonstruktion von den Anfängen im Horkheimer-Kreis bis Habermas.* Weinheim: Beltz Juventa.

Duineveld, M., van Assche, K., & Beunen, R. (2017). Re-conceptualising political landscapes after the material turn: A typology of material events. *Landscape Research, 42*(4), 375–384.

Duncan, J. (1980). The superorganic in American cultural geography. *Annals of the Association of American Geographers, 70*(2), 181–198.

Duncan, J. (1990). *The city as text: The politics of landscape interpretation in the Kandyan Kingdom.* Cambridge: Cambridge University Press.

Duncan, J., & Duncan, N. (1988). (Re)reading the landscape. *Environment and Planning D: Society and Space, 6*(2), 117–126.

Duncan, J., & Duncan, N. (2001). The aestheticization of the politics of landscape preservation. *Annals of the Association of American Geographers, 91*(2), 387–409.

Duncan, J., & Duncan, N. (2003). Can't live with them; can't landscape without them: Racism and the pastoral aesthetic in suburban New York. *Landscape Journal, 22*(2), 88–98.

Duncan, J., & Duncan, N. (2004). *Landscapes of privilege. The politics of the aesthetics in an American suburb.* New York: Routledge.

Duncan N., & Duncan, J. (2009). Doing landscape interpretation. *The SAGE handbook of qualitative geography.* http://www.sage-ereference.com/hdbk_qualgeography/Article_n13.html. Accessed 7 Jan 2019.

Dunn, K. M. (1997). Cultural geography and cultural policy. *Australian Geographical Studies, 35*(1), 1–11.

Eckardt, F. (2014). *Stadtforschung. Gegenstand und Methoden.* Wiesbaden: Springer VS.

Edler, D., & Lammert-Siepmann, N. (2017). Approaching the acoustic dimension in cartographic theory and practice. *Meta—Carto—Semiotics, 3*(1), 1–15.

Edler, D., Jebbink, K., & Dickmann, F. (2015). Einsatz audio-visueller Karten in der Schule— Eine Unterrichtsidee zum Strukturwandel im Ruhrgebiet. *Kartographische Nachrichten, 65*(5), 259–265.

Egner, H. (2006). Autopoiesis, Form und Beobachtung. *Mitteilungen der Österreichischen Geographischen Gesellschaft, 148,* 92–108.

Eichenauer, E., Reusswig, F., Meyer-Ohlendorf, L., & Lass, W. (2018). Bürgerinitiativen gegen Windkraftanlagen und der Aufschwung rechtspopulistischer Bewegungen. In O. Kühne & F. Weber (Eds.), *Bausteine der Energiewende* (pp. 633–651). Wiesbaden: SpringerVS.

Eickelmann, J. (2016). Wenn Kunst zum Ereignis wird. In M. Kauppert & H. Eberl (Eds.), *Ästhetische Praxis* (Kunst und Gesellschaft, pp. 355–376). Wiesbaden: Springer VS.

Eisel, U. (1982). Die schöne Landschaft als kritische Utopie oder als konservatives Relikt. Über die Kristallisation gegnerischer politischer Philosophien im Symbol „Landschaft". *Soziale Welt, 33*(2), 157–168.

Eisel, U. (1997). Triumph des Lebens. Der Sieg christlicher Wissenschaft über den Tod in Arkadien. *Geographisches Denken. Urbs et Regio, Kasseler Schriften zur Geographie und Planung, 65,* 39–160.

Eisel, U. (2004). Politische Schubladen als theoretische Heuristik. Methodische Aspekte politischer Bedeutungsverschiebungen in Naturbildern. In L. Fischer (Ed.), *Projektionsfläche Natur. Zum Zusammenhang von Naturbildern und gesellschaftlichen Verhältnissen* (pp. 29–44). Hamburg: Hamburg University Press.

Eisel, U. (2009). *Landschaft und Gesellschaft. Räumliches Denken im Visier: Vol. 5. Raumproduktionen: Theorie und gesellschaftliche Praxis.* Münster: Westfälisches Dampfboot.

Ellin, N. (1999). *Postmodern Urbanism.* New York: Princeton Architectural Press.

Engels, J. I. (2010). Machtfragen. Aktuelle Entwicklungen und Perspektiven der Infrastrukturgeschichte. *Neue politische Literatur, 55,* 51–70.

Entrikin, J. N. (1991). *The betweenness of place. Towards a geography of modernity.* Baltimore: Johns Hopkins University Press.

Enzensberger, H. M. (1962). Eine Theorie des Tourismus. In H. M. Enzensberger (Ed.), *Einzelheiten* (pp. 147–168). Frankfurt a. M.: Suhrkamp.

Eppler, E. (1975). *Ende oder Wende. Von der Machbarkeit des Notwendigen.* Stuttgart: Kohlhammer.

Ernstson, H. (2013). The social production of ecosystem services: A framework for studying environmental justice and ecological complexity in urbanized landscapes. *Landscape and Urban Planning, 109*(1), 7–17.

Euchner, W., Grebing, H., Stegmann, F. J., Langhorst, P., Jähnichen, T., & Friedrich, N. (2005). *Geschichte der sozialen Ideen in Deutschland. Sozialismus—Katholische Soziallehre— Protestantische Sozialethik. Ein Handbuch.* Wiesbaden: VS Verlag.

Fainstein, S. S. (2010). *The just city.* Ithaca: Cornell University Press.

Färber, A. (2014). Potenziale freisetzen: Akteur-Netzwerk-Theorie und Assemblageforschung in der interdisziplinären kritischen Stadtforschung. *Sub\urban Zeitschrift für Kritische stadtforschung, 2*(1), 95–103.

Faure, P. (1993). *Magie der Düfte. Eine Kulturgeschichte der Wohlgerüche von den Pharaonen zu den Römern.* München: Artemis & Winkler.

Fayet, R. (2003). *Reinigungen. Vom Abfall der Moderne zum Kompost der Nachmoderne.* Wien: Passagen-Verlag.

Fechner, G. T. (1876). *Vorschule der Ästhetik* (Vol. 1). Leipzig: Breitkopf & Härtel.

Fechner, G. T. (1976 [1871]). *Zur experimentalen Ästhetik* (Vol. 1). Leipzig: S. Hirzel.

Fehn, K. (1976). Historische Geographie. Eigenständige Wissenschaft und Teilwissenschaft der Geographie. *Mitteilungen der Geogrphischen Gesellschaft München, 61,* 35–51.

Fend, H. (1981). *Theorie der Schule.* München: Urban & Schwarzenberg.

Fine, A. (2000). Der Blickpunkt von niemand besonderen. In M. Sandbothe (Ed.), *Die Renaissance des Pragmatismus. Aktuelle Verflechtungen zwischen analytischer und kontinentaler Philosophie* (pp. 59–77). Weilerswist: Velbrück.

Fiske, J. (2011). *Reading the popular* (2nd ed.). New York: Routledge.

Fontaine, D. (2017a). Ästhetik simulierter Welten am Beispiel Disneylands. In O. Kühne, H. Megerle, & F. Weber (Eds.), *Landschaftsästhetik und Landschaftswandel* (pp. 105–120). Wiesbaden: Springer VS.

Fontaine, D. (2017b). *Simulierte Landschaften in der Postmoderne. Reflexionen und Befunde zu Disneyland, Wolfersheim und GTA V.* Wiesbaden: Springer VS.

Forbes, H. A. (2007). *Meaning and identity in a Greek landscape. An archaeological ethnography.* Cambridge: Cambridge University Press.

Forkel, J. A., & Grimm, M. (2014). Die Emotionalisierung durch Landschaft oder das Glück in der Natur. *Sozialwissenschaften und Berufspraxis, 37*(2), 251–266.

Foucault, M. (1977). *Überwachen und Strafen. Die Geburt des Gefängnisses, Vol. 184. Suhrkamp-Taschenbuch Wissenschaft.* Frankfurt a. M.: Suhrkamp.

Foucault, M. (1983 [1976]). *Der Wille zum Wissen. Sexualität und Wahrheit* (Suhrkamp-Taschenbuch Wissenschaft). Frankfurt a. M.: Suhrkamp taschenbuch wissenschaft.

Foucault, M. (2001). *Worte und Bilder. Schriften in 4 Bänden. Dits et Ecrits: Vol. I. 1954–1969* (pp. 794–797). Frankfurt a. M.: Suhrkamp.

Frank, S., Fürst, C., Koschke, L., Witt, A., & Makeschin, F. (2013). Assessment of landscape aesthetics—Validation of a landscape metrics-based assessment by visual estimation of the scenic beauty. *Ecological Indicators, 32,* 222–231.

Franzen, B., & Krebs, S. (Eds.). (2005). *Landschaftstheorie. Texte der Cultural Landscape Studies: Vol. 26. Kunstwissenschaftliche Bibliothek.* Köln: König.

Friesen, H. (2013). Philosophische Ästhetik und die Entwicklung der Kunst. In H. Friesen & M. Wolf (Eds.), *Kunst, Ästhetik, Philosophie. Im Spannungsfeld der Disziplinen* (pp. 71–160). Münster: Mentis.

Frohmann, E. (1997). *Gestaltungsqualitäten in Landschaft und Freiraum: Abgeleitet von den körperlich, seelisch, geistigen Wechselwirkungen zwischen Mensch und Lebensraum.* Wien: Österreichischer Kunst- und Kulturverlag.

Fuller, G. (1992). *Kitsch-Art. Wie Kitsch zur Kunst wird: Vol. 287. DuMont-Taschenbücher.* Köln: DuMont.

Gailing, L. (2015a). Die Transformation suburbaner Räume in westlichen Gesellschaften und die Perspektive der sozialwissenschaftlichen Landschaftsforschung. In O. Kühne, K. Gawroński, & J. Hernik (Eds.), *Transformation und Landschaft. Die Folgen sozialer Wandlungsprozesse auf Landschaft* (pp. 84–93). Wiesbaden: Springer VS.

Gailing, L. (2015b). Energiewende als Mehrebenen-Governance. *Nachrichten der ARL, 45*(2), 7–10.

Gailing, L., & Leibenath, M. (2012). Von der Schwierigkeit, „Landschaft" oder „Kulturlandschaft" allgemeingültig zu definieren. *Raumforschung und Raumordnung, 70*(2), 95–106.

Gailing, L., & Leibenath, M. (2015). The social construction of landscapes: Two theoretical lenses and their empirical applications. *Landscape Research, 40*(2), 123–138.

Gailing, L., & Leibenath, M. (2017). Political landscapes between manifestations and democracy, identities and power. *Landscape Research, 42*(4),1–12.

Gailing, L., Keim, K.-D., & Röhring, A. (2006). *Analyse von informellen und dezentralen Institutionen und Public Governance mit kulturlandschaftlichem Hintergrund in der Beispielregion Barnim* (Materialien no. 6), Berlin: Berlin-Brandenburgische Akademie der Wissenschaften.

Gallagher, L. (2013). *The end of the suburbs. Where the American dream is moving.* New York: Portfolio & Penguin.

Garreau, J. (1992). *Edge city: Life on the new frontier.* New York: Anchor books.

Gawroński, K. (2015). Die Veränderungen der Raumordnungspolitik Polens in den Jahren 1945–2012. In O. Kühne, K. Gawroński, & J. Hernik (Eds.), *Transformation und Landschaft. Die Folgen sozialer Wandlungsprozesse auf Landschaft* (pp. 45–59). Wiesbaden: Springer VS.

Gebhard, U. (2013). *Kind und Natur. Die Bedeutung der Natur für die psychische Entwicklung* (4th ed.). Wiesbaden: Springer VS.

Gebhardt, H. (2016). Entwicklungspfade und Perspektiven der Humangeographie im deutschsprachigen Raum—Einige Leitlinien. In: Aistleitner, J., Coy, M., & Stötter, J. (Eds.). *Die Welt verstehen—Eine geographische Herausforderung: Eine Festschrift der Geographie Innsbruck für Axel Borsdorf.* Innsbrucker geographische Studien (pp. 43–59). Innsbruck: Geographie Innsbruck.

Gebhardt, L., & Wiegandt, C.-C. (2014). Neue Stadtlust? Motive für urbanes Wohnen im Kontext der Reurbanisierungsdebatte—Die Fallstudien Köln Sülz und Leipzig Südvorstadt. In R. Danielzyk, S. Lentz, & C.-C. Wiegandt (Eds.), *Suchst du noch oder wohnst du schon? Wohnen in polyzentrischen Stadtregionen* (pp. 141–169). Berlin: LIT.

Gehlen, A. (1956). *Urmensch und Spätkultur. Philosophische Ergebnisse und Aussagen.* Bonn: Athenäum-Verlag.

Gehlen, A. (1960). *Zeit-Bilder. Zur Soziologie und Ästhetik der modernen Malerei.* Frankfurt a. M.: Athenäum.

Gehring, K., & Kohsaka, R. (2007). 'Landscape' in the Japanese language: Conceptual differences and implications for landscape research. *Landscape Research, 32*(2), 273–283.

Gelfert, H.-D. (2000). *Was ist Kitsch?: Vol. 4024.* Kleine Reihe V und R. Göttingen: Vandenhoeck & Ruprecht.

Gethmann-Siefert, A. (1995). *Einführung in die Ästhetik: Vol. 1875. UTB*. München: Fink.

Geulen, D. (2005). *Subjektorientierte Sozialisationstheorie. Sozialisation als Epigenese des Subjekts in Interaktion mit der gesellschaftlichen Umwelt*. Weinheim: Juventa.

Geulen, D., & Hurrelmann, K. (1980). Zur Programmatik einer umfassenden Sozialisationstheorie. In K. Hurrelmann & D. Ulrich (Eds.), *Handbuch der Sozialisationsforschung* (pp. 51–67). Weinheim: Beltz.

Gibson, J. J. (1979). *The ecological approach to visual perception*. Boston: Houghton Mifflin.

Giddens, A. (1990). *The consequences of modernity*. Palo Alto: Stanford University Press.

Gilbert, K. E., & Kuhn, H. (1953). *A history of esthetics*. Bloomington: Indiana University Press.

Gimblett, H. R., Itami, R. M., & Fitzgibbon, J. E. (1985). Mystery in an information processing model of landscape preference. *Landscape Journal, 4*(2), 87–95.

Glasersfeld, E. v. (1995). *Radical constructivism. A way of knowing and learning: Vol. 6. Studies in mathematics education series*. London: Falmer.

Glasze, G. (2007). Vorschläge zur Operationalisierung der Diskurstheorie von Laclau und Mouffe in einer Triangulation von lexikometrischen und interpretativen Methoden. *FQS—Forum: Qualitative Sozialforschung, 8*(2), 73 Absätze. http://www.qualitative-research.net/index.php/fqs/article/view/239/529. Accessed 30 Aug 2017.

Glasze, G. (2013). *Politische Räume. Die diskursive Konstitution eines »geokulturellen Raums«— Die Frankophonie*. Bielefeld: Transcript.

Glasze, G. (2015). Identitäten und Räume als politisch: Die Perspektive der Diskurs- und Hegemonietheorie. *Europa Regional, 21*(1–2), 23–34.

Gobster, P. H., Nassauer, J. I., Daniel, T. C., & Fry, G. (2007). The shared landscape. What does aesthetics have to do with ecology? *Landscape Ecology, 22*(7), 959–972.

Goeke, P., & Lippuner, R. (2011). Geographien sozialer Systeme. *Soziale Systeme, 17*(2), 227–233.

Gold, J. R., & Revill, G. (2003). Exploring landscapes of fear: Marginality, spectacle and surveillance. *Capital & Class, 27*(2), 27–50.

Goodman, N. (1973). *Sprachen der Kunst. Ein Ansatz zu einer Symboltheorie*. Frankfurt a. M.: Suhrkamp.

Goodman, N. (1990). *Weisen der Welterzeugung* (Suhrkamp-Taschenbuch Wissenschaft). Frankfurt a. M.: Suhrkamp.

Goodman, N. (1992). Kunst und Erkenntnis. In D. Henrich & W. Iser (Eds.), *Theorien der Kunst: Vol. 1012. Suhrkamp Taschenbuch Wissenschaft* (pp. 569–591). Frankfurt a. M.: Suhrkamp.

Gorman, R. A. (1982). *Neo-Marxism. The meanings of modern radicalism*. Westport: Greenwood.

Gottdiener, M. (2000). The consumption of space and the spaces of consumption. In M. Gottdiener (Ed.), *New forms of consumption. Consumers, culture, and commodification* (pp. 265–284). Lanham: Rowman & Littlefield.

Gräbel, C. (2015). *Die Erforschung der Kolonien. Expeditionen und koloniale Wissenskultur deutscher Geographen, 1884–1919*. Bielefeld: Transcript.

Graham, B. J. (1994). No place of the mind: Contested Protestant representations of Ulster. *Ecumene, 1*(3), 257–281.

Graham, G. (2005). *Philosophy of the arts. An introduction to aesthetics* (3rd ed.). London: Routledge.

Gratzel, G. A. (1990). Freiheit, Konflikt und Wandel. Bemerkungen zum Liberalismus-Verständnis bei Ralf Dahrendorf. In H.-G. Fleck, J. Frölich, & B.-C. Padtberg (Eds.), *Jahrbuch zur Liberalismus-Forschung. 2. Jahrgang 1990* (pp. 11–45). Baden-Baden: Nomos.

Grau, A. (2017). *Hypermoral. Die neue Lust an der Empörung* (2nd ed.). München: Claudius.

Green, N. (2003). Looking at the landscape. Class formation and the visual. In E. D. Hirsch & M. O'Hanlon (Eds.), *The anthropology of landscape. Perspectives on place and space* (pp. 31–42). Oxford: Clarendon.

Greenberg, C. (2007). Avantgarde und Kitsch. In U. Dettmar & T. Küpper (Eds.), *Kitsch. Texte und Theorien* (pp. 203–212). Stuttgart: Reclam.

Gregory, D. (1989). The crisis of modernity? Human geography and critical social theory. In R. Peet & N. Thrift (Eds.), *New models in geography: Vol. 2. The political-economy perspective* (pp. 348–385). London: Unwin Hyman.

Greider, T., & Garkovich, L. (1994). Landscapes: The social construction of nature and the environment. *Rural Sociology, 59*(1), 1–24.

Greiffenhagen, M. (1971). *Das Dilemma des Konservatismus in Deutschland*. München: Piper.

Grimm, S. (1997). Einfach hybrid!—Kulturkritische Ansätze der Postcolonial Studies (Teil 1 von 2). *iz3w, 223,* 39–42. Accessed 10 Aug 2018.

Grömer, K., Mückler, H., & Kritscher, H. (Eds.). (2012). *Bewegung—Fortbewegung: Vol. 142. Mitteilungen der Anthropologischen Gesellschaft in Wien*. Horn: Ferdinand Berger & Söhne.

Grote, L. (1950). Der Wanderer über dem Nebelmeer. Ein Beitrag zu Caspar David Friedrichs Bildgestaltung. *Die Kunst und das schöne Heim, 48,* 401–404.

Groth, P., & Wilson, C. (2005). Die Polyphonie der Cultural Landscape Studies [2003]. In B. Franzen & S. Krebs (Eds.), *Landschaftstheorie. Texte der Cultural Landscape Studies: Vol. 26. Kunstwissenschaftliche Bibliothek* (pp. 58–90). Köln: König.

Gruenter, R. (1975 [1953]). Landschaft. Bemerkungen zu Wort und Bedeutungsgeschichte. In A. Ritter (Ed.), *Landschaft und Raum in der Erzählkunst: Vol. 418. Wege der Forschung* (pp. 192–207). Darmstadt: WBG.

Grunewald, K., & Bastian, O. (2013). Ökosystemdienstleistungen (ÖSD)—Mehr als ein Modewort? In K. Grunewald & O. Bastian (Eds.), *Ökosystemdienstleistungen. Konzept, Methoden und Fallbeispiele* (pp. 1–11). Berlin: Springer Spektrum.

Ha, K. N. (2005). *Hype um Hybridität. Kultureller Differenzkonsum und postmoderne Verwertungstechniken im Spätkapitalismus: Vol. 11. Cultural studies*. Bielefeld: Transcript.

Ha, K. N. (2006). Die Grenzen überqueren? Hybridität als spätkapitalistische Logik der kulturellen Übersetzung und der nationalen Modernisierung. http://eipcp.net/transversal/1206/ha/de. Accessed 29 Nov 2018.

Haber, W. (2000). Die Kultur der Landschaft. Von der Ästhetik zur Nachhaltigkeit. In S. Appel, E. Duman, F. große Kohorst, & F. Schafranski (Eds.), *Wege zu einer neuen Planungs- und Landschaftskultur. Festschrift für Hanns Stephan Wüst* (o. S.). Kaiserslautern: Selbstverlag.

Haber, W. (2001). Kulturlandschaft zwischen Bild und Wirklichkeit. In Akademie für Raumforschung und Landesplanung (Ed.), *Die Zukunft der Kulturlandschaft zwischen Verlust, Bewahrung und Gestaltung: Vol. 215. Forschungs- und Sitzungsberichte* (pp. 6–29). Hannover: Selbstverlag.

Haber, W. (2006). Kulturlandschaften und die Paradigmen des Naturschutzes. *Stadt+Grün, 55*(12), 20–25.

Habermas, J. (1981). *Theorie des kommunikativen Handelns*. Frankfurt a. M.: Suhrkamp.

Hadjar, A., & Becker, R. (2009). Erwartete und unerwartete Folgen der Bildungsexpansion in Deutschland. In R. Becker (Ed.), *Lehrbuch der Bildungssoziologie* (pp. 195–213). Wiesbaden: VS Verlag.

Hahn, A. (2017). *Architektur und Lebenspraxis. Für eine phänomenologisch-hermeneutische Architekturtheorie: Vol. 40. Architekturen*. Bielefeld: Transcript.

Hall, S. (1994). Der Westen und der Rest: Diskurs und Macht. In S. Hall (Ed.), *Rassismus und kulturelle Identität. Ausgewählte Schriften 2* (pp. 137–179). Hamburg: Argument-Verlag.

Hall, S., & Höller, C. (1996). Terrains der Verstörung. Ein Interview mit Stuart Hall von Christian Höller. *Texte zur Kunst, 1996*(24), 47–58.

Hall, T. (1995). 'The second industrial revolution': Cultural reconstructions of industrial regions. *Landscape Research, 20*(3), 112–123.

Hammitt, W. E. (1981). The familiarity-preference component of on-site recreational experiences. *Leisure Sciences, 4*(2), 177–193.

Hampicke, U. (2013). *Kulturlandschaft und Naturschutz. Probleme—Konzepte—Ökonomie*. Wiesbaden: Springer Fachmedien.

Hank, R. (2007). Der deutsche Schotte: Wilhelm von Humboldts Grenzziehung staatlicher Wirksamkeit. In U. Ackermann (Ed.), *Welche Freiheit. Plädoyers für eine offene Gesellschaft* (Vol. 5, pp. 141–155). Berlin: Matthes & Seitz.

Hanlon, B. (2008). The decline of older, inner suburbs in metropolitan America. *Housing Policy Debate, 19*(3), 423–456.

Hanlon, B. (2010). *Once the American dream. Inner-ring suburbs of the metropolitan United States*. Philadelphia: Temple University Press.

Haraway, D. J. (1991). *Simians, Cyborgs, and women. The reinvention of nature*. New York: Routledge.

Hard, G. (1969). Das Wort Landschaft und sein semantischer Hof. Zur Methode und Ergebnis eines linguistischen Tests. *Wirkendes Wort, 19,* 3–14.

Hard, G. (1970a). *Die „Landschaft" der Sprache und die „Landschaft" der Geographen. Semantische und forschungslogische Studien*. Bonn: Ferdinand Dümmlers.

Hard, G. (1970b). „Was ist eine Landschaft?". Über Etymologie als Denkform in der geographischen Literatur. In D. Bartels (Ed.), *Wirtschafts- und Sozialgeographie: Vol. 35. Neue wissenschaftliche Bibliothek* (pp. 66–84). Köln: Kiepenheuer & Witsch.

Hard, G. (1973). *Die Geographie. Eine wissenschaftstheoretische Einführung* (Sammlung Göschen). Berlin: De Gruyter.

Hard, G. (1977). Zu den Landschaftsbegriffen der Geographie. In A. H. von Wallthor & H. Quirin (Eds.), *„Landschaft" als interdisziplinäres Forschungsproblem. Vorträge und Diskussionen des Kolloquiums am 7./8. November 1975 in Münster* (pp. 13–24). Münster: Aschendorff.

Hard, G. (1995). *Spuren und Spurenleser. Zur Theorie und Ästhetik des Spurenlesens in der Vegetation und anderswo: Vol. 16. Osnabrücker Studien zur Geographie*. Osnabrück: Universitätsverlag Rasch.

Hard, G. (2002). Zu Begriff und Geschichte von „Natur" und „Landschaft" in der Geographie des 19. und 20. Jahrhunderts [1983 erstveröffentlicht]. In G. Hard (Ed.), *Landschaft und Raum. Aufsätze zur Theorie der Geographie: Vol. 22. Osnabrücker Studien zur Geographie* (pp. 171–210). Osnabrück: Universitätsverlag Rasch.

Harker, R., Mahar, C., & Wilkes, C. (Eds.). (1990). *An introduction to the work of Pierre Bourdieu. The practice of theory*. Basingstoke: Macmillan.

Harley, J. B. (1992). Rereading the maps of the Columbian encounter. *Annals of the Association of American Geographers, 82*(3), 522–542.

Harris, N. (2002). Collaborative planning. In M. Tewdwr-Jones & P. Allmendinger (Eds.), *Planning futures. New directions for planning theory* (pp. 21–43). London: Routledge.

Hartmann, E. v. (1924). *Philosophie des Schönen* (Auswahlreihe des Volksverbandes der Bücherfreunde, 2nd ed.). Berlin: Wegweiser-Verlag.

Hartmann, N. (1953). *Ästhetik*. Berlin: De Gruyter.

Hartz, A., & Kühne, O. (2007). Der Regionalpark Saar—Eine Betrachtung aus postmoderner Perspektive. *Raumforschung und Raumordnung, 65*(1), 30–43.

Harvey, D. (1989). *The condition of postmodernity: An enquiry into the origins of cultural change*. Oxford: Blackwell.

Harvey, D. (1996). *Justice, nature and the geography of difference*. Malden: Blackwell.

Harvey, D. (2005). *A brief history of neoliberalism*. Oxford: Oxford University Press.

Harvey, D. (2008). The right to the city. *New Left Review, 53,* 23–40. https://newleftreview.org/II/53/david-harvey-the-right-to-the-city. Accessed 29 Nov 2018.

Harvey, D., Wilkinson, & Timothy J. (2018). Landscape and heritage: Emerging landscapes of heritage. In P. Howard, I. H. Thompson, E. Waterton, & M. Atha (Eds.), *The Routledge companion to landscape studies* (Routledge companions, 2nd ed., pp. 176–191). Abingdon: Routledge.

Hasse, J. (1993). *Heimat und Landschaft. Über Gartenzwerge, Center Parcs und andere Ästhetisierungen.* Wien: Passagen-Verlag.

Hasse, J. (2000). *Die Wunden der Stadt. Für eine neue Ästhetik unserer Städte.* Wien: Passagen-Verlag.

Hauck, T. E., & Hennecke, S. (2017). Die Funktionalisierung der Landschaftsästhetik für die urbane Freiraumplanung. Beispiele aus der frühen industriellen Großstadt in Deutschland und den USA. In O. Kühne, H. Megerle, & F. Weber (Eds.), *Landschaftsästhetik und Landschaftswandel* (pp. 269–282). Wiesbaden: Springer VS.

Haus, M. (2003). *Kommunitarismus. Einführung und Analyse.* Wiesbaden: VS Verlag.

Hauser, S. (2000). Modelle und Adaptionen. Planungsansätze für alte Industrieregionen. *Wolkenkuckucksheim, 4*(2). Accessed 21 Nov 2006.

Hauser, S. (2001). *Metamorphosen des Abfalls. Konzepte für alte Industrieareale.* Frankfurt a. M.: Campus.

Hauser, S. (2004). Industrieareale als urbane Räume. In W. Siebel (Ed.), *Die europäische Stadt* (pp. 146–157). Frankfurt a. M.: Suhrkamp.

Hauser, S. (2012). Kulturlandschaften—Drei Konzepte, ihre Kritik und einige Schlussfolgerungen für die urbanisierte Landschaft. In W. Schenk, M. Kühn, M. Leibenath, & S. Tzschaschel (Eds.), *Suburbane Räume als Kulturlandschaften: Vol. 236. Forschungs- und Sitzungsberichte* (pp. 197–209). Hannover: Selbstverlag.

Hauser, S., & Kamleithner, C. (2006). *Ästhetik der Agglomeration: Vol. 8. Zwischenstadt.* Wuppertal: Müller + Busmann.

Hauskeller, M. (2005). *Was ist Kunst? Positionen der Ästhetik von Platon bis Danto* (Beck'sche Reihe, 8th ed.). München: Beck.

Häußermann, H., & Siebel, W. (2004). *Stadtsoziologie. Eine Einführung.* Frankfurt a. M.: Campus.

Hayden, D. (2004). *Building Suburbia. Green fields and urban growth, 1820–2000.* New York: Vintage Books.

Healey, P. (1997). *Collaborative planning. Shaping places in fragmented societies.* Basingstoke: Macmillan.

Hegel, G. W. F. (1970 [1835–1838]). *Vorlesungen über die Ästhetik I* (20 vols.). Frankfurt a. M.: Suhrkamp.

Heidegger, M. (2005 [1927]). *Die Grundprobleme der Phänomenologie.* Frankfurt a. M.: Klostermann.

Heiland, S. (1999). *Voraussetzungen erfolgreichen Naturschutzes: Individuelle und gesellschaftliche Bedingungen umweltgerechten Verhaltens, ihre Bedeutung für den Naturschutz und die Durchsetzbarkeit seiner Ziele.* Landsberg/Lech: Ecomed-Verlag.

Heiland, S. (2006). Zwischen Wandel und Bewahrung, zwischen Sein und Sollen: Kulturlandschaft als Thema und Schutzgut in Naturschutz und Landschaftsplanung. In U. Matthiesen, R. Danielzyk, S. Heiland, & S. Tzschaschel (Eds.), *Kulturlandschaften als Herausforderung für die Raumplanung. Verständnisse—Erfahrungen—Perspektiven: Vol. 228. Forschungs- und Sitzungsberichte* (pp. 43–70). Hannover: Selbstverlag.

Hein, K. (2006). *Hybride Identitäten. Bastelbiografien im Spannungsverhältnis zwischen Lateinamerika und Europa.* Bielefeld: Transcript.

Hellpach, W. (1950 [1911]). *Geopsyche. Die Menschenseele unter dem Einfluss von Wetter und Klima, Boden und Landschaft.* Stuttgart: Enke.

Henderson, G., & Sheppard, E. (2006). Marx and the spririt of Marx. In S. C. Aitken & G. Valentine (Eds.), *Approaches to human geography* (pp. 57–74). London: Sage.

Henderson, G. L. (2003). What (else) we talk about when we talk about landscape: For a return to a social imagination. In C. Wilson & P. Groth (Eds.), *Everyday America. Cultural landscape studies after J. B. Jackson* (pp. 178–198). Berkeley: University of California Press.

Henderson, V., & Mitra, A. (1996). The new urban landscape. Developers and edge cities. *Regional Science and Urban Economics, 26*(6), 613–643.

Henning, C. (2016). Grenzen der Kunst. In M. Kauppert & H. Eberl (Eds.), *Ästhetische Praxis* (Kunst und Gesellschaft, pp. 303–327). Wiesbaden: Springer VS.

Hernik, J., & Dixon-Gough, R. (2013). The concept and importance of landscape in Polish language and in Poland. In D. Bruns & O. Kühne (Eds.), *Landschaften: Theorie, Praxis und internationale Bezüge* (pp. 83–98). Schwerin: Oceano.

Herring, P. (2018). Valuing the whole historic landscape. In P. Howard, I. H. Thompson, E. Waterton, & M. Atha (Eds.), *The Routledge companion to landscape studies* (Routledge companions, 2nd ed., pp. 192–205). Abingdon: Routledge.

Herrington, S. (2006). Framed again: The picturesque aesthetics of contemporary landscapes. *Landscape Journal, 25*(1), 22–37.

Herrington, S. (2016). *Landscape theory in design*. London: Routledge.

Herzog, L. (2004). Globalization of the Barrio: Transformation of the Latino cultural landscapes of San Diego, California. In D. D. Arreola (Ed.), *Hispanic spaces, Latino places. Community and cultural diversity in contemporary America* (pp. 103–124). Austin: University of Texas Press.

Herzog, L. (2013). *Freiheit gehört nicht nur den Reichen—Plädoyer für einen zeitgemäßen Liberalismus: Vol. 6127. C.-H.-Beck Paperback* (Orig.-Ausg). München: Beck.

Herzog, T. R., Herbert, E. J., Kaplan, R., & Crooks, C. L. (2000). Cultural and developmental comparisons of landscape perceptions and preferences. *Environment and Behavior, 32*(3), 323–346.

Hesse, M. (2008). Resilient Suburbs? Ungleiche Entwicklungsdynamiken suburbaner Räume in Nordamerika im Zeichen der Kreditkrise. *Geographische Zeitschrift, 96*(4), 228–249.

Hesse, M. (2010). Suburbs: The next slum? Explorations into the contested terrain of social construction and political discourse. *articulo. Journal of Urban Research, (Special issue 3*, 43 Absätze).https://articulo.revues.org/1552. Accessed 20 June 2016.

Hesse, M., & Siedentop, S. (2018). Suburbanisation and suburbanisms—Making sense of Continental European developments. *Raumforschung und Raumordnung, 76*(2), 97–108.

Hetherington, K. (1998). *Expressions of identity. Space, performance, politics*. London: Sage.

Hilbig, H. (2014). Warum es keine Architekturethik braucht—Und warum vielleicht doch. *Ausdruck und Gebrauch, 12,* 96–106.

Hirsch, J., & Roth, R. (1986). *Das neue Gesicht des Kapitalismus. Vom Fordismus zum Post-Fordismus*. Hamburg: VSA-Verl.

Hoch, K.-L. (1996). *Caspar David Friedrich in der Sächsischen Schweiz*. Dresden: Verlag der Kunst.

Hoeft, C., Messinger-Zimmer, S., & Zilles, J. (Eds.). (2017). *Bürgerproteste in Zeiten der Energiewende. Lokale Konflikte um Windkraft, Stromtrassen und Fracking*. Bielefeld: Transcript.

Hoesterey, I. (2001). *Pastiche. Cultural memory in art, film, literature*. Bloomington: Indiana University Press.

Hoffmann-Lange, U. (2000). Bildungsexpansion, politisches Interesse und politisches Engagement in den alten Bundesländern. In O. Niedermayer & B. Westle (Eds.), *Demokratie und Partizipation. Festschrift für Max Kaase* (pp. 46–64). Wiesbaden: Westdeutscher Verlag.

Hofinger, G. (2001). *Denken über Umwelt und Natur*. Weinheim: Beltz.

Hofmann, W. (2013). *Caspar David Friedrich. Naturwirklichkeit und Kunstwahrheit* (3rd ed.). München: Beck.

Hofmeister, S. (2008). Verwildernde Naturverhältnisse. Versuch über drei Formen der Wildnis. *Das Argument, 50*(6), 813–826.

Hofmeister, S., & Kühne, O. (2016). StadtLandschaften: Die neue Hybridität von Stadt und Land. In S. Hofmeister & O. Kühne (Eds.), *StadtLandschaften. Die neue Hybridität von Stadt und Land* (pp. 1–10). Wiesbaden: Springer VS.

Hohl, H. (1977). Das Thema Landschaft in der deutschen Malerei des ausgehenden 18. und beginnenden 19. Jahrhunderts. In A. H. von Wallthor & H. Quirin (Eds.), *„Landschaft" als interdisziplinäres Forschungsproblem. Vorträge und Diskussionen des Kolloquiums am 7./8. November 1975 in Münster* (pp. 45–53). Münster: Aschendorff.

Hoisl, R., Nohl, W., Zekorn, S., & Zöllner, G. (1987). *Landschaftsästhetik in der Flurbereinigung. Empirische Grundlagen zum Erleben der Agrarlandschaft.* München: Ministerielle Veröffentlichung.

Hokema, D. (2013). *Landschaft im Wandel? Zeitgenössische Landschaftsbegriffe in Wissenschaft, Planung und Alltag.* Wiesbaden: Springer VS.

Hokema, D. (2015). Landscape is everywhere. The construction of landscape by US-American laypersons. *Geographische Zeitschrift, 103*(3), 151–170.

Hook, S. (2018). ‚Energiewende': Von internationalen Klimaabkommen bis hin zum deutschen Erneuerbaren-Energien-Gesetz. In O. Kühne & F. Weber (Eds.), *Bausteine der Energiewende* (pp. 21–54). Wiesbaden: Springer VS.

Hoppmann, H. (2000). *Pro:Vision—Postmoderne Taktiken in einer strategischen Gegenwartsgesellschaft. Eine soziologische Analyse.* Berlin: wvb.

Horkheimer, M. (1963). *Über das Vorurteil.* Köln: Opladen.

Horkheimer, M. (1976). Vernunft und Selbsterhaltung. In H. Ebeling (Ed.), *Subjektivität und Selbsterhaltung. Beiträge zur Diagnose der Moderne* (Theorie-Diskussion, pp. 41–75). Frankfurt a. M.: Suhrkamp.

Horkheimer, M. (1977 [1937]). *Traditionelle und kritsiche Theorie. Fünf Aufsätze.* Frankfurt a. M.: Fischer Wissenschaft.

Horkheimer, M. (1982). *Critical theory. Selected essays.* New York: continuum.

Horkheimer, M., & Adorno, T. W. (1969). *Dialektik der Aufklärung. Philosophische Fragmente.* Frankfurt a. M.: Fischer.

Hoskins, W. G. (2005 [1955]). *The making of the english landscape.* London: The Folio Society.

Howard, P. J. (2011). *An introduction to landscape.* Farnham: Routledge.

Howley, P. (2011). Landscape aesthetics: Assessing the general publics' preferences towards rural landscapes. *Ecological Economics, 72,* 161–169.

Hugill, P. J. (1995). *Upstate Arcadia. Landscape, aesthetics, and the triumph of social differentiation in America.* Lanham, Maryland: Rowman & Littlefield.

Hügin, U. (1996). *Individuum, Gemeinschaft, Umwelt. Konzeption einer Theorie der Dynamik anthropogener Systeme.* Bern: Lang.

Hülz, M., & Kühne, O. (2015). Handlungsbedarfe und -empfehlungen an die räumliche Planung vor dem Hintergrund einer zunehmenden Internationalisierung der Gesellschaft. In B. Nienaber & U. Roos (Eds.), *Internationalisierung der Gesellschaft und die Auswirkungen auf die Raumentwicklung. Beispiele aus Hessen, Rheinland-Pfalz und dem Saarland: Vol. 13. Arbeitsberichte der ARL* (pp. 131–135). Hannover: Selbstverlag.

Hume, D. (2003 [1738]). *A treatise of human nature.* http://www.acatholic.org/wp-content/uploads/A-Treatise-of-Human-Nature-by-David-Hume.pdf. Accessed 24 Jan 2019.

Hunt, D. M. (2004). Representing "Los Angeles": Media, space, and place. In M. J. Dear (Ed.), *From Chicago to L.A. Making sense of urban theory* (pp. 321–346). Thousand Oaks: Sage.

Huntington, S. P. (2011). *The clash of civilizations and the remaking of world order* (Simon & Schuster). New York: Simon & Schuster Paperbacks.

Hunziker, M. (2010). Die Bedeutung der Landschaft für den Menschen: Objektive Eigenschaften der Landschaft oder individuelle Wahrnehmung des Menschen? In WSL (Ed.), *Landschaftsqualität. Konzepte, Indikatoren und Datengrundlagen* (Forum für Wissen, pp. 33–41). Birmensdorf: Eidgenössische Forschungsanstalt WSL.

Hunziker, M., & Kienast, F. (1999). Potential impacts of changing agricultural activities on scenic beauty—A prototypical technique for automated rapid assessment. *Landscape Ecology, 14*(2), 161–176.

Hunziker, M., Felber, P., Gehring, K., Buchecker, M., Bauer, N., & Kienast, F. (2008). Evaluation of landscape change by different social groups. Results of two empirical studies in Switzerland. *Mountain Research and Development, 28*(2), 140–147.

Hupke, K.-D. (2015). *Naturschutz. Ein kritischer Ansatz*. Berlin: Springer Spektrum.

Hüppauf, B. (2007). Heimat—Die Wiederkehr eines verpönten Wortes. Ein Populärmythos im Zeitalter der Globalisierung. In G. Gebhard, O. Geisler, & S. Schröter (Eds.), *Heimat. Konturen und Konjunkturen eines umstrittenen Konzepts* (pp. 109–140). Bielefeld: Transcript.

Husserl, E. (1913). *Ideen zu einer reinen Phänomenologie und phänomenologischen Philosopie. Erster Buch: Allgemeine Einführung in die reine Phänomenologie*. Halle (Saale): Niemeyer.

Hutcheson, F. (1986 [1725]). *Eine Untersuchung über den Ursprung unserer Ideen von Schönheit und Tugend. Über moralisch Gutes und Schlechtes: Vol. 364. Philosophische Bibliothek*. Hamburg: Meiner.

Illing, F. (2006). *Kitsch, Kommerz und Kult. Soziologie des schlechten Geschmacks*. Konstanz: UVK.

Imbusch, P. (2002). Macht und Herrschaft. In H. Korte & B. Schäfers (Eds.), *Einführung in Hauptbegriffe der Soziologie* (6th ed., pp. 161–182). Opladen: Leske + Budrich.

Ingold, T. (1993). The temporality of the landscape. *World Archaeology, 25*(2), 152–174.

Ingold, T. (2002). *The perception of the environment. Essays on livelihood, dwelling and skill*. London: Routledge.

Ipsen, D. (1992). Stadt und Land—Metamorphosen einer Beziehung. In H. Häußermann, D. Ipsen, R. Krämer-Badoni, D. Läpple, M. Rodenstein, & W. Siebel (Hrsg.), *Stadt und Raum. Soziologische Analysen* (2nd ed, pp. 117–156). Pfaffenweiler: Centaurus.

Ipsen, D. (2006). *Ort und Landschaft*. Wiesbaden: VS Verlag.

Jackson, J. B. (1997). Landscape revisions. In H. L. Horowitz (Ed.), *Landscape in sight. Looking at America* (pp. 333–371). London: Yale University Press.

Jedicke, E. (2013). Die Ästhetik von Landschaften—Was ist „schön"? *Naturschutz und Landschaftsplanung, 45*(9), 261.

Joas, H. (1988). Symbolischer Interaktionismus. Von der Philosophie des Pragmatismus zu einer soziologischen Forschungstradition. *Kölner Zeitschrift für Soziologie und Sozialpsychologie, 40*, 417–446.

Johnson, M. H. (2012). Phenomenological approaches in landscape archaeology. *Annual Review of Anthropology, 41*(1), 269–284.

Jones, M. (1991). The elusive reality of landscape. Concepts and approaches in landscape research. *Norsk Geografisk Tidsskrift, 45*(4), 229–244.

Jones, M., & Daugstad, K. (1997). Usages of the "cultural landscape" concept in Norwegian and Nordic landscape administration. *Landscape Research, 22*(3), 267–281.

Jones, M., Howard, P., Olwig, K. R., Primdahl, J., & Sarlöv Herlin, I. (2007). Multiple interfaces of the European landscape convention. *Norsk Geografisk Tidsskrift, 61*(4), 207–216.

Jongen, M. (Ed.). (2008). *Philosophie des Raumes. Standortbestimmungen ästhetischer und politischer Theorie*. München: Fink.

Jorgensen, A. (2011). Beyond the view. Future directions in landscape aesthetics research. *Landscape and Urban Planning, 100*(4), 353–355.

Jörke, D. (2010). Die Versprechen der Demokratie und die Grenzen der Deliberation. *Zeitschrift für Politikwissenschaft, 20*(3–4), 269–290.

Jung, A. (2009). *Identität und Differenz. Sinnprobleme der differenzlogischen Systemtheorie* (Sozialtheorie). Bielefeld: Transcript.

Jurt, J. (2012). Bourdieus Kapital-Theorie. In M. M. Bergman, S. Hupka-Brunner, T. Meyer, & R. Samuel (Eds.), *Bildung—Arbeit—Erwachsenwerden. Ein interdisziplinärer Blick auf die Transition im Jugend und jungen Erwachsenenalter* (pp. 21–41). Wiesbaden: Springer.

Kamlage, J.-H., Nanz, P., & Fleischer, B. (2014). Dialogorientierte Bürgerbeteiligung im Netzausbau. In H. Rogall, H.-C. Binswanger, F. Ekardt, A. Grothe, W.-D. Hasenclever, I. Hauchler, et al. (Eds.), *Im Brennpunkt: Die Energiewende als gesellschaftlicher Transformationsprozess: Vol. 4. Jahrbuch Nachhaltige Ökonomie* (pp. 195–216). Marburg: Metropolis-Verlag.

Kant, I. (1959a [1781]). *Kritik der reinen Vernunft*. Hamburg: Felix Meiner.

Kant, I. (1959b [1790]). *Kritik der Urteilskraft* (Philosophische Bibliothek, Unveränd. Neudr. der Ausg. von 1924). Hamburg: Meiner.

Kant, I. (1983 [1793]). *Kant. Werke* (Vol. 9). Darmstadt: WBG.

Kaplan, S., & Kaplan, R. (1982). *Cognition and environment. Functioning in an uncertain world.* New York: Praeger.

Kaplan, R., & Kaplan, S. (1989). *The experience of nature. A psychological perspective.* Cambridge: Cambridge University Press.

Kaplan, R., Kaplan, S., & Ryan, R. L. (1998). *With people in mind. Design and management of everyday nature.* Washington: Island.

Kastner, J. (2002). Existenzgeld statt Unsicherheit? Zygmunt Bauman und die Krise globaler Politik angesichts der neoliberalen Globalisierung. In M. Junge & T. Kron (Eds.), *Zygmunt Bauman. Soziologie zwischen Postmoderne und Ethik: Vol. 2221. UTB* (pp. 225–254). Opladen: Leske + Budrich.

Kaufmann, S. (2005). *Soziologie der Landschaft*. Wiesbaden: VS Verlag.

Kaymaz, I. C. (2012). Landscape perception. In M. Ozyavuz (Ed.), *Landscape planning* (pp. 251–276). London: InTech.

Kazig, R. (2007). Atmosphären—Konzept für einen nicht repräsentationellen Zugang zum Raum. In C. Berndt & R. Pütz (Eds.), *Kulturelle Geographien. Zur Beschäftigung mit Raum und Ort nach dem Cultural Turn* (pp. 167–187). Bielefeld: Transcript.

Kazig, R. (2008). Typische Atmosphären städtischer Plätze. Auf dem Weg zu einer anwendungsorientierten Atmosphärenforschung. *Die alte Stadt, 35*(2), 148–160.

Kazig, R. (2013). Landschaft mit allen Sinnen—Zum Wert des Atmosphärenbegriffs für die Landschaftsforschung. In D. Bruns & O. Kühne (Eds.), *Landschaften: Theorie, Praxis und internationale Bezüge* (pp. 221–232). Schwerin: Oceano.

Kazig, R. (2016). Die Bedeutung von Alltagsästhetik im Kontext der Polarisierung und Hybridisierung von Städten. Eine Spurensuche. In F. Weber & O. Kühne (Eds.), *Fraktale Metropolen. Stadtentwicklung zwischen Devianz, Polarisierung und Hybridisierung* (pp. 215–230). Wiesbaden: Springer VS.

Kazig, R. (2019). Für ein alltagsästhetisches Verständnis von Heimat. In M. Hülz, O. Kühne, & F. Weber (Eds.), *Heimat. Ein vielfältiges Konstrukt*. Wiesbaden: Springer VS (in press).

Kazig, R., & Weichhart, P. (2009). Die Neuthematisierung der materiellen Welt in der Humangeographie. *Berichte zur deutschen Landeskunde, 83*(2), 109–128.

Kearney, A. R., & Bradley, G. A. (2011). The effects of viewer attributes on preference for forest scenes. Contributions of attitudes, knowledge, demographic factors, and stakeholder group membership. *Environment and Behavior, 43*(2), 147–181.

Kebeck, G., & Schroll, H. T. (2011). *Experimentelle Ästhetik: Vol. 3474. UTB*. Wien: facultas wuv.

Kersting, W. (2005). Gerechtigkeit und Sozialstaatsbegründung. In O. Neumaier, C. Sedmak, & M. Zichy (Eds.), *Gerechtigkeit. Auf der Suche nach einem Gleichgewicht*(pp. 57–88). Frankfurt a. M.: Ontos.

Kersting, W. (2009). *Verteidigung des Liberalismus*. Hamburg: Murmann.

Kirchhoff, T., & Trepl, L. (2009). Landschaft, Wildnis, Ökosystem: Zur kulturbedingten Vieldeutigkeit ästhetischer, moralischer und theoretischer Naturauffassungen. Einleitender Überblick. In T. Kirchhoff & L. Trepl (Eds.), *Vieldeutige Natur. Landschaft, Wildnis und Ökosystem als kulturgeschichtliche Phänomene* (Sozialtheorie, pp. 13–68). Bielefeld: Transcript.

Kitchin, R. (2015). Positivist geography. In S. C. Aitken & G. Valentine (Eds.), *Approaches to human geography. Philosophies, theories, people and practices* (2nd ed., pp. 23–34). Los Angeles: Sage.

Kloock, D., & Spahr, A. (2007 [1986]). *Medientheorien. Eine Einführung* (UTB). München: Fink.

Klotz, H. (1985). *Moderne und Postmoderne. Architektur der Gegenwart 1960–1980* (Schriften des Deutschen Architekturmuseums zur Architekturgeschichte und Architekturtheorie, 2nd ed.). Wiesbaden: Vieweg+Teubner.

Kneer, G. (2009a). Akteur-Netzwerk-Theorie. In G. Kneer & M. Schroer (Eds.), *Handbuch Soziologische Theorien* (pp. 19–39). Wiesbaden: VS Verlag.

Kneer, G. (2009b). Jenseits von Realismus und Antirealismus. Eine Verteidigung des Sozialkonstruktivismus gegenüber seinen postkonstruktivistischen Kritikern. *Zeitschrift für Soziologie, 38*(1), 5–25.

Kneer, G., & Nassehi, A. (1997). *Niklas Luhmanns Theorie sozialer Systeme. Eine Einführung*. München: Fink.

Kniffen, F. (1965). Folk housing: Key to diffusion. *Annals of the Association of American Geographers, 55*(4), 549–576.

Knoll, J. H. (1981). Liberalismus. In J. H. Schoeps, J. H. Knoll, & C.-E. Bärsch (Eds.), *Konservativismus, Liberalismus, Sozialismus. Einführung, Texte, Bibliographien: Vol. 1032. Uni-Taschenbücher Politologie, Neuere Geschichte, Soziologie* (pp. 87–139). München: Fink.

Koch, F. (2010). *Die europäische Stadt in Transformation. Stadtplanung und Stadtentwicklungspolitik im postsozialistischen Warschau*. Wiesbaden: VS Verlag (Zugl.: Berlin, Humboldt-Univ., Diss, 2009).

Köhler, W. (1969). *The task of Gestalt psychology* (Princeton Legacy Library). Princeton: Princeton University Press.

Kölsche, C. (2015). Herausforderungen der Energiewende: Zur Konstruktion von ‚Energieregionen'. In O. Kühne & F. Weber (Eds.), *Bausteine der Regionalentwicklung* (pp. 137–148). Wiesbaden: Springer VS.

Konermann, M. (2001). Das Schutzgut Landschaftsbild in der Landschaftsrahmenplanung Rheinland-Pfalz. *Natur und Landschaft, 76*(7), 311–317.

Konold, W. (1996). Vorwort. In W. Konold (Ed.), *Naturlandschaft—Kulturlandschaft. Die Veränderung der Landschaften nach der Nutzbarmachung durch den Menschen* (p. 5). Landsberg: Ecomed.

Kook, K. (2008). Zum Landschaftsverständnis von Kindern: Aussichten—Ansichten—Einsichten. In R. Schindler, J. Stadelbauer, & W. Konold (Eds.), *Points of View. Landschaft verstehen— Geographie und Ästhetik, Energie und Technik* (pp. 107–124). Freiburg: modo.

Körner, S. (2006). Die neue Debatte über Kulturlandschaft in Naturschutz und Stadtplanung. www.bfn.de/fileadmin/MDB/documents/service/perspektivekultur_koerner.pdf. Accessed 10 May 2017.

Körner, S., & Eisel, U. (2006). Nachhaltige Landschaftsentwicklung. In D. D. Genske (Ed.), *Fläche—Zukunft—Raum. Strategien und Instrumente für Regionen im Umbruch: Vol. 37.*

Schriftenreihe der Deutschen Gesellschaft für Geowissenschaften (pp. 45–60). Hannover: Deutsche Gesellschaft für Geowissenschaften.

Kortländer, B. (1977). Die Landschaft in der Literatur des ausgehenden 18. und beginnenden 19. Jahrhunderts. In A. H. von Wallthor & H. Quirin (Eds.), *„Landschaft" als interdisziplinäres Forschungsproblem. Vorträge und Diskussionen des Kolloquiums am 7./8. November 1975 in Münster.* Münster: Aschendorff.

Kost, S. (2017). Raumbilder und Raumwahrnehmung von Jugendlichen. In O. Kühne, H. Megerle, & F. Weber (Eds.), *Landschaftsästhetik und Landschaftswandel* (pp. 69–85). Wiesbaden: Springer VS.

Kost, S., & Schönwald, A. (Eds.). (2015). *Landschaftswandel—Wandel von Machtstrukturen.* Wiesbaden: Springer VS.

Kötzle, M. (1999). Eigenart und Eigentum. Zur Genese und Struktur konservativer und liberaler Weltbilder. In S. Körner, T. Heger, A. Nagel, & U. Eisel (Eds.), *Naturbilder in Naturschutz und Ökologie: Vol. 111. Landschaftsentwicklung und Umweltforschung* (pp. 19–36). Berlin: TU Berlin.

Kraidy, M. M. (2005). *Hybridity, or the cultural logic of globalization.* Philadelphia: Temple University Press.

Krätke, S. (1995). *Stadt—Raum—Ökonomie. Einführung in aktuelle Problemfelder der Stadtökonomie und Wirtschaftsgeographie: Vol. 53. Stadtforschung aktuell.* Basel: Birkhäuser.

Krauss, K. O. (1974). Ästhetische Bewertungsprobleme in der Landschaftsplanung. *Landschaft + Stadt, 1974*(1), 27–38.

Krauss, W. (2018). Postenvironmental landscapes in the Anthropocene. In P. Howard, I. H. Thompson, E. Waterton, & M. Atha (Eds.), *The Routledge companion to landscape studies* (2nd ed., pp. 94–105). Abingdon: Routledge.

Krebs, H. (2014). *Klassischer Liberalismus. Die Staatsfrage—Gestern, heute, morgen.* Norderstedt: Books on Demand.

Kreuzer, F., Hayek, F. A. v., & Dahrendorf, R. (1983). *Markt, Plan, Freiheit. Franz Kreuzer im Gespräch mit Friedrich von Hayek und Ralf Dahrendorf.* Wien: Deuticke.

Kristol, I. (1995). *Neoconservatism. The autobiography of an idea.* New York: Free Press (Selected Essays 1949–1995).

Kropp, C. (2015). Regionale StadtLandschaften—Muster der lebensweltlichen Erfahrung postindustrieller Raumproduktion zwischen Homogenisierung und Fragmentierung. *Raumforschung und Raumordnung, 73*(2), 91–106.

Kruse-Graumann, L. (1996). Umweltschutz aus psychologischer Perspektive. Bewusstsein und Verhalten. In K.-H. Erdmann & J. Nauber (Eds.), *Beiträge zur Ökosystemforschung und Umwelterziehung: Vol. 38. MAB-Mitteilungen* (pp. 171–179). Bonn: Selbstverlag.

Krysmanski, R. (1996). Die Nützlichkeit der Landschaft [1971]. In G. Gröning & U. Herlyn (Eds.), *Landschaftswahrnehmung und Landschaftserfahrung* (Arbeiten zur sozialwissenschaftlich orientierten Freiraumplanung, pp. 223–242). Münster: LIT.

Kubsch, R. (2007). *Die Postmoderne. Abschied von der Eindeutigkeit.* Holzgerlingen: Hänssler.

Kühne, O. (2005a). *Landschaft als Konstrukt und die Fragwürdigkeit der Grundlagen der konservierenden Landschaftserhaltung—Eine konstruktivistisch-systemtheoretische Betrachtung. 2005: Vol. 4. Beiträge zur Kritischen Geographie.* Wien: Selbstverlag.

Kühne, O. (2005b). Stadt-Land-Beziehungen zwischen Moderne und Postmoderne. *Ländlicher Raum, 56*(6), 45–50.

Kühne, O. (2006a). *Landschaft in der Postmoderne. Das Beispiel des Saarlandes.* Wiesbaden: DUV.

Kühne, O. (2006b). Landschaft und ihre Konstruktion. Theoretische Überlegungen und empirische Befunde. *Naturschutz und Landschaftsplanung, 38*(5), 146–152.

Kühne, O. (2006c). Soziale Distinktion und Landschaft. Eine landschaftssoziologische Betrachtung. *Stadt+Grün, 56*(12), 42–45.

Kühne, O. (2007). Soziale Akzeptanz und Perspektiven der Altindustrielandschaft. Ergebnisse einer empirischen Studie im Saarland. *RaumPlanung, 2007*(132/133), 156–160.

Kühne, O. (2008a). Die Sozialisation von Landschaft—Sozialkonstruktivistische Überlegungen, empirische Befunde und Konsequenzen für den Umgang mit dem Thema Landschaft in Geographie und räumlicher Planung. *Geographische Zeitschrift, 96*(4), 189–206.

Kühne, O. (2008b). *Distinktion—Macht—Landschaft. Zur sozialen Definition von Landschaft.* Wiesbaden: VS Verlag.

Kühne, O. (2008c). Kritische Geographie der Machtbeziehungen—Konzeptionelle Überlegungen auf der Grundlage der Soziologie Pierre Bourdieus. *geographische revue, 10*(2), 40–50.

Kühne, O. (2008d). Landschaft und Kitsch—Anmerkungen zu impliziten und expliziten Landschaftsvorstellungen. *Naturschutz und Landschaftsplanung, 44*(12), 403–408.

Kühne, O. (2009a). Grundzüge einer konstruktivistischen Landschaftstheorie und ihre Konsequenzen für die räumliche Planung. *Raumforschung und Raumordnung, 67*(5/6), 395–404.

Kühne, O. (2009b). Heimat und Landschaft—Zusammenhänge und Zuschreibungen zwischen Macht und Mindermacht. Überlegungen auf sozialkonstruktivistischer Grundlage. *Stadt+Grün, 58*(9), 17–22.

Kühne, O. (2009c). Landschaft und Heimat—Überlegungen zu einem geographischen Amalgam. *Berichte zur deutschen Landeskunde, 83*(3), 223–240.

Kühne, O. (2011a). Akzeptanz von regenerativen Energien—Überlegungen zur sozialen Definition von Landschaft und Ästhetik. *Stadt+Grün, 60*(8), 9–13.

Kühne, O. (2011b). Heimat und sozial nachhaltige Landschaftsentwicklung. *Raumforschung und Raumordnung, 69*(5), 291–301.

Kühne, O. (2012a). Landschaft, Ästhetik und der Abbau mineralischer Rohstoffe. Überlegungen zur gesellschaftlichen Akzeptanz des Abbaus mineralischer Rohstoffe aus Perspektive der sozialwissenschaftlichen Landschaftsforschung. *GesteinsPerspektiven, 4*, 40–43. http://www.bv-miro.org/downloads/forschung%20GP-4-12%20S1-54.pdf. Accessed 20 Feb 2018.

Kühne, O. (2012b). *Stadt—Landschaft—Hybridität. Ästhetische Bezüge im postmodernen Los Angeles mit seinen modernen Persistenzen.* Wiesbaden: Springer VS.

Kühne, O. (2012c). Urban nature between modern and postmodern aesthetics: Reflections based on the social constructivist approach. *Quaestiones Geographicae, 31*(2), 61–70.

Kühne, O. (2013a). Landschaft zwischen Objekthaftigkeit und Konstruktion—Überlegungen zur inversen Landschaft. In D. Bruns & O. Kühne (Eds.), *Landschaften: Theorie, Praxis und internationale Bezüge* (pp. 181–193). Schwerin: Oceano.

Kühne, O. (2013b). Landschaftsästhetik und regenerative Energien—Grundüberlegungen zu De- und Re-Sensualisierungen und inversen Landschaften. In L. Gailing & M. Leibenath (Eds.), *Neue Energielandschaften—Neue Perspektiven der Landschaftsforschung* (pp. 101–120). Wiesbaden: Springer VS.

Kühne, O. (2013c). *Landschaftstheorie und Landschaftspraxis. Eine Einführung aus sozialkonstruktivistischer Perspektive.* Wiesbaden: Springer VS.

Kühne, O. (2014a). Das Konzept der Ökosystemdienstleistungen als Ausdruck ökologischer Kommunikation. Betrachtungen aus der Perspektive Luhmannscher Systemtheorie. *Naturschutz und Landschaftsplanung, 46*(1), 17–22.

Kühne, O. (2014b). Motive für zivilgesellschaftliche Partizipation—Zur Notwendigkeit eines gewandelten Verständnisses zum Umgang mit Landschaft. In BHU (Ed.), *Energielandschaften gestalten. Leitlinien und Beispiele für Bürgerpartizipation* (pp. 121–130). Bonn: BHU.

Kühne, O. (2015a). Das studentische Verständnis von Landschaft Ergebnisse einer qualitativen und quantitativen Studie bei Studierenden der Fakultät Landschaftsarchitektur der Hochschule Weihenstephan-Triesdorf. *Morphé. Rural—Suburban—Urban, 1,* 50–59. www.hswt.de/fkla-morphe. Accessed 21 March 2017.

Kühne, O. (2015b). Historical developments: The evolution of the concept of landscape in German linguistic areas. In D. Bruns, O. Kühne, A. Schönwald, & S. Theile (Eds.), *Landscape culture—Culturing landscapes. The differentiated construction of landscapes* (pp. 43–52). Wiesbaden: Springer VS.

Kühne, O. (2015c). The streets of Los Angeles: Power and the infrastructure landscape. *Landscape Research, 40*(2), 139–153.

Kühne, O. (2015d). Was ist Landschaft? Eine Antwort aus sozialkonstruktivistischer Perspektive. *Morphé. Rural—Suburban—Urban, 1,* 27–32. http://www.hswt.de/fileadmin/Dateien/Hochschule/Fakultaeten/LA/Dokumente/MORPHE/MORPHE-Band-01-Juni-2015.pdf. Accessed 21 March 2017.

Kühne, O. (2015e). Weltanschauungen in regionalentwickelndem Handeln—Die Beispiele liberaler und konservativer Ideensysteme. In O. Kühne & F. Weber (Eds.), *Bausteine der Regionalentwicklung* (pp. 55–69). Wiesbaden: Springer VS.

Kühne, O. (2016a). Transformation, Hybridisierung, Streben nach Eindeutigkeit und Urbanizing former Suburbs (URFSURBS): Entwicklungen postmoderner Stadtlandhybride in Südkalifornien und in Altindustrieräumen Mitteleuropas—Beobachtungen aus der Perspektive sozialkonstruktivistischer Landschaftsforschung. In S. Hofmeister & O. Kühne (Eds.), *StadtLandschaften. Die neue Hybridität von Stadt und Land* (pp. 13–36). Wiesbaden: Springer VS.

Kühne, O. (2016b). Warschau—Das postsozialistische Raumpastiche und seine spezifische Ästhetik. In F. Weber & O. Kühne (Eds.), *Fraktale Metropolen. Stadtentwicklung zwischen Devianz, Polarisierung und Hybridisierung* (pp. 271–294). Wiesbaden: Springer VS.

Kühne, O. (2017a). Der intergenerationelle Wandel landschaftsästhetischer Vorstellungen—Eine Betrachtung aus sozialkonstruktivistischer Perspektive. In O. Kühne, H. Megerle, & F. Weber (Eds.), *Landschaftsästhetik und Landschaftswandel* (pp. 53–67). Wiesbaden: Springer VS.

Kühne, O. (2017b). Hybridisierungstendenzen, Raumpastiches und URFSURBs in Südkalifornien als Herausforderung für die Planung. In K. Berr (Ed.), *Architektur- und Planungsethik. Zugänge, Perspektiven, Standpunkte* (pp. 15–32). Wiesbaden: Springer VS.

Kühne, O. (2017c). *Zur Aktualität von Ralf Dahrendorf. Einführung in sein Werk* (Aktuelle und klassische Sozial- und Kulturwissenschaftlerlinnen). Wiesbaden: Springer VS.

Kühne, O. (2018a). ‚Neue Landschaftskonflikte'—Überlegungen zu den physischen Manifestationen der Energiewende auf der Grundlage der Konflikttheorie Ralf Dahrendorfs. In O. Kühne & F. Weber (Eds.), *Bausteine der Energiewende* (pp. 163–186). Wiesbaden: Springer VS.

Kühne, O. (2018b). Der doppelte Landschaftswandel. Physische Räume, soziale Deutungen, Bewertungen. *Nachrichten der ARL, 48*(1), 14–17. https://shop.arl-net.de/media/direct/pdf/nachrichten/2018-1/NR_1-18_K%C3%BChne_S14-17_online.pdf. Accessed 8 Oct 2018.

Kühne, O. (2018c). *Landscape and power in geographical space as a social-aesthetic construct.* Dordrecht: Springer International Publishing.

Kühne, O. (2018d). *Landschaft und Wandel. Zur Veränderlichkeit von Wahrnehmungen.* Wiesbaden: Springer VS.

Kühne, O. (2018e). *Landschaftstheorie und Landschaftspraxis. Eine Einführung aus sozialkonstruktivistischer Perspektive* (2., aktualisierte und überarbeitete Aufl.). Wiesbaden: Springer VS.

Kühne, O. (2018f). Macht, Herrschaft und Landschaft: Landschaftskonflikte zwischen Dysfunktionalität und Potenzial. Eine Betrachtung aus Perspektive der Konflikttheorie Ralf Dahrendorfs. In K. Berr (Ed.), *Transdisziplinäre Landschaftsforschung. Grundlagen und Perspektiven* (pp. 155–170). Wiesbaden: Springer VS.

Kühne, O. (2018g). Postmodernisierung und Großschutzgebiete—Überlegungen zu Natur, Raum und Planung aus sozialkonstruktivistischer Perspektive. In F. Weber, F. Weber, & C. Jenal (Eds.), *Wohin des Weges? Regionalentwicklung in Großschutzgebieten: Vol. 21. Arbeitsberichte der ARL* (pp. 44–55). Hannover: Selbstverlag.

Kühne, O. (2019). Vom ,Bösen' und ,Guten' in der Landschaft—Das Problem moralischer Kommunikation im Umgang mit Landschaft und ihren Konflikten. In K. Berr & C. Jenal (Eds.), *Landschaftskonflikte* (folgen). Wiesbaden: Springer VS.

Kühne, O., & Hernik, J. (2015). Zur Bedeutung materieller Objekte bei der Konstitution von Heimat—Unter besonderer Berücksichtigung von Objekten deutschen Ursprungs aus der Teilungsära Polens. In O. Kühne, K. Gawroński, & J. Hernik (Eds.), *Transformation und Landschaft. Die Folgen sozialer Wandlungsprozesse auf Landschaft* (pp. 221–229). Wiesbaden: Springer VS.

Kühne, O., & Schönwald, A. (2013). Zur Frage der sozialen Akzeptanz von Landschaftsveränderungen—Hinweise zum Ausbau von Energienetzen in Deutschland. *UMID—Umwelt und Mensch-Informationsdienst, 2013*(2), 82–88. https://www.umweltbundesamt.de/sites/default/files/medien/419/publikationen/umid_2_2013.pdf. Accessed 22 Aug 2017.

Kühne, O., & Schönwald, A. (2015). *San Diego. Eigenlogiken, Widersprüche und Hybriditäten in und von ,America's finest city'*. Wiesbaden: Springer VS.

Kühne, O., & Schönwald, A. (2018). Hybridisierung und Grenze: das Beispiel San Diego/Tijuana. In M. Heintel, R. Musil, & N. Weixlbaumer (Eds.), *Grenzen. Theoretische, konzeptionelle und praxisbezogene Fragestellungen zu Grenzen und deren Überschreitungen* (pp. 401–417). Wiesbaden: Springer VS.

Kühne, O., & Spellerberg, A. (2010). *Heimat und Heimatbewusstsein in Zeiten erhöhter Flexibilitätsanforderungen. Empirische Untersuchungen im Saarland*. Wiesbaden: VS Verlag.

Kühne, O., & Weber, F. (2015). Der Energienetzausbau in Internetvideos—Eine quantitativ ausgerichtete diskurstheoretisch orientierte Analyse. In S. Kost & A. Schönwald (Eds.), *Landschaftswandel—Wandel von Machtstrukturen* (pp. 113–126). Wiesbaden: Springer VS.

Kühne, O., & Weber, F. (2017). Geographisches Problemlösen: das Beispiel des Raumkonfliktes um die Gewinnung mineralischer Rohstoffe. *Geographie Aktuell und Schule, 39*(225), 16–24.

Kühne, O., & Weber, F. (Eds.). (2018). *Bausteine der Energiewende*. Wiesbaden: Springer VS.

Kühne, O., & Weber, F. (2018 [online first 2017]). Conflicts and negotiation processes in the course of power grid extension in Germany. *Landscape Research, 43*(4), 529–541.

Kühne, O., Weber, F., & Weber, F. (2013). Wiesen, Berge, blauer Himmel. Aktuelle Landschaftskonstruktionen am Beispiel des Tourismusmarketings des Salzburger Landes aus diskurstheoretischer Perspektive. *Geographische Zeitschrift, 101*(1), 36–54.

Kühne, O., Weber, F., & Jenal, C. (2016a). Der Stromnetzausbau in Deutschland: Formen und Argumente des Widerstands. *Geographie Aktuell und Schule, 38*(222), 4–14.

Kühne, O., Jenal, C., & Weber, F. (2016b). Die soziale Definition von Heimat. In Bund Heimat und Umwelt in Deutschland (BHU) (Ed.), *Heimat—Vergangenheit verstehen, Zukunft gestalten. Dokumentation der zwei Veranstaltungen „Workshop zur Vermittlung des römischen Kulturerbes" (17. November 2016, Bonn) und „Heimat neu finden" (23. bis 24. November 2016, Bensberg)* (pp. 21–27). Bonn: Selbstverlag.

Kühne, O., Schönwald, A., & Weber, F. (2016c). Urban/rural hybrids: The Urbanisation Of Former Suburbs (URFSURBS). *Quaestiones Geographicae, 35*(4), 23–34.

Kühne, O., Schönwald, A., & Weber, F. (2017a). Die Ästhetik von Stadtlandhybriden: URFSURBS (*Urbanizing former suburbs*) in Südkalifornien und im Großraum Paris. In O. Kühne, H. Megerle, & F. Weber (Eds.), *Landschaftsästhetik und Landschaftswandel* (pp. 177–198). Wiesbaden: Springer VS.

Kühne, O., Megerle, H., & Weber, F. (2017b). Landschaft—Landschaftswandel—Landschaftsästhetik: Einführung—Überblick—Ausblick. In O. Kühne, H. Megerle, & F. Weber (Eds.), *Landschaftsästhetik und Landschaftswandel* (pp. 1–22). Wiesbaden: Springer VS.

Kühne, O., Weber, F., & Jenal, C. (2018). *Neue Landschaftsgeographie. Ein Überblick* (Essentials). Wiesbaden: Springer VS.

Kühne, O., Weber, F., Berr, K., & Jenal, C. (Hrsg.). (2019). *Handbuch Landschaft*. Wiesbaden: Springer VS (in press).

Küster, H. (2013 [1995]). *Geschichte der Landschaft in Mitteleuropa. Von der Eiszeit bis zur Gegenwart*. München: Beck.

Laclau, E., & Mouffe, C. (1985). *Hegemony and socialist strategy. Towards a radical democratic politics*. London: Verso.

Lamla, J. (2008). Die Konflikttheorie als Gesellschaftstheorie. In T. Bonacker (Ed.), *Sozialwissenschaftliche Konflikttheorien. Eine Einführung* (4th ed., pp. 207–248). Wiesbaden: VS Verlag.

Lang, R. (2003). *Edgeless cities. Exploring the elusive metropolis* (Brookings metro series). Washington, D.C.: Brookings Institution Press.

Lang, R. E., Sanchez, T. W., & Oner, A. C. (2013). Beyond edge city. Office geography in the new metropolis. *Urban Geography, 30*(7), 726–755.

Lankheit, K. (1978). Caspar David Friedrich. In R. Brinkmann (Ed.), *Romantik in Deutschland. Ein interdisziplinäres Symposium* (pp. 683–707). Stuttgart: Metzler.

Lanz, S. (1996). *Demokratische Stadtplanung in der Postmoderne: Vol. 15. Wahrnehmungsgeographische Studien*. Oldenburg: BIS-Verlag.

Läpple, D. (1992). Essay über den Raum. Für ein gesellschaftswissenschaftliches Raumkonzept. In H. Häußermann, D. Ipsen, R. Krämer-Badoni, D. Läpple, M. Rodenstein, & W. Siebel (Eds.), *Stadt und Raum. Soziologische Analysen* (2nd ed., pp. 157–207). Pfaffenweiler: Centaurus.

Larner, W. (2003). Neoliberalism? *Environment and Planning D: Society and Space, 21*(5), 509–512.

Latour, B. (1996). *Der Berliner Schlüssel. Erkundungen eines Liebhabers der Wissenschaften*. Berlin: Akademie.

Latour, B. (2002 [1999]). *Die Hoffnung der Pandora. Untersuchungen zur Wirklichkeit der Wissenschaft*. Frankfurt a. M.: Suhrkamp.

Lautensach, H. (1973). Über die Erfassung und Abgrenzung von Landschaftsräumen [Erstveröffentlichung 1938]. In K. Paffen (Ed.), *Das Wesen der Landschaft: Vol. 39. Wege der Forschung* (pp. 20–38). Darmstadt: WBG.

Law, J., & Hassard, J. (Eds.). (1999). *Actor network theory and after* (Sociological review Monographs). Oxford: Blackwell.

Lehmann, D. (2009). Die Verdinglichung der Natur. Über das Verhältnis von Vernunft und die Unmöglichkeit der Naturbeherrschung. *Phase 2, Zeitschrift gegen die Realität, 2009*(33, 36 Absätze). https://phase-zwei.org/hefte/artikel/die-verdinglichung-der-natur-255/. Accessed 5 Dec 2018.

Lehmann, H. (2016). *Ästhetische Erfahrung. Eine Diskursanalyse*. Paderborn: Wilhelm Fink.

Leibenath, M. (2014a). Landschaft im Diskurs: Welche Landschaft? Welcher Diskurs? Praktische Implikationen eines alternativen Entwurfs konstruktivistischer Landschaftsforschung. *Naturschutz und Landschaftsplanung, 46*(4), 124–129.

Leibenath, M. (2014b). Landschaftsbewertung im Spannungsfeld von Expertenwissen, Politik und Macht. *UVP-report, 28*(2), 44–49. https://www2.ioer.de/recherche/pdf/2014_leibenath_uvp-report.pdf. Accessed 26 Jan 2017.

Leibenath, M. (2015). Landschaften und Macht. In S. Kost & A. Schönwald (Eds.), *Landschaftswandel—Wandel von Machtstrukturen* (pp. 17–26). Wiesbaden: Springer VS.

Leibenath, M., & Otto, A. (2012). Diskursive Konstituierung von Kulturlandschaft am Beispiel politischer Windenergiediskurse in Deutschland. *Raumforschung und Raumordnung, 70*(2), 119–131.

Leibenath, M., & Otto, A. (2013). Windräder in Wolfhagen—Eine Fallstudie zur diskursiven Konstituierung von Landschaften. In M. Leibenath, S. Heiland, H. Kilper, & S. Tzschaschel (Eds.), *Wie werden Landschaften gemacht? Sozialwissenschaftliche Perspektiven auf die Konstituierung von Kulturlandschaften* (pp. 205–236). Bielefeld: Transcript.

Leibenath, M., & Otto, A. (2014). Competing wind energy discourses, contested landscapes. *Landscape Online, 38,* 1–18.

Lekan, T., & Zeller, T. (2005). The landscape of German environmental history. In T. Lekan & T. Zeller (Eds.), *Germany's nature. Cultural landscapes and environmental history* (pp. 1–16). New Brunswick: Rutgers University Press.

Lenk, K. (1989). *Deutscher Konservatismus*. Frankfurt a. M.: Campus.

Leonhard, J. (2001). *Liberalismus. Zur historischen Semantik eines europäischen Deutungsmusters* (Veröffentlichungen des Deutschen Historischen Instituts London/ Publications of the German Historical Institute London). München: Oldenbourg.

Liessmann, K. P. (1999). *Philosophie der modernen Kunst. Eine Einführung: Vol. 2088. UTB für Wissenschaft Mittlere Reihe Philosophie, Kunstwissenschaft.* Wien: WUV-Universitätsverlag.

Liessmann, K. P. (2002). *Kitsch! oder Warum der schlechte Geschmack der eigentlich gute ist.* Wien: Brandstätter.

Liessmann, K. P. (2009). *Ästhetische Empfindungen. Eine Einführung: Vol. 3133. UTB.* Stuttgart: UTB.

Lindström, K. (2008). Landscape image as a mnemonic tool in cultural change: The case of two phantom sceneries. In E. Näripea, V. Sarapik, & J. Tomberg (Eds.), *Koht ja Paik/place and location. Studies in environmental aesthetics and semiotics VI* (pp. 227–238). Tallinn: Estonian Academy of Arts.

Lindström, K., Palang, H., & Kull, K. (2018). Landscape semiotics. In P. Howard, I. H. Thompson, E. Waterton, & M. Atha (Eds.), *The Routledge companion to landscape studies* (2nd ed., pp. 74–90). Abingdon: Routledge.

Linke, S. (2017a). Ästhetik, Werte und Landschaft—Eine Betrachtung zwischen philosophischen Grundlagen und aktueller Praxis der Landschaftsforschung. In O. Kühne, H. Megerle, & F. Weber (Eds.), *Landschaftsästhetik und Landschaftswandel* (pp. 23–40). Wiesbaden: Springer VS.

Linke, S. (2017b). Neue Landschaften und ästhetische Akzeptanzprobleme. In O. Kühne, H. Megerle, & F. Weber (Eds.), *Landschaftsästhetik und Landschaftswandel* (pp. 87–104). Wiesbaden: Springer VS.

Lipietz, A. (1991). Zur Zukunft der städtischen Ökologie. In M. Wentz (Ed.), *Stadt-Räume* (pp. 129–136). Frankfurt: Campus.

Lippard, L. (2005). Park-Plätze [1999]. In B. Franzen & S. Krebs (Eds.), *Landschaftstheorie. Texte der Cultural Landscape Studies: Vol. 26. Kunstwissenschaftliche Bibliothek* (pp. 110–138). Köln: König.

Lippuner, R. (2007). Kopplung, Steuerung, Differenzierung. Zur Geographie sozialer Systeme. *Erdkunde, 61*(2), 174–185.

Lippuner, R. (2008). Raumbilder der Gesellschaft. Zur Räumlichkeit des Sozialen in der Systemtheorie. In J. Döring & T. Thielmann (Eds.), *Spatial Turn. Das Raumparadigma in den Kultur- und Sozialwissenschaften* (pp. 341–363). Bielefeld: Transcript.

Löfgren, O. (2002). *On holiday. A history of vacationing.* Berkeley: University of California Press.

Loidl, H. J. (1981). Landschaftsbildanalyse—Ästhetik in der Landschaftsgestaltung. *Landschaft + Stadt, 13*(1), 7–19.

Lorberg, F. (2006). Metaphern und Metamorphosen der Landschaft. Die Funktion von Leitbildern in der Landespflege. https://kobra.uni-kassel.de/bitstream/handle/123456789/2007110719590/DissertationFrankLorberg.pdf?sequence=3&isAllowed=y. Accessed 11 Dec 2018.

Lorimer, H. (2005). Cultural geography: The busyness of being 'more-than-representational'. *Progress in Human Geography, 29*(1), 83–94.

Lothian, A. (1999). Landscape and the philosophy of aesthetics. Is landscape quality inherent in the landscape or in the eye of the beholder? *Landscape and Urban Planning, 44*(4), 177–198.

Löw, M. (2001). *Raumsoziologie*. Frankfurt a. M.: Suhrkamp.

Löw, M. (2008). Wenn Sex zum Image wird. Über die Leistungsfähigkeit vergeschlechtlichter Großstadtbilder. In D. Schott& M. Toyka-Seid (Eds.), *Die europäische Stadt und ihre Umwelt* (pp. 193–206). Darmstadt: Wissenschaftliche Buchgesellschaft.

Löw, M. (2010). *Soziologie der Städte* (Vol. 1976). Frankfurt a. M.: Suhrkamp.

Luhmann, N. (1984). *Soziale Systeme. Grundriß einer allgemeinen Theorie*. Frankfurt a. M.: Suhrkamp.

Luhmann, N. (1986). *Ökologische Kommunikation. Kann die moderne Gesellschaft sich auf ökologische Gefährdungen einstellen?* Opladen: Westdeutscher Verlag.

Luhmann, N. (1988). *Die Wirtschaft der Gesellschaft* (1st ed.). Frankfurt a. M.: Suhrkamp.

Luhmann, N. (1989 [1980]). *Gesellschaftsstruktur und Semantik. Studien zur Wissenssoziologie der modernen Gesellschaft* (Vol. 1). Frankfurt a. M.: Suhrkamp.

Luhmann, N. (1993). Die Moral des Risikos und das Risiko der Moral. In G. Bechmann (Ed.), *Risiko und Gesellschaft. Grundlagen und Ergebnisse interdisziplinärer Risikoforschung* (pp. 327–338). Opladen: Westdeutscher Verlag.

Luhmann, N. (1996). *Die Realität der Massenmedien*. Opladen: Westdeutscher Verlag.

Luhmann, N. (2001 [1997]). *Die Gesellschaft der Gesellschaft*. Frankfurt a. M.: Suhrkamp.

Luhmann, N. (2002). *Die Politik der Gesellschaft: Vol. 1582. Suhrkamp-Taschenbuch Wissenschaft*. Frankfurt a. M.: Suhrkamp.

Luhmann, N. (2017). *Systemtheorie der Gesellschaft*. Berlin: Suhrkamp.

Lundmark, T. (1997). *Landscape, recreation, and takings in German and American Law: Vol. 6. American German studies*. Stuttgart: Heinz.

Lyons, E. (1983). Demographic correlates of landscape preference. *Environment and Behavior, 15*(4), 487–511.

Lyotard, J.-F. (1987). Das Erhabene und die Avantgarde. In J. Le Rider & G. Raulet (Eds.), *Verabschiedung von der (Post-)Moderne?* (pp. 251–269). Tübingen: G. Narr.

Macpherson, H. (2010). Non-representational approaches to body-landscape relations. *Geography Compass, 4*(1), 1–13.

Maischatz, K. (2010). Eine Einführung in das Sozialkapital-Konzept anhand der zentralen Vertreter. In A. Fischer (Ed.), *Die soziale Dimension von Nachhaltigkeit—Beziehungsgeflecht zwischen Nachhaltigkeit und Benachteiligtenförderung. Berufliche Bildung und zukünftige Entwicklung: Vol. 3. Leuphana-Schriften zur Berufs- und Wirtschaftspädagogik* (pp. 31–54). Baltmannsweiler: Schneider-Verlag Hohengehren.

Majetschak, S. (2016). *Ästhetik zur Einführung* (4., vollständig überarbeitete Aufl.). Hamburg: Junius.

Makhzoumi, J. M. (2002). Landscape in the Middle East: An inquiry. *Landscape research, 27*(3), 213–228.

Makhzoumi, J. M. (2015). Borrowed or rooted? The discourse of 'landscape' in the Arab Middle East. In D. Bruns, O. Kühne, A. Schönwald, & S. Theile (Eds.), *Landscape culture—Culturing landscapes. The differentiated construction of landscapes* (pp. 111–126). Wiesbaden: Springer VS.

Manzo, L. C., & Devine-Wright, P. (Eds.). (2014). *Place attachment. Advances in theory, methods and applications*. London: Routledge.

Mason, K., & Milbourne, P. (2014). Constructing a 'landscape justice' for windfarm development: The case of Nant Y Moch, Wales. *Geoforum, 53*, 104–115.

Masotti, L. H., & Hadden, J. K. (Eds.). (1974). *Suburbia in transition*. New York: New Viewpoints.

Matheis, A. (2016). Vernunft, Moral, Handeln—Grenzverläufe. Anmerkungen zu einem abend-ländischen kulturellen Selbstverständnis. In A. Schaffer, E. Lang, & S. Hartard (Eds.), *An und in Grenzen—Entfaltungsräume für eine nachhaltige Entwicklung* (pp. 107–126). Marburg: Metropolis-Verlag.

Mathewson, K. (2009). Carl Sauer and his critics. In W. M. Denevan & K. Mathewson (Eds.). *Carl Sauer on culture and landscape: Readings and commentaries*. Baton Rouge: Louisiana State University Press.

Mattissek, A., & Wiertz, T. (2014). Materialität und Macht im Spiegel der Assemblage-Theorie: Erkundungen am Beispiel der Waldpolitik in Thailand. *Geographica Helvetica, 69*(3), 157–169.

Maturana, H. R., & Varela, F. J. (1987). *The tree of knowledge. The biological roots of human understanding* (Revised ed.). Boston: Shambhala.

Matys, T., & Brüsemeister, T. (2012). Gesellschaftliche Universalien versus bürgerliche Freiheit des Einzelnen—Macht, Herrschaft und Konflikt bei Ralf Dahrendorf. In P. Imbusch (Ed.), *Macht und Herrschaft. Sozialwissenschaftliche Theorien und Konzeptionen* (2nd ed., pp. 195–216). Wiesbaden: Springer VS.

McCormack, D. P. (2003). An event of geographical ethics in spaces of affect. *Transactions of the institute of British geographers, 28*(4), 488–507.

Mecheril, P. (2009). *Politik der Unreinheit. Ein Essay über Hybridität* (2., durchgesehene Aufl.). Wien: Passagen-Verlag.

Meijer, G. (1987). The history of neo-liberalism: Affinity to some developments in economics in Germany. *International Journey of Social Economics, 14*(7, 8, 9), 142–155.

Merleau-Ponty, M. (1962). *Phenomenology of perception*. London: Routledge & Kegan.

Michaeli, M. (2008). Verstädterte Landschaft—Landschaftliche Stadt. Der unbeabsichtigte Selbstmord der Planung im uneindeutigen Raum metropolitaner Kulturlandschaften. In Bayerische Akademie für Naturschutz und Landschaftspflege, & Lehrstuhl für Landschaftsbau und Vegetationstechnik (Eds.), *Die Zukunft der Kulturlandschaft—Entwicklungsräume und Handlungsfelder* (pp. 46–55). Laufen: ANL.

Michaelis, J., Schuz, J., Meinert, R., Menger, M., Grigat, J. P., Kaatsch, P., et al. (1997). Childhood leukemia and electromagnetic fields: Results of a population-based case-control study in Germany. *Cancer Causes Control, 8*, 167–174.

Michelsen, D., & Walter, F. (2013). *Unpolitische Demokratie. Zur Krise der Repräsentation: Vol. 2668. Edition Suhrkamp* (1st ed.). Berlin: Suhrkamp.

Miller, P. A. (1984). A comparative study of the BLM scenic quality rating procedure and land-scape preference dimensions. *Landscape Journal, 3*(2), 123–135.

Mises, L. von. (1927). *Liberalismus*. Jena: Verlag von Gustav Fischer.

Mitchell, D. (2003). Cultural landscapes: Just landscapes or landscapes of justice? *Progress in Human Geography, 27*(6), 787–796.

Mitchell, D. (2007). Work, struggle, death, and geographies of justice: The transformation of land-scape in and beyond California's imperial valley. *Landscape Research, 32*(5), 559–577.

Mitchell, D. (2008). New axioms for reading the landscape: Paying attention to political economy and social justice. In J. L. Wescoat & D. M. Johnston (Eds.), *Political economies of landscape change. Places of integrative power: Vol. 89. The geojournal library* (pp. 29–50). Dordrecht: Springer.

Mitchell, W. J. T. (2002a). Imperial landscape. In W. J. T. Mitchell (Ed.), *Landscape and power* (2nd ed., pp. 5–34). Chicago: University of Chicago Press.

Mitchell, W. J. T. (2002b). Introduction. In W. J. T. Mitchell (Ed.), *Landscape and power* (2nd ed., pp. 1–4). Chicago: University of Chicago Press.

Mölders, T., Othengrafen, F., Stock, K., & Zibell, B. (2016). Zwischen Stadt und Land: Hybride Räume verstehen und gestalten. In S. Hofmeister & O. Kühne (Eds.), *StadtLandschaften. Die neue Hybridität von Stadt und Land* (pp. 37–61). Wiesbaden: Springer VS.

Moran, D. (2000). *Introduction to phenomenology*. Abingdon: Routledge.

Morgan, R. (1999). Some factors affecting coastal landscape aesthetic quality assessment. *Landscape Research, 24*(2), 167–184.

Morris, J. (2002). Los Angeles: The know-how city. In D. L. Ulin (Ed.), *Writing Los Angeles. A literary anthology* (pp. 596–613). New York: Library of America.

Morrow, R. A., & Brown, D. D. (1994). *Critical theory and methodology: Vol. 3 Contemporary social theory*. Thousand Oaks: Sage.

Mouffe, C. (2000). Deliberative Democracy or Agonistic Pluralism. Reihe Politikwissenschaft Political Science Series: 72. https://www.ihs.ac.at/publications/pol/pw_72.pdf. Accessed 13 Oct 2017.

Mouffe, C. (2005). *On the political*. London: Routledge.

Moulaert, F., & Swyngedouw, E. (1989). Survey 15. A regulation approach to the geography of flexible production systems. *Environment and Planning D: Society and Space, 7*(3), 327–345.

Muir, R. (1998). Reading the landscape, rejecting the present. *Landscape Research, 23*(1), 71–82.

Muir, R. (2000). *The new reading the landscape. Fieldwork in landscape history*. Exeter: University of Exeter Press.

Müller, G. (1977). Zur Geschichte des Wortes Landschaft. In A. H. von Wallthor & H. Quirin (Eds.), *„Landschaft" als interdisziplinäres Forschungsproblem. Vorträge und Diskussionen des Kolloquiums am 7./8. November 1975 in Münster* (pp. 3–13). Münster: Aschendorff.

Müller, W. (1998). Erwartete und unerwartete Folgen der Bildungsexpansion. In J. Friedrichs, M. R. Lepsius, & K. U. Mayer (Eds.), *Die Diagnosefähigkeit der Soziologie: Vol. 38. Kölner Zeitschrift für Soziologie und Sozialpsychologie: Sonderhefte* (pp. 81–112). Opladen: Westdeutscher Verlag.

Murdoch, J. (1998). The spaces of actor-network theory. *Geoforum, 29*(4), 357–374.

Myga-Piątek, U. (2012). *Krajobrazy Kulturowe. Aspekty Ewolucyjne I Typologiczne*. Katowice: Uniwersytet Śląski (Cultural landscape. Evotionary and typological aspects).

Naranjo, F. Z. (2006). Landscape and spatial planning policies. In Council of Europe (Ed.), *Landscape and sustainable development. Challenges of the European landscape convention* (pp. 53–79). Strasbourg: Council of Europe Publishing.

Nassauer, J. I. (1995). Culture and changing landscape structure. *Landscape Ecology, 10*(4), 229–237.

Nederveen Pieterse, J. (2005). Hybridität, na und? In L. Allolio-Näcke, B. Kalscheuer, & A. Manzeschke (Eds.), *Differenzen anders denken. Bausteine zu einer Kulturtheorie der Transdifferenz* (pp. 396–430). Frankfurt a. M.: Campus.

Niedenzu, H.-J. (2001). Kapitel 8: Konflikttheorie: Ralf Dahrendorf. In J. Morel, E. Bauer, T. Maleghy, H.-J. Niedenzu, M. Preglau, & H. Staubmann (Eds.), *Soziologische Theorie. Abriß ihrer Hauptvertreter* (7th ed., pp. 171–189). München: Oldenbourg.

Nissen, U. (1998). *Kindheit, Geschlecht und Raum. Sozialisationstheoretische Zusammenhänge geschlechtsspezifischer Raumaneignung*. Weinheim: Beltz Juventa.

Nogué i Font, J. (1993). Toward a phenomenology of landscape and landscape experience: An example from Catalonia. In D. Seamon (Ed.), *Dwelling, seeing, and designing. Toward a phenomenological ecology* (pp. 159–180). Albany: State University of New York Press.

Nohl, W. (2001a). *Landschaftsplanung. Ästhetische und reaktive Aspekte. Konzept, Begründungen und Verfahrensweisen auf Ebene des Landschaftsplans*. Berlin: Patzer.

Nohl, W. (2001b). Sustainable landscape use and aesthetic perception—Preliminary reflections on future landscape aesthetics. *Landscape and Urban Planning, 54*(1–4), 223–237.

Nohl, W. (2015). *Landschaftsästhetik heute. Auf dem Wege zu einer Landschaftsästhetik des guten Lebens; ausgewählte Aufsätze aus vier Jahrzehnten*. München: Oekom.

Nowotny, H. (2005). Experten, Expertisen und imaginierte Laien. In A. Bogner & H. Torgersen (Eds.), *Wozu Experten? Ambivalenzen der Beziehung von Wissenschaft und Politik* (pp. 33–44). Wiesbaden: VS Verlag.

Olessak, E. (1981). *Kalifornien*. München: Prestel.

Olwig, K. (2008). The Jutland Ciper: Unlocking the meaning and power of a contested landscape. In M. Jones & K. Olwig (Eds.), *Nordic landscapes. Region and belonging on the northern edge of Europe* (pp. 12–52). Minneapolis: University of Minnesota Press (Published in cooperation with the Center for American Places).

Olwig, K. F. (2003). "Transnational" socio-cultural systems and ethnographic research: Views from an extended field site. *International Migration Review, 37*(3), 787–811.

Olwig, K. R. (2002). *Landscape, nature, and the body politic. From Britain's renaissance to America's new world*. Madison: University of Wisconsin Press.

Olwig, K. R. (2007). The practice of landscape 'Conventions' and the just landscape: The case of the European landscape convention. *Landscape Research, 32*(5), 579–594.

Olwig, K. R. (2011). The earth is not a globe: Landscape versus the 'globalist' agenda. *Landscape Research, 36*(4), 401–415.

Olwig, K. R., & Lowenthal, D. (Eds.). (2006). *The nature of cultural heritage and the culture of natural heritage. Northern perspectives on a contested Patrimony*. Abingdon: Routledge.

Olwig, K. R., & Mitchell, D. (Eds.). (2009). *Justice, power and the political landscape*. Abingdon: Routledge.

Opielka, M. (2004). *Sozialpolitik. Grundlagen und vergleichende Perspektiven: Vol. 55662. Rororo Rowohlts Enzyklopädie*. Reinbek bei Hamburg: Rowohlt Taschenbuch.

Orians, G. H. (1980). Habitat selection: General theory and applications to human behavior. In J. S. Lockard (Ed.), *The evolution of human social behavior* (pp. 3–25). New York: Elsevier.

Orians, G. H. (1986). An ecological and evolutionary approach to landscape aesthetics. In E. C. Penning-Rowsell & D. Lowenthal (Eds.), *Landscape meanings and values* (pp. 3–25). London: Allen & Unwin.

Paasi, A. (2008). Finnish landscape as social practice. Mapping identity and scale. In M. Jones & K. R. Olwig (Eds.), *Nordic landscapes. Region and belonging on the northern edge of Europe* (pp. 511–539). Minneapolis: University of Minnesota Press.

Paffen, K. (1973a). Der Landschaftsbegriff als Problemstellung (1953). In K. Paffen (Ed.), *Das Wesen der Landschaft: Vol. 39. Wege der Forschung* (pp. 71–112). Darmstadt: WBG.

Paffen, K. (1973b). Einleitung. In K. Paffen (Ed.), *Das Wesen der Landschaft: Vol. 39. Wege der Forschung* (pp. IX–XXXVII). Darmstadt: WBG.

Paris, R. (2005). *Normale Macht. Soziologische Essays*. Konstanz: UVK.

Parsons, T. (1991 [1951]). *The social system*. London: Routledge.

Parsons, R., & Daniel, T. C. (2002). Good looking. In defense of scenic landscape aesthetics. *Landscape and Urban Planning, 60*(1), 43–56.

Pasqualetti, M. J. (2001). Wind energy landscapes: Society and technology in the California desert. *Society & Natural Resources: An International Journal, 14*(8), 689–699.

Pasqualetti, M. J., Gipe, P., & Righter, R. W. (Eds.). (2002). *Wind power in view: Energy landscapes in a crowded world*. San Diego: Academic.

Passarge, S. (1929). *Beschreibende Landschaftskunde* (2., erweiterte und verbesserte Aufl.). Hamburg: Friedrichsen & De Gruyter.

Pedroli, B., & van Mansvelt, J. D. (2006). Landscape and awareness-raising, training and education. In Council of Europe (Ed.), *Landscape and sustainable development. Challenges of the European landscape convention* (pp. 117–140). Strasbourg: Council of Europe Publishing.

Peet, R. (1996). Discursive idealism in the "landscape-as-text" school. *The Professional Geographer, 48*(1), 96–98.

Pennington, M. (2002). A Hayekian liberal critique of collaborative planning. In M. Tewdwr-Jones & P. Allmendinger (Eds.), *Planning futures. New directions for planning theory* (pp. 187–205). London: Routledge.

Peres, C. (2013). Philosophische Ästhetik. Eine Standortbestimmung. In H. Friesen & M. Wolf (Eds.), *Kunst, Ästhetik, Philosophie. Im Spannungsfeld der Disziplinen* (pp. 13–69). Münster: Mentis.

Pfütze, H. (2016). Das ist doch keine Kunst—Das kann ich auch. In M. Kauppert & H. Eberl (Eds.), *Ästhetische Praxis* (Kunst und Gesellschaft, pp. 83–102). Wiesbaden: Springer VS.

Piechocki, R. (2010). *Landschaft—Heimat—Wildnis. Schutz der Natur—Aber welcher und warum?* München: Beck.

Piepmeier, R. (1980). Das Ende der ästhetischen Kategorie „Landschaft". Zu einem Aspekt neuzeitlichen Naturverhältnisses. *Westfälische Forschungen, 30,* 8–46.

Platon. (2005 [im 4. Jh. v. u. Z.]). *Werke in 8 Bänden* (9 vols.). Darmstadt: WBG.

Plessner, H. (1924). *Grenzen der Gemeinschaft. Eine Kritik des sozialen Radikalismus.* Bonn: Cohen.

Pohl, J. (1993). *Regionalbewusstsein als Thema der Sozialgeographie. Theoretische Überlegungen und empirische Untersuchungen am Beispiel Friaul: Vol. 70 Münchener geographische Hefte.* Kallmünz: Lassleben.

Pöltner, G. (2008). *Philosophische Ästhetik: Vol. 400. Kohlhammer-Urban-Taschenbücher.* Stuttgart: Kohlhammer.

Popitz, H. (1992). *Phänomene der Macht* (2., stark erweiterte Aufl.). Tübingen: Mohr.

Popper, K. R. (1973). *Objektive Erkenntnis. Ein evolutionärer Entwurf.* Hamburg: Hoffmann & Campe.

Popper, K. R. (2002). *The logic of scientific discovery.* Abingdon: Routledge.

Popper, K. R. (2011). *The open society and its enemies.* Abingdon: Routledge.

Porteous, J. D. (1985). Smellscape. *Progress in Physical Geography, 9*(3), 356–378.

Porteous, J. D. (2013). *Environmental aesthetics. Ideas, politics and planning.* Abingdon: Routledge.

Poschlod, P. (2017). *Geschichte der Kulturlandschaft. Entstehungsursachen und Steuerungsfaktoren der Entwicklung der Kulturlandschaft, Lebensraum- und Artenvielfalt in Mitteleuropa* (2., aktualisierte Aufl.). Stuttgart: Eugen Ulmer KG.

Pott, A. (2007). *Orte des Tourismus. Eine raum- und gesellschaftstheoretische Untersuchung.* Bielefeld: Transcript.

Potthoff, K. (2013). The use of 'cultural landscape' in 19th century German geographical literature. *Norsk Geografisk Tidsskrift—Norwegian Journal of Geography, 67*(1), 49–54.

Pregill, P., & Volkman, N. (1999). *Landscapes in history. Design and planning in the eastern and western traditions.* New York: Wiley.

Price, M., & Lewis, M. (1993). The reinvention of cultural geography. *Annals of the Association of American Geographers, 83*(1), 1–17.

Pries, C. (1989). Einleitung. In C. Pries (Ed.), *Das Erhabene. Zwischen Grenzerfahrung und Größenwahn* (pp. 1–30). Weinheim: VCH Acta Humaniora.

Prigge, W., & Herterich, F. (1988). Skyline: Zeichen der Stadt. Moderner und Postmoderner Städtebau. In K. R. Scherpe (Ed.), *Die Unwirklichkeit der Städte. Großstadtdarstellungen zwischen Moderne und Postmoderne* (pp. 304–324). Reinbek bei Hamburg: Rowohlt Taschenbuch.

Prominski, M. (2004). *Landschaft entwerfen. Zur Theorie aktueller Landschaftsarchitektur*. Berlin: Reimer.

Proshansky, H. M., Fabian, A. K., & Kaminoff, R. (1983). Place-identity. Physical world socialization of the self. *Journal of Environmental Psychology, 3*(1), 57–83.

Purcell, A. T. (1992). Abstract and specific physical attributes and the experience of landscape. *Journal of Environmental Management, 34*(3), 159–177.

Pütz, G. (2007). Landschaft als Logo. Die Inszenierung postindustrieller Landschaften. In U. Eisel & S. Körner (Eds.), *Landschaft in einer Kultur der Nachhaltigkeit: Vol. 2. Landschaftsgestaltung im Spannungsfeld zwischen Ästhetik und Nutzen* (Arbeitsberichte des Fachbereichs Architektur, Stadtplanung, Landschaftsplanung, Vol. 166, pp. 125–135). Kassel: Kassel University Press.

Quasten, H. (1997). Grundsätze und Methoden der Erfassung und Bewertung kulturhistorischer Phänomene der Kulturlandschaft. In W. Schenk, K. Fehn, & D. Denecke (Eds.), *Kulturlandschaftspflege. Beiträge der Geographie zur räumlichen Planung* (pp. 19–34). Berlin: Borntraeger.

Raab, J. (1998). Die soziale Konstruktion olfaktorischer Wahrnehmung. Eine Soziologie des Geruchs. http://kops.uni-konstanz.de/bitstream/handle/123456789/11429/260_1.pdf?sequence=1&isAllowed=y. Accessed 20 Dec 2018.

Rademacher, C. (1999). Ein „Liebeslied für Bastarde"? Anmerkungen zum Hybridisierungskonzept im Globalisierungsdiskurs. In C. Rademacher, M. Schroer, & P. Wiechens (Eds.), *Spiel ohne Grenzen? Ambivalenzen der Globalisierung* (pp. 255–269). Opladen: Westdeutscher Verlag.

Raffestin, C. (2005). *Dalla Nostalgia Del Territorio Al Desiderio Di Paesaggio. Elementi Per Una Teroria Del Paesaggio* (Architettura del paesaggio). Florenz: Alinea Editrice.

Rebay-Salisbury, K. (2013). Phänomenologie und Landschaft: der menschliche Körper in Bewegung. In R. Karl & J. Leskovar (Eds.), *Interpretierte Eisenzeiten. Fallstudien, Methoden, Theorie: Tagungsbeträge der 5. Linzer Gespräche zur interpretativen Eisenzeitarchäologie* (Studien zur Kulturgeschichte von Oberösterreich, Folge 37, pp. 61–70). Linz: Oberösterreichisches Landesmuseum.

Recki, B. (2009). *Freiheit: Vol. 3233. Grundbegriffe der europäischen Geistesgeschichte*. Wien: Facultas Verlags- & Buchhandels AG.

Recki, B. (2013). Stil im Handeln oder die Aufgaben der Urteilskraft. In H. Friesen & M. Wolf (Eds.), *Kunst, Ästhetik, Philosophie. Im Spannungsfeld der Disziplinen* (pp. 221–244). Münster: Mentis.

Reckwitz, A. (2001). Multikulturalismustheorien und der Kulturbegriff. Vom Homogenitätsmodell zum Modell kultureller Interferenzen. *Berliner Journal für Soziologie, 11*(2), 179–200.

Reckwitz, A. (2012). *Die Erfindung der Kreativität. Zum Prozess gesellschaftlicher Ästhetisierung: Vol. 1995. Suhrkamp-Taschenbuch Wissenschaft*. Berlin: Suhrkamp.

Redepenning, M. (2006). *Wozu Raum? Systemtheorie, critical geopolitics und raumbezogene Semantiken: Vol. 62. Beiträge zur Regionalen Geographie*. Leipzig: Selbstverlag.

Redepenning, M. (2009). Inszenierung im/des Ländlichen: Feste, raumbezogene Semantiken, lokale Kultur und ein Elefant in Niederroßla. *Berichte zur deutschen Landeskunde, 83*(4), 367–388.

Redfern, P. A. (2003). What makes gentrification 'gentrification'? *Urban Studies, 40*(12), 2351–2366.

Reese-Schäfer, W. (1992). *Luhmann zur Einführung: Vol. 82. Zur Einführung*. Hamburg: Junius.

Reicher, M. E. (2015). *Einführung in die philosophische Ästhetik* (Einführungen Philosophie, 3., überarbeitete Aufl.). Darmstadt: WBG.

Relph, E. (1967). *Place and placelessness*. London: Pion Limited.

Renfrew, C., & Zubrow, E. B. W. (Eds.). (1994). *The ancient mind. Elements of cognitive archaeology* (New directions in archaeology). New York: Cambridge University Press.

Renn, O. (2012). Wissen und Moral. Stadien der Risikowahrnehmung. In M.-D. Weitze, A. Pühler, W. M. Heckl, W. Müller-Röber, O. Renn, P. Weingart, et al. (Eds.), *Biotechnologie-Kommunikation. Kontroversen, Analysen, Aktivitäten* (Acatech DISKUSSION, pp. 367–375). Berlin: Springer Vieweg.

Reuter, W. (2001). Öffentliches-privates Partnerschaftsprojekt „Stuttgart 21". Konflikte, Krisen, Machtkalküle. *disP—The Planning Review, 145*(37), 29–40.

Revill, G. (2018). Landscape, music and sonic environments. In P. Howard, I. H. Thompson, E. Waterton, & M. Atha (Eds.), *The Routledge companion to landscape studies* (2nd ed., pp. 264–274). Abingdon: Routledge.

Riehl, W. H. (1854). *Die Naturgeschichte des Volkes als Grundlage einer deutschen Social-Politik. Land und Leute* (Vol. 1). Stuttgart: Klett-Cotta.

Riley, R. B. (1994). Gender, landscape, culture: Sorting out some questions. *Landscape Journal, 13*(2), 153–163.

Ritter, J. (1996). Landschaft. Zur Funktion des Ästhetischen in der modernen Gesellschaft. In G. Gröning & U. Herlyn (Eds.), *Landschaftswahrnehmung und Landschaftserfahrung* (Arbeiten zur sozialwissenschaftlich orientierten Freiraumplanung, pp. 28–68). Münster: LIT.

Rivera López, E. (1995). *Die moralischen Voraussetzungen des Liberalismus*. Freiburg: Alber.

Robertson, R. (1995). Glocalization: Time-space and homogeneity-heterogeneity. In M. Featherstone, S. Lash, & R. Robertson (Eds.), *Global modernities* (pp. 25–44). London: Sage.

Robertson, I., & Richards, P. (Eds.). (2003). *Studying cultural landscapes*. London: Arnold.

Rodewald, R. (2001). *Sehnsucht Landschaft. Landschaftsgestaltung unter ästhetischem Gesichtspunkt* (2nd ed.). Zürich: Chronos.

Rodaway, P. (2011). *Sensuous geographies. Body, sense, and place*. London: Routledge.

Roe, M. (2018). Landscape and participation. In P. Howard, I. H. Thompson, E. Waterton, & M. Atha (Eds.), *The Routledge companion to landscape studies* (2nd ed., pp. 402–417). Abingdon: Routledge.

Roger, A. (Ed.). (1995). *La théorie du paysage en France. 1974–1994*. Seyssel: Champ Vallon.

Rolle, A. F. (1977). Simon Rodia. In J. Caughey & L. Caughey (Eds.), *Los Angeles. Biography of a city* (pp. 317–319). Berkeley: University of California Press.

Rose, G. (1995). Place and identitiy: A sense of place. In D. B. Massey & P. M. Jess (Eds.), *A Place in the world? Places, cultures and globalization: Vol. 4. The shape of the world* (pp. 87–132). Oxford: Oxford University Press.

Rosa, H. (2005). *Beschleunigung. Die Veränderung der Zeitstrukturen in der Moderne* (Suhrkamp-Taschenbuch Wissenschaft). Frankfurt a. M.: Suhrkamp.

Rosenkranz, K. (1996 [1853]). *Ästhetik des Häßlichen* (2., überarbeitete Aufl.). Leipzig: Reclam.

Roth, M. (2012). *Landschaftsbildbewertung in der Landschaftsplanung. Entwicklung und Anwendung einer Methode zur Validierung von Verfahren zur Bewertung des Landschaftsbildes durch internetgestützte Nutzerbefragungen: Vol. 59. IÖR-Schriften*. Berlin: Rhombos-Verlag.

Roth, M., & Bruns, E. (2016). *Landschaftsbildbewertung in Deutschland. Stand von Wissenschaft und Praxis: Vol. 439. BfN-Skripten*. Bonn-Bad Godesberg: Selbstverlag.

Sachsse, H. (1971). *Einführung in die Kybernetik unter besonderer Berücksichtigung von technischen und biologischen Wirkungsgefügen*. Braunschweig: Vieweg + Sohn.

Safranski, R. (2007). *Romantik. Eine deutsche Affäre*. München: Hanser.

Sahraoui, Y., Clauzel, C., & Foltête, J.-C. (2016). Spatial modelling of landscape aesthetic potential in urban-rural fringes. *Journal of Environmental Management, 181,* 623–636.

Said, E. W. (1979). *Orientalism.* New York: Vintage Books.

Samers, M., Bigger, P., & Belcher, O. (2015). To build another world: Activism in the light of Marxist geographical thougt. In S. C. Aitken & G. Valentine (Eds.), *Approaches to human geography. Philosophies, theories, people and practices* (2nd ed., pp. 344–360). Los Angeles: Sage.

Satter, E. (2000). Ästhetik. In J. Bretschneider & H.-G. Eschke (Eds.), *Lexikon freien Denkens* (lose Blattsammlung ohne Seitenangabe). Neustadt am Rübenberge: Angelika Lenz.

Sauer, C. O. (1969 [1925]). The morphology of landscape. In J. Leighly (Ed.), *Land and life: A selection from the writings of Carl Ortwin Sauer* (Vol. 2, pp. 19–53). Berkeley: University of California Press.

Schaal, G. S., & Heidenreich, F. (2006). *Einführung in die Politischen Theorien der Moderne: Vol. 2791. UTB Politikwissenschaft.* Opladen: Budrich.

Schafer, R. M. (1994). *The soundscape. Our sonic environment and the tuning of the world.* Rochester: Destiny Books.

Scheer, B. (2015 [1997]). *Einführung in die philosophische Ästhetik.* Darmstadt: WBG.

Schein, R. H. (1997). The place of landscape. A conceptual framework for interpreting an American scene. *Annals of the Association of American Geographers, 87*(4), 660–680.

Schenk, W. (2001). Kulturlandschaft in Zeiten verschärfter Nutzungskonkurrenz: Genese, Akteure, Szenarien. In Akademie für Raumforschung und Landesplanung (Ed.), *Die Zukunft der Kulturlandschaft zwischen Verlust, Bewahrung und Gestaltung: Vol. 215. Forschungs- und Sitzungsberichte* (pp. 30–44). Hannover: Selbstverlag.

Schenk, W. (2006). Der Terminus „gewachsene Kulturlandschaft" im Kontext öffentlicher und raumwissenschaftlicher Diskurse zu „Landschaft" und Kulturlandschaft". In U. Matthiesen, R. Danielzyk, S. Heiland, & S. Tzschaschel (Eds.), *Kulturlandschaften als Herausforderung für die Raumplanung. Verständnisse—Erfahrungen—Perspektiven: Vol. 228. Forschungs- und Sitzungsberichte* (pp. 9–21). Hannover: Selbstverlag.

Schenk, W. (2011). *Historische Geographie* (Geowissen kompakt). Darmstadt: WBG.

Schenk, W. (2013). Landschaft als zweifache sekundäre Bildung—Historische Aspekte im aktuellen Gebrauch von Landschaft im deutschsprachigen Raum, namentlich in der Geographie. In D. Bruns & O. Kühne (Eds.), *Landschaften: Theorie, Praxis und internationale Bezüge* (pp. 23–36). Schwerin: Oceano.

Schenk, W. (2017). Landschaft. In L. Kühnhardt & T. Mayer (Eds.), *Bonner Enzyklopädie der Globalität* (Vols. 1 and 2, pp. 671–684). Wiesbaden: Springer VS.

Schenk, W., Fehn, K., & Denecke, D. (Eds.). (1997). *Kulturlandschaftspflege. Beiträge der Geographie zur räumlichen Planung.* Berlin: Borntraeger.

Schenker, H. M. (1994). Feminist interventions in the histories of landscape architecture. *Landscape Journal, 13*(2), 107–112.

Scherle, N. (2016). *Kulturelle Geographien der Vielfalt. Von der Macht der Differenzen zu einer Logik der Diversität* (Sozial- und Kulturgeographie). Bielefeld: Transcript.

Schildberg, C. (2010). *Politische Identität und Soziales Europa. Parteikonzeptionen und Bürgereinstellungen in Deutschland, Großbritannien und Polen.* Wiesbaden: VS Verlag.

Schirpke, U., Tasser, E., & Tappeiner, U. (2013). Predicting scenic beauty of mountain regions. *Landscape and Urban Planning, 111,* 1–12.

Schlink, B. (2000). *Heimat als Utopie* (Edition Suhrkamp Sonderdruck). Frankfurt a. M.: Suhrkamp.

Schmithüsen, J. (1973). Was ist eine Landschaft? (1963). In K. Paffen (Ed.), *Das Wesen der Landschaft: Vol. 39. Wege der Forschung* (pp. 156–174). Darmstadt: WBG.

Schneider, N. (2005). *Geschichte der Ästhetik von der Aufklärung bis zur Postmoderne. Eine paradigmatische Einführung: Vol. 9457. Universal-Bibliothek* (4th ed.). Stuttgart: Reclam.

Schneider, M. (2016). Der Raum—Ein Gemeingut? Die Grenzen einer marktorientierten Raumverteilung. In F. Weber & O. Kühne (Eds.), *Fraktale Metropolen. Stadtentwicklung zwischen Devianz, Polarisierung und Hybridisierung* (pp. 179–214). Wiesbaden: Springer VS.

Schoeps, J. H. (1981). Konservativismus. In J. H. Schoeps, J. H. Knoll, & C.-E. Bärsch (Eds.), *Konservativismus, Liberalismus, Sozialismus. Einführung, Texte, Bibliographien: Vol. 1032. Uni-Taschenbücher Politologie, Neuere Geschichte, Soziologie* (pp. 11–86). München: Fink.

Schönwald, A. (2015). Die Transformation von Altindustrielandschaften. In O. Kühne, K. Gawroński, & J. Hernik (Eds.), *Transformation und Landschaft. Die Folgen sozialer Wandlungsprozesse auf Landschaft* (pp. 63–73). Wiesbaden: Springer VS.

Schönwald, A. (2017). Ästhetik des Hybriden. Mehr Bedeutungsoffenheit für Landschaften durch Hybridisierungen. In O. Kühne, H. Megerle, & F. Weber (Eds.), *Landschaftsästhetik und Landschaftswandel* (pp. 161–175). Wiesbaden: Springer VS.

Schröter-Schlaack, C. (2012). Das Konzept der Ökosystemleistungen. In B. Hansjürgens, C. Neßhöver, & I. Schniewind (Eds.), *Der Nutzen von Ökonomie und Ökosystemleistungen für die Naturschutzpraxis. Workshop I: Einführung und Grundlagen.* Erste Veranstaltung der Workshop-Reihe des Bundesamtes für Naturschutz … 07.–11. November 2011, Internationale Naturschutzakademie Insel Vilm (BfN-Skripten, Vol. 318, pp. 8–15). Bonn: Bundesamt für Naturschutz.

Schubert, H.-J., Joas, H., & Wenzel, H. (2010). *Pragmatismus zur Einführung. Kreativität, Handlung, Deduktion, Induktion, Abduktion, Chicago School, Sozialreform, symbolische Interaktion: Vol. 382. Zur Einführung.* Hamburg: Junius.

Schultheiß, G. (2007). Alles Landschaft? Zur Konjunktur eines Begriffes in der Urbanistik. In U. Eisel & S. Körner (Eds.), *Landschaft in einer Kultur der Nachhaltigkeit: Vol. 2. Landschaftsgestaltung im Spannungsfeld zwischen Ästhetik und Nutzen* (Arbeitsberichte des Fachbereichs Architektur, Stadtplanung, Landschaftsplanung, Vol. 166, pp. 86–104). Kassel: Kassel University Press.

Schultze, J. H. (1973). Landschaft (1966/1970). In K. Paffen (Ed.), *Das Wesen der Landschaft: Vol. 39. Wege der Forschung* (pp. 202–219). Darmstadt: WBG.

Schulze, G. (1993). *Die Erlebnisgesellschaft. Kultursoziologie der Gegenwart.* Frankfurt a. M.: Campus.

Schulz-Schaeffer, I. (2000). Akteur-Netzwerk-Theorie: Zur Koevolution von Gesellschaft, Natur und Technik. In J. Weyer & J. Abel (Eds.), *Soziale Netzwerke. Konzepte und Methoden der sozialwissenschaftlichen Netzwerkforschung* (Lehr- und Handbücher der Soziologie, pp. 187–210). München: Oldenbourg.

Schütz, A. (1960 [1932]). *Der sinnhafte Aufbau der sozialen Welt. Eine Einleitung in die Verstehende Soziologie* (2nd ed.). Wien: Julius Springer (Original work published 1932).

Schütz, A. (1971a [1962]). *Gesammelte Aufsätze 1. Das Problem der Wirklichkeit.* Den Haag: Martinus Nijhoff.

Schütz, A. (1971b). *Gesammelte Aufsätze 3. Studien zur phänomenologischen Philosophie.* Den Haag: Martinus Nijhoff.

Schwarzer, M. (2014). *Von Mondlandschaften zur Vision eines neuen Seenlandes. Der Diskurs über die Gestaltung von Tagebaubrachen in Ostdeutschland.* Wiesbaden: Springer VS.

Schweppenhäuser, G. (2007). *Ästhetik. Philosophische Grundlagen und Schlüsselbegriffe.* Frankfurt a. M.: Campus.

Scott, A. J., & Soja, E. W. (Eds.). (1996). *The city: Los Angeles and urban theory at the end of the twentieth century.* Berkeley:University of California Press.

Seel, M. (1985). *Die Kunst der Entzweiung. Zum Begriff der ästhetischen Rationalität*. Frankfurt a. M.: Suhrkamp.

Seel, M. (1996). *Eine Ästhetik der Natur* (Vol. 1231). Frankfurt a. M.: Suhrkamp.

Selman, P. (2010). Learning to love the landscapes of carbon-neutrality. *Landscape Research, 35*(2), 157–171.

Sen, A. (2009). *The idea of justice*. Cambridge: Harvard University Press.

Sen, A. (2016). 'What do we want from a theorie of justice?'. In T. Campbell & A. Mancilla (Eds.), *Theories of justice* (pp. 27–50). Abingdon: Routledge.

Setten, G., Brown, K. M., & Rørtveit, H. N. (2018). Landscape and social justice. In P. Howard, I. H. Thompson, E. Waterton, & M. Atha (Eds.), *The Routledge companion to landscape studies* (2nd ed., pp. 418–428). Abingdon: Routledge.

Shepard, P. (1967). *Man in the landscape. A historic view of the esthetics of nature*. New York: Knopf.

Shusterman, R. (2001). Tatort: Kunst als Dramatisieren. In J. Früchtl & Z. Jörg (Eds.), *Ästhetik der Inszenierung. Dimensionen eines künstlerischen, kulturellen und gesellschaftlichen Phänomens: Vol. 2196. Edition Suhrkamp* (pp. 126–143). Frankfurt a. M.: Suhrkamp.

Siekmann, R. (2004). *Eigenartige Senne. Zur Kulturgeschichte der Wahrnehmung einer peripheren Landschaft: Vol. 20. Lippische Studien*. Lemgo: Landesverband Lippe Inst. für Lippische Landeskunde.

Sieverts, T. (1998 [1997]). *Zwischenstadt. Zwischen Ort und Welt, Raum und Zeit, Stadt und Land: Vol. 118. Bauwelt Fundamente* (2., durchgesehene und um ein Nachwort ergänzte Aufl.). Braunschweig: Vieweg + Sohn.

Sofsky, W. (2007). *Verteidigung des Privaten. Eine Streitschrift*. München: Beck.

Soja, E. W. (1989). *Postmodern geographies. The reassertion of space in critical social theory*. London: Verso.

Soja, E. W. (1996). *Thirdspace. Journeys to Los Angeles and other real-and-imagined places*. Malden: Blackwell.

Soja, E. W. (2003). Thirdspace—Die Erweiterung des Geographischen Blicks. In H. Gebhardt, P. Reuber, & G. Wolkersdorfer (Eds.), *Kulturgeographie. Aktuelle Ansätze und Entwicklungen* (Spektrum Lehrbuch, pp. 269–288). Heidelberg: Spektrum Akademischer.

Soja, E. W. (2007). Verräumlichungen: Marxistische Geographie und kritische Gesellschaftstheorie. In B. Belina & B. Michel (Eds.), *Raumproduktionen. Beiträge der Radical Geography. Eine Zwischenbilanz: Vol. 1. Raumproduktionen* (pp. 77–110). Münster: Westfälisches Dampfboot.

Somerville, M., Power, K., & Carteret, P. d. (2009). *Landscapes and learning. Place studies for a global world: Vol. 57. Transgressions*. Rotterdam: Sense.

Sopher, D. E. (1979). The landscape of home. Myth, experience, social meaning. In D. W. Meinig (Ed.), *The interpretation of ordinary landscapes. Geographical essays* (pp. 129–151). New York: Oxford University Press.

Sørensen, M. L. S., & Rebay-Salisbury, K. (Eds.). (2012). *Embodied knowledge. Perspectives on believe and technology*. Oxford: Oxbow Books.

Sorkin, M. (1992). See you In Disneyland. In M. Sorkin (Ed.), *Variations on a theme park. The new American city and the end of public space* (pp. 205–232). New York: Noonday Press.

Spanier, H. (2006). Pathos der Nachhaltigkeit. Von der Schwierigkeit, „Nachhaltigkeit" zu kommunizieren. *Stadt+Grün, 55*(12), 26–33.

Spencer-Brown, G. (1971). *Laws of form*. London: George Allen & Unwin.

Spengler, O. (1950a). *Der Untergang des Abendlandes. Umrisse einer Morphologie der Weltgeschichte* (2 vols.). München: Beck'sche Verlagsbuchhandlung (Zweiter Band: Welthistorische Perspektiven).

Spengler, O. (1950b). *Der Untergang des Abendlandes. Umrisse einer Morphologie der Weltgeschichte* (2 vols.). München: Beck'sche Verlagsbuchhandlung (Erster Band: Gestalt und Wirklichkeit).

Sperling Cockcroft, E., & Barnet-Sánchez, H. (Eds.). (1993). *Signs from the heart: California Chicano murals* (Art/Chicano studies). Albuquerque: University of New Mexico Press.

Staubmann, H., & Wenzel, H. (Eds.). (2000). *Talcott Parsons. Zur Aktualität eines Theorieprogramms: Vol. 6. Österreichische Zeitschrift für Soziologie: Sonderband*. Wiesbaden: VS Verlag.

Steffe, L. P., & Thompson, P. W. (Eds.). (2000). *Radical constructivism in action. Building on the pioneering work of Ernst von Glasersfeld: Vol. 15. Studies in mathematics education series*. New York: Falmer.

Stemmer, B. (2016). *Kooperative Landschaftsbewertung in der räumlichen Planung. Sozialkonstruktivistische Analyse der Landschaftswahrnehmung der Öffentlichkeit*. Wiesbaden: Springer VS.

Stemmer, B., & Bruns, D. (2017). Kooperative Landschaftsbewertung in der räumlichen Planung—Planbare Schönheit? Partizipative Methoden, (Geo-)Soziale Medien. In O. Kühne, H. Megerle, & F. Weber (Eds.), *Landschaftsästhetik und Landschaftswandel* (pp. 283–302). Wiesbaden: Springer VS.

Stern, P. C., Dietz, T., & Kalof, L. (1993). Value orientations, gender, and environmental concern. *Environment and Behavior, 25*(5), 322–348.

Stevens, G. (2002). *The favored circle. The social foundations of architectural distinction*. Cambridge: MIT Press.

Stiles, R. (1994). Landscape theory: A missing link between landscape planning and landscape design? *Landscape and Urban Planning, 30*(3), 139–149.

Stobbelaar, D. J., & Pedroli, B. (2011). Perspectives on landscape identity: A conceptual challenge. *Landscape Research, 36*(3), 321–339.

Stotten, R. (2013). Kulturlandschaft gemeinsam verstehen—Praktische Beispiele der Landschaftssozialisation aus dem Schweizer Alpenraum. *Geographica Helvetica, 68*(2), 117–127.

Stotten, R. (2015). *Das Konstrukt der bäuerlichen Kulturlandschaft. Perspektiven von Landwirten im Schweizerischen Alpenraum: Vol. 15. Alpine space—Man & environment*. Innsbruck: Innsbruck University Press.

Stremke, S. (2010). *Designing sustainable energy landscapes. Concepts, principles and procedures*. Wageningen: Wageningen University.

Swaffield, S. R. (Ed.). (2002). *Theory in landscape architecture. A reader* (Penn studies in landscape architecture). Philadelphia: University of Pennsylvania Press.

Swyngedouw, E., Moulaert, F., & Rodriguez, A. (2002). Neoliberal urbanization in Europe: Large-scale urban development projects and the new urban policy. *Antipode, 34*(3), 542–577.

Tänzler, D. (2007). Politisches Charisma in der entzauberten Welt. In P. Gostmann & P.-U. Merz-Benz (Eds.), *Macht und Herrschaft. Zur Revision zweier soziologischer Grundbegriffe* (pp. 107–137). Wiesbaden: VS Verlag.

Tapsell, S. M. (1997). Rivers and river restoration: A child's-eye view. *Landscape Research, 22*(1), 45–65.

Taylor, K., & Xu, Q. (2018). Challenging landscape Eurocentrism: An Asian perspective. In P. Howard, I. H. Thompson, E. Waterton, & M. Atha (Eds.), *The Routledge companion to landscape studies* (2nd ed., pp. 311–328). Abingdon: Routledge.

Teaford, J. C. (1997). *Post-suburbia. Government and politics in the edge cities*. Baltimore: Johns Hopkins University Press.

TEEB. (2009). The Economics of Ecosystems and Biodiversity for National and International Policy Makers, Europäische Kommission. http://www.teebweb.org/wp-content/uploads/Study%20and%20Reports/Reports/National%20and%20International%20Policy%20Making/TEEB%20for%20National%20Policy%20Makers%20report/TEEB%20for%20National.pdf. Accessed 16 May 2018.

Terkenli, T. S. (2001). Towards a theory of the landscape: The Aegean landscape as a cultural image. *Landscape and Urban Planning, 57*(3–4), 197–208.

Termeer, M. (2007). Natur unter Kontrolle—Landschaften als Bilder dritter Ordnung. In L. Engell, B. Siegert, & J. Vogl (Eds.), *Stadt—Land—Fluss. Medienlandschaften: Vol. 7. Archiv für Mediengeschichte* (pp. 171–180). Weimar: Universitätsverlag.

Tewdwr-Jones, M. (2002). Personal dynamics, distinctive frames and communicative planning. In M. Tewdwr-Jones & P. Allmendinger (Eds.), *Planning futures. New directions for planning theory* (pp. 65–92). London: Routledge.

Thibaud, J.-P. (2003). Die sinnliche Umwelt von Städten. Zum Verständnis urbaner Atmosphären. In M. Hauskeller (Ed.), *Die Kunst der Wahrnehmung. Beiträge zu einer Philosophie der sinnlichen Erkenntnis* (pp. 280–297). Kusterdingen: SFG-Servicecenter Fachverlage.

Thiem, N., & Weber, F. (2011). Von eindeutigen Uneindeutigkeiten—Grenzüberschreitungen zwischen Geografie und Literaturwissenschaft im Hinblick auf Raum und Kartografie. In M. Gubo, M. Kypta, & F. Öchsner (Eds.), *Kritische Perspektiven: „Turns", Trends und Theorien* (pp. 171–193). Berlin: LIT.

Thompson, C. W. (2018). Landscape perception and environmental psychology. In P. Howard, I. H. Thompson, E. Waterton, & M. Atha (Eds.), *The Routledge companion to landscape studies* (2nd ed., pp. 19–38). Abingdon: Routledge.

Thompson, E. A. (2004). *The soundscape of modernity. Architectural acoustics and the culture of listening in America, 1900–1933.* Cambridge: MIT Press.

Thrift, N. (2008). *Non-representational theory. Space, politics, affect* (International library of sociology). Abingdon: Routledge.

Tiezzi, E. (2005). *Beauty and science: Vol. 10. The sustainable world.* Southampton: WIT.

Tilley, C. (1997). *A phenomenology of landscape. Places, paths and monuments* (Explorations in anthropology). Oxford: Berg.

Tilley, C. (2005). Phenomenological archaeology. In C. Renfrew & P. Bahn (Eds.), *Archaeology. The key concepts* (Routledge key guides, pp. 151–155). Abingdon: Routledge.

Tillmann, K.-J. (2007). *Sozialisationstheorien. Eine Einführung in den Zusammenhang von Gesellschaft, Institution und Subjektwerdung: Vol. 55476. Rororo Rowohlts Enzyklopädie* (15th ed.). Reinbek bei Hamburg: Rowohlt.

Toro, A. d. (2007). Escenificación de nuevas hibridaciones, nuevas identidades. Repensar Las Americas. In A. d. Toro, C. Gronemann, R. Ceballos, & C. Sieber (Eds.), *Estrategias de la hibridez en América Latina. Del descubrimiento al siglo XXI* (pp. 367–394). Frankfurt a. M.: Lang.

Treibel, A., Korte, H., & Schäfers, B. (Eds.). (1997). *Einführung in soziologische Theorien der Gegenwart: Vol. 3. UTB für Wissenschaft Große Reihe* (4., verbesserte Aufl.). Opladen: Leske + Budrich.

Trepl, L. (2012). *Die Idee der Landschaft. Eine Kulturgeschichte von der Aufklärung bis zur Ökologiebewegung.* Bielefeld: Transcript.

Tress, B., & Tress, G. (2001). Begriff, Theorie und System der Landschaft. Ein transdisziplinärer Ansatz zur Landschaftsforschung. *Naturschutz und Landschaftsplanung, 33*(2/3), 52–58.

Trigg, D. (2006). *The aesthetics of decay. Nothingness, Nostalgia, and the absence of reason: Vol. 37. New studies in aesthetics.* New York: Lang.

Trudeau, D. (2006). Politics of belonging in the construction of landscapes: Place-making, boundary-drawing and exclusion. *Cultural Geographies, 13*(3), 421–443.

Tschernokosheva, E. (2005). Geschichten vom hybriden Leben: Begriffe und Erfahrungswege. In E. Tschernokosheva & M. Jurić Pahor (Eds.), *Auf der Suche nach hybriden Lebensgeschichten. Theorie—Feldforschung—Praxis* (pp. 9–42). Münster: Waxmann.

Tuan, Y.-F. (1974). *Topophilia: A study of environmental perception, attitudes and values*. Englewood Cliffs: Prentice-Hall.

Tuan, Y.-F. (1976). Humanistic geography. *Annals of the Association of American Geographers, 66*(2), 266–276.

Tuan, Y.–F. (1989). Surface phenomena and aesthetic experience. *Annals of the Association of American Geographers, 79*(2), 233–241.

Tunstall, S., Tapsell, S., & House, M. (2004). Children's perceptions of river landscapes and play: What children's photographs reveal. *Landscape Research, 29*(2), 181–204.

Türer-Baskaya, F. A. (2013). Landscape concepts in Turkey. In D. Bruns & O. Kühne (Eds.), *Landschaften: Theorie, Praxis und internationale Bezüge* (pp. 101–113). Schwerin: Oceano.

Turner, M. G., Gardner, R. H., O'Neill, R. (2001). *Landscape ecology in theory and practice*. New York: Springer.

Tveit, M. S. (2009). Indicators of visual scale as predictors of landscape preference; a comparison between groups. *Journal of Environmental Management, 90*(9), 2882–2888.

Ueda, H. (2009). *A study on residential landscape perception through landscape image. Four case studies in German and Japanese rural communities*. Kassel: Universität Kassel.

Ueda, H. (2013). The concept of landscape in Japan. In D. Bruns & O. Kühne (Eds.), *Landschaften: Theorie, Praxis und internationale Bezüge* (pp. 115–130). Schwerin: Oceano.

Urry, J. (2002 [1990]). *The tourist gaze* (2nd ed.). London: Sage.

Vaïsse, J. (2010). *Neoconservatism. The biography of a movement*. Cambridge: Belknap Press of Harvard University Press.

van Assche, K. (2010). Landscape of the year, or, taking Luhmann to the marshes. Social systems theory and the analysis of ecological and cultural adaptation. *Studia Politica, 42*(3), 110–132.

van Assche, K., & Verschraegen, G. (2008). The limits of planning: Niklas Luhmann's systems theory and the analysis of planning and planning ambitions.*Planning Theory, 7*(3), 263–283.

van Noy, R. (2003). *Surveying the interior. Literary cartographers and the sense of place* (Environmental arts and humanities series). Reno: University of Nevada Press.

van Wezemael, J., & Loepfe, M. (2009). Veränderte Prozesse der Entscheidungsfindung in der Raumentwicklung. *Geographica Helvetica, 64*(2), 106–118.

van der Jagt, A. P.N., Craig, T., Anable, J., Brewer, M. J., & Pearson, D. G. (2014). Unearthing the picturesque. The validity of the preference matrix as a measure of landscape aesthetics. *Landscape and Urban Planning, 124*, 1–13.

Vervloet, J. A. J., van Beek, R., & Keunen, L. J. (2010). A biography of the cultural landscape in the eastern Netherlands: Theory and practice of acquisition and propagation of knowledge. In T. Bloemers, H. Kars, A. van der Valk, & M. Wijnen (Eds.), *The cultural landscape & heritage paradox. Protection and development of the Dutch archaeological-historical landscape and its European dimension* (pp. 131–148). Amsterdam: Amsterdam University Press.

Vester, H.-G. (1991). *Emotion, Gesellschaft und Kultur. Grundzüge einer soziologischen Theorie der Emotionen*. Opladen: Westdeutscher Verlag.

Vester, H.-G. (1993). *Soziologie der Postmoderne*. München: Quintessenz.

Vicenzotti, V. (2006). Kulturlandschaft und Stadt-Wildnis. In I. Kazal, A. Voigt, A. Weil, & A. Zutz (Eds.), *Kulturen der Landschaft. Ideen von Kulturlandschaft zwischen Tradition und Modernisierung: Vol. 127. Landschaftsentwicklung und Umweltforschung* (pp. 221–236). Berlin: Technische Universität Berlin.

Vicenzotti, V. (2011). *Der »Zwischenstadt«-Diskurs. Eine Analyse zwischen Wildnis, Kulturlandschaft und Stadt.* Bielefeld: Transcript.

Vicenzotti, V. (2012). Gestalterische Zugänge zum suburbanen Raum—Eine Typisierung. In W. Schenk, M. Kühn, M. Leibenath, & S. Tzschaschel (Eds.), *Suburbane Räume als Kulturlandschaften: Vol. 236. Forschungs- und Sitzungsberichte* (pp. 252–275). Hannover: Selbstverlag.

Vicenzotti, V. (2017). Thomas Sieverts: Zwischenstadt. In F. Eckardt (Ed.), *Schlüsselwerke der Stadtforschung* (pp. 127–143). Wiesbaden: Springer VS.

Vining, J. (1992). Environmental emotions and decisions. A comparison of the responses and expectations of forest managers, an environmental group, and the public. *Environment and Behavior, 24*(1), 3–34.

Virden, R. J., & Walker, G. J. (1999). Ethnic/racial and gender variations among meanings given to, and preferences for, the natural environment. *Leisure Sciences, 21*(3), 219–239.

Vischer, F. T. v. (1922). *Kritische Gänge* (2., verm. Aufl.). München: Meyer & Jessen.

Vöckler, K. (1998). Psychoscape. In W. Prigge (Ed.), *Peripherie ist überall: Vol. 1. Edition Bauhaus* (pp. 276–288). Frankfurt a. M.: Campus.

Vogel, H. (1993). Landschaftserleben, Landschaftswahrnehmung, Naturerlebnis, Naturwahrnehmung. In H. Hahn & H. J. Kagelmann (Eds.), *Tourismuspsychologie und Tourismussoziologie. Ein Handbuch zur Tourismuswissenschaft* (Quintessenz Tourismuswissenschaft, pp. 286–293). München: Quintessenz.

Voigt, A. (2009a). ›Wie sie ein Ganzes bilden‹—Analoge Deutungsmuster in ökologischen Theorien und politischen Philosophien der Vergesellschaftung. In T. Kirchhoff & L. Trepl (Eds.), *Vieldeutige Natur. Landschaft, Wildnis und Ökosystem als kulturgeschichtliche Phänomene* (Sozialtheorie, pp. 331–348). Bielefeld: Transcript.

Voigt, A. (2009b). *Die Konstruktion der Natur. Ökologische Theorien und politische Philosophien der Vergesellschaftung: Vol. 12. Sozialgeographische Bibliothek.* Stuttgart: Steiner.

Wagner, P. L., & Mikesell, M. W. (Eds.). (1962). *Readings in cultural geography.* Chicago: University of Chicago Press.

Walker, P., & Fortmann, L. (2003). Whose landscape? A political ecology of the 'exurban' Sierra. *Cultural Geographies, 10*(4), 469–491.

Walter, F., Marg, S., Geiges, L., & Butzlaff, F. (Eds.). (2013). *Die neue Macht der Bürger. Was motiviert die Protestbewegungen? BP-Gesellschaftsstudie.* Reinbek bei Hamburg: Rowohlt.

Wardenga, U. (2002). Alte und neue Raumkonzepte für den Geographieunterricht. *Geographie Heute, 23*(200), 8–11.

Wardenga, U. (2006). Raum- und Kulturbegriffe in der Geographie. In M. Dickel & D. Kanwischer (Eds.), *TatOrte. Neue Raumkonzepte didaktisch inszeniert: Vol. 3. Praxis Neue Kulturgeographie* (pp. 21–47). Berlin: LIT.

Warnke, M. (1992). *Politische Landschaft. Zur Kunstgeschichte der Natur.* München: Hanser.

Warren, S. (1994). Disneyfication of the metropolis: Popular resistance in seattle. *Journal of Urban Affairs, 16*(2), 89–107.

Waterton, E. (2013). Landscape and non-representational theories. In P. Howard, I. H. Thompson, & E. Waterton (Eds.), *The Routledge companion to landscape studies* (pp. 66–75). Abingdon: Routledge.

Wattchow, B., & Prins, A. (2018). Learning a landscape: Enskilment, pedagogy and a sense of place. In P. Howard, I. H. Thompson, E. Waterton, & M. Atha (Eds.), *The Routledge companion to landscape studies* (2nd ed., pp. 102–112). Abingdon: Routledge.

Watzlawick, P. (1995). *Vom Unsinn des Sinns.* München: Piper.

Wayand, G. (1998). Pierre Bourdieu: Das Schweigen der Doxa aufbrechen. In P. Imbusch (Ed.), *Macht und Herrschaft. Sozialwissenschaftliche Konzeptionen und Theorien* (pp. 221–237). Opladen: VS Verlag.

Weber, F. (2015a). Diskurs—Macht—Landschaft. Potenziale der Diskurs- und Hegemonietheorie von Ernesto Laclau und Chantal Mouffe für die Landschaftsforschung. In S. Kost & A. Schönwald (Eds.), *Landschaftswandel—Wandel von Machtstrukturen* (pp. 97–112). Wiesbaden: Springer VS.

Weber, F. (2015b). Landschaft aus diskurstheoretischer Perspektive. Eine Einordnung und Perspektiven. *Morphé. Rural—Suburban—Urban, 1,* 39–49. http://www.hswt.de/fileadmin/ Dateien/Hochschule/Fakultaeten/LA/Dokumente/MORPHE/MORPHE-Band-01-Juni-2015. pdf. Accessed 30 Aug 2017.

Weber, F. (2016a). Extreme Stadtlandschaften: Die französischen ‚banlieues'. In S. Hofmeister & O. Kühne (Eds.), *StadtLandschaften. Die neue Hybridität von Stadt und Land* (pp. 85–109). Wiesbaden: Springer VS.

Weber, F. (2016b). The potential of discourse theory for landscape research. *Dissertations of Cultural Landscape Commission, 31,* 87–102. http://www.krajobraz.kulturowy.us.edu.pl/ publikacje.artykuly/31/6.weber.pdf. Accessed 30 Aug 2017.

Weber, F. (2017a). Landschaftsreflexionen am Golf von Neapel. *Déformation profession-nelle, Meer-Stadtlandhybride und Atmosphäre.* In O. Kühne, H. Megerle, & F. Weber (Eds.), *Landschaftsästhetik und Landschaftswandel* (pp. 199–214). Wiesbaden: Springer VS.

Weber, F. (2017b). Widerstände im Zuge des Stromnetzausbaus—Eine diskurstheoretische Analyse der Argumentationsmuster von Bürgerinitiativen in Anschluss an Laclau und Mouffe. *Berichte. Geographie und Landeskunde, 91*(2), 139–154.

Weber, F. (2018). *Konflikte um die Energiewende. Vom Diskurs zur Praxis.* Wiesbaden: Springer VS.

Weber, F., & Kühne, O. (2016). Räume unter Strom. Eine diskurstheoretische Analyse zu Aushandlungsprozessen im Zuge des Stromnetzausbaus. *Raumforschung und Raumordnung, 74*(4), 323–338.

Weber, F., & Kühne, O. (2017). Hybrid suburbia: New research perspectives in France and Southern California. *Quaestiones Geographicae, 36*(4), 17–28.

Weber, F., Kühne, O., Jenal, C., Sanio, T., Langer, K., & Igel, M. (2016a). Analyse des öffent-lichen Diskurses zu gesundheitlichen Auswirkungen von Hochspannungsleitungen— Handlungsempfehlungen für die strahlenschutzbezogene Kommunikation beim Stromnetzausbau. Ressortforschungsbericht. https://doris.bfs.de/jspui/bitstream/urn:n-bn:de:0221-2016050414038/3/BfS_2016_3614S80008.pdf. Accessed 17 Oct 2018.

Weber, F., Jenal, C., & Kühne, O. (2016b). Der Stromnetzausbau als konfliktträchtiges Terrain. The German power grid extension as a terrain of conflict. *UMID—Umwelt und Mensch-Informationsdienst, 2016*(1), 50–56. http://www.umweltbundesamt.de/sites/default/files/ medien/378/publikationen/umid_01_2016_internet.pdf. Accessed 30 Aug 2017.

Weber, F., Jenal, C., Roßmeier, A., & Kühne, O. (2017a). Conflicts around Germany's *Energiewende*: Discourse patterns of citizens' initiatives. *Quaestiones Geographicae, 36*(4), 117–130.

Weber, F., Roßmeier, A., Jenal, C., & Kühne, O. (2017b). Landschaftswandel als Konflikt. Ein Vergleich von Argumentationsmustern beim Windkraft- und beim Stromnetzausbau aus diskurstheoretischer Perspektive. In O. Kühne, H. Megerle, & F. Weber (Eds.), *Landschaftsästhetik und Landschaftswandel* (pp. 215–244). Wiesbaden: Springer VS.

Weber, F., Kühne, O., Jenal, C., Aschenbrand, E., & Artuković, A. (2018). *Sand im Getriebe. Aushandlungsprozesse um die Gewinnung mineralischer Rohstoffe aus konflikttheoretischer Perspektive nach Ralf Dahrendorf.* Wiesbaden: Springer VS.

Weber, M. (1976 [1922]). *Wirtschaft und Gesellschaft. Grundriß der verstehenden Soziologie.* Tübingen: Mohr.

Weber, M. (2008). *Alltagsbilder des Klimawandels. Zum Klimabewusstsein in Deutschland.* Wiesbaden: VS Verlag.

Weber, P., Wardenga, U., & Petzold, C. (1999). Vielfalt, Eigenart und Schönheit der Landschaft. In O. Bastian & K.-F. Schreiber (Eds.), *Analyse und ökologische Bewertung der Landschaft. Mit 164 Tabellen* (2nd ed., pp. 348–353). Heidelberg: Spektrum Akademischer.

Weingart, P. (2001). *Die Stunde der Wahrheit? Zum Verhältnis der Wissenschaft zu Politik, Wirtschaft und Medien in der Wissensgesellschaft.* Weilerswist: Velbrück Wissenschaft.

Weingart, P. (2003). *Wissenschaftssoziologie* (Einsichten). Bielefeld: Transcript.

Weingart, P., Engels, A., & Pansegrau, P. (2008). *Von der Hypothese zur Katastrophe. Der anthropogene Klimawandel im Diskurs zwischen Wissenschaft, Politik und Massenmedien* (2., leicht veränderte Aufl.). Opladen & Farmington Hills: Budrich.

Welsch, W. (1987). *Unsere postmoderne Moderne.* Weinheim: VCH Acta Humaniora.

Welsch, W. (1988). Einleitung. In W. Welsch (Ed.), *Wege aus der Moderne. Schlüsseltexte der Postmoderne-Diskussion* (pp. 1–46). Weinheim: VCH Acta Humaniora.

Welsch, W. (1993). Das Ästhetische—Eine Schlüsselkategorie unserer Zeit? In W. Welsch (Ed.), *Die Aktualität des Ästhetischen* (pp. 13–47). München: Fink.

Welsch, W. (2006). *Ästhetisches Denken.* Stuttgart: Reclam.

Werlen, B., & Weingarten, M. (2005). Tun, Handeln, Strukturieren—Gesellschaft, Struktur, Raum. In M. Weingarten (Ed.), *Strukturierung von Raum und Landschaft. Konzepte in Ökologie und der Theorie gesellschaftlicher Naturverhältnisse* (pp. 177–221). Münster: Westfälisches Dampfboot.

Wescoat, J. L. (2008). Introduction: Three faces of power in landscape change. In J. L. Wescoat & D. M. Johnston (Eds.), *Political economies of landscape change. Places of integrative power: Vol. 89. The geojournal library* (pp. 1–25). Dordrecht: Springer.

Whatmore, S. (2002). *Hybrid geographies. Natures cultures spaces.* London: Sage.

Whatmore, S. (2016). Hybrid geographies: Rethinking the 'human' in human geography. In K. Anderson & B. P. Braun (Eds.), *Environment. Critical essays in human geography* (Contemporary foundations of space and place, pp. 411–428). Abingdon: Routledge.

Wilson, C., & Groth, P. (Eds.). (2003). *Everyday America. Cultural landscape studies after J. B. Jackson.* Berkeley: University of California Press.

Wilson, E. O. (1984). *Biophilia.* Cambridge: Harvard University Press.

Winchester, H. P. M., Kong, L., & Dunn, K. (2003). *Landscapes. Ways of imagining the world.* London: Routledge.

Winkler, J. (2005). Raumzeitphänomen Klanglandschaften. In V. Denzer, J. Hasse, K.-D. Kleefeld, & U. Recker (Eds.), *Kulturlandschaft. Wahrnehmung—Inventarisation—Regionale Beispiele: Vol. 14. Kulturlandschaft* (pp. 77–88). Bonn: Habelt.

Wirth, U. (2012). LowHigh. Hybridität und Pfropfung als Modelle einer Vermischung von Hoch und Tief. In T. Wegmann & N. C. Wolf (Eds.), *„High" und „low". Zur Interferenz von Hoch- und Populärkultur in der Gegenwartsliteratur: Vol. 130. Studien und Texte zur Sozialgeschichte der Literatur* (pp. 27–42). Berlin: De Gruyter.

Wöbse, H.-H. (1999). „Kulturlandschaft" und „historische Kulturlandschaft". *Informationen zur Raumentwicklung, 26*(5), 269–278.

Wöbse, H.-H. (2002). *Landschaftsästhetik. Über das Wesen, die Bedeutung und den Umgang mit landschaftlicher Schönheit.* Stuttgart: Ulmer.

Wohlwill, J. F. (1976). Environmental aesthetics: The environment as a source of affect. In I. Altman & J. F. Wohlwill (Eds.), *Human behavior and environment. advances in theory and research* (Vol. 1, pp. 37–86). New York: Springer US.

Wojtkiewicz, W. (2015). *Sinn—Bild—Landschaft. Landschaftsverständnisse in der Landschaftsplanung: Eine Untersuchung von Idealvorstellungen und Bedeutungszuweisungen.* Berlin: Technische Universität Berlin.

Wojtkiewicz, W., & Heiland, S. (2012). Landschaftsverständnisse in der Landschaftsplanung. Eine semantischeAnalyse der Verwendung des Wortes „Landschaft" in kommunalen Landschaftsplänen. *Raumforschung und Raumordnung, 70*(2), 133–145.

Wood, G. (2003). Die postmoderne Stadt: Neue Formen der Urbanität im Übergang vom zweiten ins dritte Jahrtausend. In H. Gebhardt, P. Reuber, & G. Wolkersdorfer (Eds.), *Kulturgeographie. Aktuelle Ansätze und Entwicklungen* (Spektrum Lehrbuch, pp. 131–148). Heidelberg: Spektrum Akademischer.

Wormbs, B. (1996). Über den Umgang mit Natur [1976]. In G. Gröning & U. Herlyn (Eds.), *Landschaftswahrnehmung und Landschaftserfahrung* (Arbeiten zur sozialwissenschaftlich orientierten Freiraumplanung, pp. 243–257). Münster: LIT.

Wylie, J. (2005). A single day's walking: Narrating self and landscape on the South West Coast Path. *Transactions of the Institute of British Geographers, 30*(2), 234–247.

Wylie, J. (2007). *Landscape.* Abingdon: Routledge.

Wylie, J. (2015). Poststructuralist approaches: Deconstruction and discourse analysis. In S. C. Aitken & G. Valentine (Eds.), *Approaches to human geography. Philosophies, theories, people and practices* (2nd ed., pp. 373–384). Los Angeles: Sage.

Wylie, J. (2018). Landscape and phenomenology. In P. Howard, I. H. Thompson, E. Waterton, & M. Atha (Eds.), *The Routledge companion to landscape studies* (2nd ed., pp. 127–138). Abingdon: Routledge.

Zapf, H. (2002). *Dekonstruktion des Reinen. Hybridität und ihre Manifestationen im Werk von Ishmael Reed.* Würzburg: Königshausen & Neumann.

Zhang, K., Zhao, J., & Bruns, D. (2013). Landschaftsbegriffe in China. In D. Bruns & O. Kühne (Eds.), *Landschaften: Theorie, Praxis und internationale Bezüge* (pp. 133–150). Schwerin: Oceano.

Zierhofer, W. (2003). Natur—Das Andere der Kultur? Konturen einer nicht-essentialistischen Geographie. In H. Gebhardt, P. Reuber, & G. Wolkersdorfer (Eds.), *Kulturgeographie. Aktuelle Ansätze und Entwicklungen* (Spektrum Lehrbuch, pp. 193–212). Heidelberg: Spektrum Akademischer.

Zube, E. H., & Pitt, D. G. (1981). Cross-cultural perceptions of scenic and heritage landscapes. *Landscape Planning, 8*(1), 69–87.

Zube, E. H., Sell, J. L., & Taylor, J. G. (1982). Landscape perception: Research, application and theory. *Landscape Planning, 9*(1), 1–33.

Zukin, S. (1992). Postmodern urban landscapes: Mapping culture and power. In S. Lash & J. Friedman (Eds.), *Modernity and identity* (pp. 221–247). Oxford: Blackwell.

The manufacturer's authorised representative in the EU is Springer
Nature Customer Service Centre GmbH, Europaplatz 3, 69115 Heidelberg,
Germany. If you have any concerns regarding our products, please
contact ProductSafety@springernature.com

Printed and bound by CPI Group (UK) Ltd, Croydon, CR0 4YY
27/04/2026
02097618-0001